When men and women are mature enough to discuss the issues intelligently, lawmakers will be able to consider changing the laws. We are grateful to Congressman Danny Davis, Illinois 7th Congressional District, for sending the following letter of support to members of Congress.

****

Dear Colleague:

By no stretch of the imagination am I promoting polygamy; however, I am encouraging you to read this book, "The Female Solution," which was written by Ms. Naimah Latif whom I have known and worked with in the same or similar venues for years.

Ms. Latif is a serious minded social worker and educator who has succinctly delineated many of the problems and much of the difficulty experienced by children growing up in single parent female headed households and the negative impact of no father being present.

It is my belief that this publication makes a strong case for finding ways to strengthen dual parent child-rearing as a way of promoting strong family development.

I trust that you will read it.

Sincerely,

Danny K. Davis
Member of Congress
Illinois, 7th District

D1617364

The Female Solution

A Vision for the Future

By Naimah Latif

For my daughter Zakiyya,
who taught me the
joy of motherhood

Published by

Latif Communications Group, Inc.
Phone: (312) 849-3456
E-mail: latifmediagroup@yahoo.com
Website: www.latifmedia.com

Send inquiries to:
Naimah Latif
P.O. Box 87251
Chicago, IL 60680-0251

Cover design by
Jason Warfield

The Female Solution
A Vision for the Future

By Naimah Latif

ISBN 978-1-60461-911-9

Printed in the United States of America

Dedication

To all the mothers of the world, the first teachers of the children, who risk their own lives to bring new life into existence; to the mothers of the prophets, the scholars, the warriors, the doctors, the scientists, the builders, the farmers, the artists, and the musicians; to the women who raise orphaned and abandoned children, providing them with the love, guidance, and security they need to grow into productive men and women; to the women who understand the power of their sexuality, the sacredness of their bodies, and the importance of their Divine responsibility to protect the unborn souls entrusted to them; to the women who pass this wisdom on to their daughters to ensure the survival of the family, the community, and the entire human species ...this book is dedicated to you.

Acknowledgements

First and foremost, I thank Almighty God for making it possible for me to finish this book. I don't say that in any pretentious way; it's just that as each day passes, I realize that tomorrow is not promised, and I am grateful to have completed a work that will exist long after I am gone and, God willing, will be of help to future generations.

Next, I thank my husband, Sultan Abdul Latif, my friend and partner, for years of patience, support, encouragement, forgiveness, understanding, compassion and all the other things necessary to make a marriage work, and for offering that unique male perspective that helps me maintain a balanced view. May our love continue from this life to the next life.

I thank my daughter, Zakiyya Latif, for her insight, wisdom and sensitivity at such a young age, and for inspiring me to try to be a better mother, wife, daughter, sister and friend.

I thank my sisters, Barbara Pement and Cheryl Charles, for their editing expertise, constructive criticism, and for incredible patience in putting up with me, their little sister, these many years.

And I thank my parents, Anderson and Leatha Charles, who inspired me by demonstrating that marriage can last forever, even after death parts you.

I realize that acknowledgements are like the credits at the end of a movie; people don't tend to read them, unless they or some people they know are listed there. Nevertheless, there are a number of people that I must acknowledge, whose help, support, feedback, and expertise contributed to this book:

Thanks to my friends and colleagues at Betty Shabazz International School, Chicago, Illinois: Karen Auset Nelson, Karen Abena Calhoun, Rodney Cummings, Makita Kheperu, Fred Kheperu, Sunjata Mason, Cazembe Muganda, Darryl Pulliam, and Charles S. Holley, Jr. And thanks to my friends and sisters Rafia Karim and Lucia Kukoyi for their valuable suggestions.

Thanks to the 7th and 8th Grade students at Betty Shabazz for their helpful critique of Chapter 2: Nosakhe're Beecham, Maurice Bell, Tezrah Billingsley, Londen Buckner, Eugene Najee Butler, Joslyn Harris, Olivia Hatch, Richard Hobson, Jonathan Honesty, Antasia Jaynes, Megan Kelton, Shelby Kukoyi, Brian King, Dana Leggette, Ephraim Mahou, Anthony Malone, Christopher McGhee, Salahuddin Muhammad, Mariah Mullen, Samantha Piper, Charles Russell, Sonya Sims, Tyreik Smith, Kadija Stallings, Cinnamon Stewart, Sidney Tukes, Emmanuel Tyler, Cory Williams, Trae Anderson, Nana Arkorful, Adeniji Bowden, Javonn Boykin, Lauren Conner, Malik Dean, Xavier Glover, Devin Hampton, Jr., Larry Heath, Carl Hicks, Amanda Hill, Maryxenia Jenkins, Denikko Johnson, Stephen Mack II, Yavonne McCray, Sydoni O'Conner, Sally Monette Owusu, Keenan Pearson, Bryan Ray, Anthony Robinson, Ravyn Shelton, Jazmyne Thomas, Brandon West, Precious Wilson, and Jawanza Wright.

And thanks to these 7th Grade students for their helpful critique of Chapter 3: Quwann Bradley, Diamond Brown, Akyla Buie, Adam Cole, Brijai Davis, Aaron Ellerson, Yaofi Eshun, Rahimah Gaither, Rashad Hatcher, Jordan Henry, Naomi Macklin, Ahmad Malone, Jeremiah McGhee, Safiyyah Muhammad, Shakeri Murphy, Erica Patterson, Jasmine Porter, Ariel Rayburn, Jamal Stallings, China Stewart, Dionne Smith and Kendra Wright.

Thanks to students at King College Prep High School and DuSable Leadership Academy in Chicago who participated in the opinion survey.

The nature scenes described in this book are actual events observed on various wildlife programs. I wish to thank the producers of *The Most Extreme*, Animal Planet TV, and *Nature,* PBS TV, for providing a close up view of animal life through their television shows.

Special thanks to all of the individuals quoted in this book, either as subjects of personal interviews or as authors whose research provided important documentation and information. Thanks to Granville Ware and Eric Pement for essential technical support. (You can't finish a book if your computer won't work, can you?) And, as always, thanks to Robert Porter for expert advice.

Contents

Chapter 3
The Skill of The Sparrow

Chapter 4
Contest of the Caribou

Foreword

By Sultan Abdul Latif

When I considered writing the Foreword to this book, *The Female Solution*, I thought about what I could say that would appeal to men.

As men, we are only half of who we are until we enter into the sacred bonds of marriage. In analyzing this, we look at the world today and wonder what has happened to men, where they no longer set a good example for their families, their communities or for mankind.

If I used as ink all the tears I shed grieving over the way we have treated women and children, this foreword would be a thousand pages long... because I would have to write about the condition in South Africa, where black men, in their own nation, with their own people, rape little eight-month-old babies. They are encouraged by the witch doctors, who, for few dollars, are willing to mislead men and tell them that if they rape an innocent baby they can get rid of their dreadful disease, AIDS. In South Africa, AIDS is spreading at such a rapid rate, and the rate of rape is spreading just as fast. About 1 out of every 3 women in South Africa is raped – a horrific figure, too overwhelming to contemplate.

I would have to write about the condition in Central Africa, in places like Uganda and the Congo, where young girls are forced to enter the military at age 8 or 9 years old and are turned into trained assassins and sent out to brutally take lives over petty tribal differences. The government steals the innocence of these young girls and crushes the motherly instincts of those who grow into womanhood.

I would have to write about countries in West Africa, where families sell their daughters into slavery abroad to serve a rich aristocracy that, under the pretence of providing for them, end up exploiting them as house servants, and turning them into virtual prisoners and slaves...

And the region of Daffur, where Northern Sudanese men regularly go and rape the women in the Southern regions of the Sudan and government officials look the other way in order to suit their own political interests...

And in Southeast Asia where 250 thousand people died in the recent Tsunami disaster, and rather than coming to help the poor helpless orphans, pedophiles came to the stricken areas to steal and molest the children. Many of those regions where the Tsunami hit were known places of recruitment for child prostitution, where adults groomed children to serve a large clientele of pedophiles.

I would have to write about the conditions in Eastern Europe, where pedophilia is so rampant among the wealthy that they make regular trips to countries like Romania, seeking out poor boys and girls to pay so they can exploit them for sexual pleasure...

And I would have to write about America, the crown jewel of today's modern world, the place where people of all nations want to come, as if the streets were paved with gold. For those privileged classes of immigrants, this nation holds the promise of prosperity and untold wealth.

However, if you look at the foundation of this nation that claims to glorify democracy and freedom and liberty for all, you will see that at its very roots is the horrendous Trans-Atlantic slave trade, where the massive rape of African women took place on slave ships bound for Northern and Central America. The evidence of the rape still exists in the many colors and shades of the descendants of those unfortunate African captives.

And yet, one particular aspect of that atrocious experience has not been told, and it is so painful that people don't want to face the reality of it. Many young boys that were forcibly brought to America were raped as well. The practice was so common that before they were sold, the boys were forced to bend over to be examined, so that buyers could determine whether or not they had, in fact, been "altered."

Alter: to cause to be different; change; modify; transform.

The young men that were victims of homosexual rape were

forever altered. Their manhood was taken away along with their freedom and dignity.

These are the things that history shows us that men have done. If you analyze the tragic events of history, you would think there is no hope for mankind. However, this book, *The Female Solution*, has presented an entirely different approach and focuses on an entirely different type of man. Real manhood is not measured by how much power you have or how much you can exploit other people.

This book challenges men to step up and address those important issues of our survival. It addresses that wonderful quality in a man that encourages him to look at himself in a divine light and rise above his petty personal needs. It presents him with some ideas that may correct some of the terrible ills we face in this modern day society.

This book encourages us to look into the future, to have a vision. It encourages us to be responsible. It encourages us to look at ourselves and our relationships with our wives. It encourages us to look at the condition of other women and the responsibility of taking care of them also.

We have become quite familiar with the phrase, "It takes a village to raise a child." I would like to add to that, "It takes a father, it takes a mother and it takes a commitment by the father and the mother."

To solve our problems will require a willingness to take bold steps and employ new ideas, many of them controversial. I think that a workable formula just might be written on the pages of what I believe is one of the most outstanding, most provocative books ever written, *The Female Solution*.

And if we study these pages, we may discover that perhaps this book does present a solution.

Sultan Abdul Latif is co-author of the book <u>Slavery The African American Psychic Trauma</u> and author of the book <u>When Nations Gather.</u>

Introduction
What Happened to Our Families?
The Crisis in Male-Female Relationships

"Mama! Mama!"

"Shut up your mouth, or I'll give you something to cry about!"

How does one stop crying when lashes from a leather belt are stinging ones bare legs?

"Mama! Mama!" I sobbed, my hand vainly trying to block the blows, my body trying to twist out of the way as her left hand firmly gripped my arm, her right hand flailing away at my legs with the strap.

"Shut up!" She bit her lip, her face twisting in an angry scowl, as if this somehow gave more power to her arm.

"Mamaaaa!" was all I could cry out in an anguished reply. Because, although a four year old understands in her head, she does not yet have the words to express her thoughts.

What I meant was, Mama, why are you always beating me? Mama, why are you so angry? Mama, how could you be so cruel to a little child for making such a small mistake? Mama, how could you betray my love and trust like this?

How could I know that her face was twisted in anger, not at me, but at my father, the man who left her? How could I know that each lash of the belt was a lash out at the man who broke her heart, disappointed her, forced her to struggle alone with children, and made her feel ugly and unwanted? How could I know that, as a four year old child? I could only know my own pain.

As the whipping subsided, I crumpled to the floor in word-less sobs. A leather belt leaves minor welts that quickly fade away. Deeper are the scars on the soul. Hurt quickly turns to anger at the sense of injustice. But you can't fight back, you can only bury the anger deep inside, where it festers and grows into rage, a rage that will one day explode.

This is where all of our hurt and pain begins. In childhood.

How many times have we watched this scene – an angry mother beating her young child for some minor offense? We cringe. We want to intervene on the child's behalf, but usually we decide to mind our own business. We judge the mother harshly in our minds, because often we can identify with the child's anguish.

But what about the mother? Why is she so angry? Perhaps this is the child she didn't really intend to have – an accidental pregnancy from a casual affair. Perhaps she doesn't even know who the father is. Or perhaps this child reminds her so much of the father – a man who left her for another woman and broke her heart. Or perhaps she is still upset at her husband who, in a drunken tirade, slapped her around and called her some ugly names. Or perhaps she herself was beaten as a child, by her own angry mother.

Women are angry. They are angry at men who won't make commitments, won't be honest, won't work, won't take care of their children, and won't treat them with respect.

Do any of these sound like issues you have had to deal with in your relationships? These are common problems for many women. But this is not a book to bash men. This is a book to help us understand what we are doing to our children.

This is not another "you don't need a man, learn how to enjoy being by yourself" book. Because the fact is, we do need each other. We are designed for each other, two halves of a whole, created to be joined together as one. We need each other so badly it hurts. That's why women are so angry. They are in pain.

And what about the fathers of the children? Why are so many men reluctant to commit to marriage, dishonest about relationships with other women, unwilling to provide financial support for their families, and disdainful of women in general?

Men are also in pain. They are frustrated, angry, confused, lonely and hurt. They have been hurt by fathers who left them, mothers who beat them, and women who rejected them. They are haunted by memories of angry mothers who derisively told them they were "Just like your no-good Daddy."

They are wounded by memories of absent fathers who gave so little positive input into their lives, fathers who failed to define manhood. Men want to express love. But what they have inside is the hurt and anger from a painful childhood.

Emotionally scarred men and women form relationships and have children together. Then their own unresolved pain surfaces, causing them to attack and destroy each other. A marriage that begins with love ends in bitterness and hate. Families are shattered. And in the process, parents take their frustrations out on innocent children, destroying them as well.

What happened to our children? They are the products of unhappy homes, violent homes, broken homes, where nurturing from a happy, loving couple is absent. In his book *A Season of Afflictions*, Dr. Kenneth Nave observes:

A total falling away from things spiritual and divine has besieged our communities and is showing up in the behaviors of our children, who demonstrate greater and greater levels of perversity each day. Social graces and respect appear to have abandoned our people, and the future seems dim indeed. Can destruction be far away?

A Season of Afflictions, page v

We have a problem. And we can only solve it together. We need each other. And yet, we can't do something as simple as keep our families together. What went wrong? In the past marriage was the natural progression from adolescence, the symbol of adulthood and responsibility. Marriage is more than a legal partnership; it is a spiritual union that binds two souls into one unit, just as two atoms join to form a single molecule.

Something has happened to disrupt the natural order of things. In American society today, 62% of all marriages end in divorce. That means that more than half of all marriages do not last. Sociological studies have proven over and over again that all of society's social problems begin with the break down of the family.

Broken Homes Lead to Increase in Crime

The weakening of the family unit has a domino effect on all of society's social institutions. When a man and woman divorce, they create a broken home and leave children vulnerable to the negative forces that prey upon unprotected, unsupervised youth.

Across the country, crime and violence is on the rise among youth of all races and nationalities. Some blame the nation's economy and many others blame the public school system. But internationally renowned, award winning entertainer Bill Cosby pointed out during a 2004 address in Washington, D.C. that every social ill is caused by the failure of parents to raise their children properly. In an editorial published in the *Chicago Defender* newspaper, he stated:

What can the future hold for us with a 50 percent high school dropout rate in many cities and a 60 percent illiteracy rate among inmates and a 45 percent Black prison population?

I recently tried to address these issues at Constitution Hall in Washington, D.C., commemorating the 50th anniversary of Brown vs. Board of Education. *In Washington, I made reference to parents whose children had been arrested. And I wondered aloud: "Where were you when he was 2, when he was 12, when he was 18, and how come you didn't know that he had a pistol?"*

Now those are important questions, even if they make people angry. Too often, the answer from across the United States - regardless of race, color or creed – is: "I can't do nothin' with him." Teenage girls become unwed mothers while males are allowed to walk away without taking any responsibility.

The incarceration of our youth is accelerating with devastating consequences for families and neighborhoods. Children are being killed by stray bullets in territorial gang and drug wars. Many of us feel shocked and helpless.

Bill Cosby
Chicago Defender editorial,
Thursday, June 10, 2004, page 9

Mothers are often blamed for the condition of the children. But today's culture places women with families in difficult and sometimes impossible situations. Women are expected to pursue professional careers after high school and become independent wage earners the same as men. When two working people enter into marriage, they expect to be able to afford a decent lifestyle. Then, when women begin to have children, the physical demands of childbirth and early parenting of an infant require that they take time off. Rarely are women prepared for the extreme physical exhaustion following those first few weeks after the birth of a child. Yet, most jobs offer little more than six weeks of paid maternity leave, hardly enough time to spend with an infant before leaving home to return to work.

Even if mothers desire to remain full time homemakers after they have children, the American economy does not support a two-parent household in which only one parent works, unless the working parent has a very lucrative career. The high cost of living forces many women to resume working full time jobs whether they are ready or not. They often have to pay someone for childcare.

To make matters worse, when companies relocate abroad, leading to the loss of factory jobs traditionally held by men, many men end up unemployed while their wives continue to work full time. Rarely are men prepared to function in the role of homemaker while their wives work. So, when men lose jobs, women, who are already tired and overworked as both mothers and employees, come home to a dirty house and no dinner prepared for them. They become angry and frustrated at their husbands. Day after day arguments erupt. Eventually, couples get divorced.

Some men and women, after growing up in broken homes themselves, decide never to marry at all. Men may father several children and never marry the mothers. Women may have several children and never marry the fathers. Children are raised in homes where the roles and responsibilities of husbands and wives are undefined. And so when they reach adulthood and form relationships that don't last, their children also end up in single parent homes, and the cycle continues, generation after generation.

As divorce and broken homes increase, gang membership and gang violence increase across the country. Law enforcement officials say that the statistics are staggering: In 1995, more than thirteen hundred of America's cities and towns reported evidence of gang activity. A decade later, many cities now estimate that 70% or more of reported murders are gang related. In her book, *The Other America: Gangs*, author Gail Stewart observes:

Gang violence has escalated in the years since the first gangs roamed the neighborhoods of New York City, as automatic and semiautomatic weapons have replaced brass knuckles and switchblades. Changed, too, are the ways gangs make money.

Gangs today control a large share of the drug market, the same way in which the Mafia controlled the trade in liquor during the days of Prohibition. As crack cocaine has become the drug of choice in the bleakest neighborhoods of the city, gangs have become distributors.

"On any city block, in any bar or pool hall, any of the apartment buildings and projects in the inner city, there are the sellers," says one youth counselor. "The kids can be as young as nine or ten; all they have to do is hand over a little bag and hold on to the money. Every hour or so an overseer comes and takes the money, makes sure the dealer has more crack to sell if he needs it, and the whole thing starts over again."

There seems to be no limit to the amount of money to be made in the selling and distribution of drugs, primarily because the supply of customers is endless...

Some experts see the increased violence as a result of the drug trade. They point to the fierce competition for territory among drug dealers, where the income from a single city block can make a huge difference in profits...

As people grapple to understand the violence and mayhem that gangs produce, they also seek answers. Who are the young people who join gangs? If, as one gang member suggests, there are only three futures available for kids in gangs—"a tomb, a cell, or a drug box (coffin)"—why would being part of a gang appeal to anyone?...

  One reason is very clear to those who have worked with young people in gangs: security. In a time when, as many people believe, most of our culture's institutions—church, family, school—have crumbled, the gang remains a powerful force. "Within the gang you're somebody," one gang counselor observes. "People respect you; you've got a name. Most of the kids I see are from one-parent or no-parent families. Nobody notices them, nobody really cares about them, and nobody has time for them. But the gang has time for them; their 'homies' have time. Sometimes it's as simple as that."

The Other America: Gangs,
by Gail B. Stewart, pages 9-11

It's much too simplistic to blame the current drug related gang crime epidemic only on the rise in single parent families. Poverty is also a factor in the increasing popularity of drug trafficking. But poverty itself is often a consequence of a broken home. After a marital breakup, a couple's combined financial resources must then be divided between two residences, often creating economic hardship for the custodial parent, usually the mother.

Prison Industry Profits From Drug Related Arrests

As the gang member quoted by Gail Stewart observed, gang members can expect to end up either dead or in jail. Jail has, unfortunately, become a way of life for a large segment of society. The prison industry is now a multi-billion dollar business, and many prisoners, warehoused in pens for months and years, emerge emotionally scarred and unprepared to earn a living. They return to the only trade they know – crime. They become repeat offenders, returning to the prison system like a repeat customer returns to his or her favorite restaurant.

Drug trafficking reached a high point during the 1970s. This had a tremendous effect on the prison industry. In just ten years, from 1975 to 1985, America's prison population doubled from less than 200,000 inmates to more than 400,000. This had a devastating effect on the generation of children born during the 1980s and 1990s. Many were raised in families where one parent, often the father, was absent because he was serving time in prison.

Despite longer sentences imposed for those convicted and more stringent standards for parole and probation, the prison population continues to increase steadily. Current statistics indicate a startling rise in the female prison population. Now children are being raised in families where the mother is serving time in prison.

More prisons and more prisoners mean more people are committing crime, creating more victims and more hurt and devastated families. Society's goal should be the elimination of crime, not the increased punishment for it.

In the book *America's Prisons, Opposing Viewpoints,* in the chapter entitled *Prisons Should Rehabilitate,* United States Supreme Court Chief Justice Warren E. Burger states:

Plainly, if we can divert more people from lives of crime we would benefit both those who are diverted and the potential victims. All that we have done in improved law enforcement, in new laws for mandatory minimum sentences, and changing parole and probation practices has not prevented 30% of America's homes from being touched by crime every year...

Prison inmates, by definition, are for the most part maladjusted people. From whatever cause, whether too little discipline or too much; too little security or too much; broken homes or whatever, these people lack self-esteem. They are insecure, they are at war with themselves as well as with society...They did not learn, either at home or in the schools, the moral values that lead people to have respect and concern for the rights of others...

Today the cost of confinement of the 400,000 inmates of American prisons costs the taxpayers of this country, including the innocent victims of crimes, who help pay for it, more than twelve million dollars a day!

America's Prisons, Opposing Viewpoints,
edited by Bonnie Szumski, pages 18-21

The breakdown of the family triggers a host of societal ills. The increased prison population is just one symptom of the illness.

Hostile Parents Abuse and Neglect Children

When families fall apart, children are often caught in the middle of a hostile battle between husband and wife. They may receive hostile treatment from one or both parents. In the midst of conflict, adults tend to inflict their emotional distress on the innocent children. When parents are angry, they are more likely to abuse their children, verbally and physically.

Just as a healthy plant cannot grow in soil that has been poisoned by toxic waste, an emotionally healthy child cannot grow in a family that is poisoned by bitterness and hostility. The purpose of a family is to provide a safe, secure, loving environment in order to raise healthy, well-adjusted children.

Children need love. They need love just like they need air, water and food. When children are abused, neglected and deprived of love, they grow into emotionally sick adults. Like the carriers of an infectious disease, these emotionally sick adults spread their illness throughout society, bringing pain to the lives they touch.

The escalating prison population is not a signal that the country needs more police or stricter penalties for committing crimes. It is a signal that we as a society are failing to raise good children. If all children were raised properly, under the safety and protection of a loving family, there would be no need for prisons. There would be no victims of crime.

While America's prison population is racially disproportionate, reflecting a racially biased criminal justice system, the problems of crime and violence are not restricted to any particular race. Poverty may be presumed to be a motivating factor behind many crimes of theft or drug sales. But even poverty is not the greatest cause of social dysfunction.

In his book, *State of Emergency: We Must Save African American Males*, author Dr. Jawanza Kunjufu states:

Research confirms that the most significant factor in the life of a child is not race or family income, but whether the father is at home. I want you to meditate on that statement for a moment. As significant as race and economics are in America, they do not compare to the destructive impact of fatherlessness in America.

- *Sixty-three percent of youth that commit suicide are from fatherless homes.*
- *Ninety percent of all homeless and runaway children are from fatherless homes.*
- *Eighty-five percent of all children that exhibit behavioral disorders come from fatherless homes.*
- *Eighty percent of rapists motivated with displaced anger come from fatherless homes.*
- *Seventy-one percent of all high school dropouts come from fatherless homes.*
- *Seventy-five percent of all adolescent patients in chemical abuse centers come from fatherless homes.*
- *Seventy percent of juveniles in state-operated institutions come from fatherless homes.*
- *Eighty-five percent of all youths sitting in prisons grew up in fatherless homes.*
- *Eighty-two percent of teenage girls who get pregnant come from fatherless homes.*

(State of Emergency: We Must Save African American Males, page 157)

Men are leaving their children unprotected. We have failed to form families that keep our children safe and secure.

Where did we go wrong?

Women blame men for being irresponsible for the children they produce. Men argue that women should not expect legal and financial commitments in exchange for sex. Pharmaceutical companies say that the solution is to use more birth control pills. Some blame religious leaders for a lack of clear moral guidance, noting that many of them differ on issues regarding sex and marriage.

Religion Seen as a Tool to Oppress Women

Religion has often defined the social roles of males and females in relation to marriage, family, and responsibilities for raising children. But according to many feminists and advocates for women's rights, most of the world's religions promote repression of women.

In her *book, The Women's Movement, Political, Socioeconomic and Psychological Issues,* author Barbara Deckard asserts:

Religion has had a particularly important role in advancing and perpetuating sexist notions. The great religions of the world have mostly been pervaded to the core by sexism. Examples:

"...And the Lord God said unto the woman, What is this that thou hast done? And the woman said, The serpent beguiled me, and I did eat...Unto the woman He said, I will greatly multiply thy sorrow and thy conception; in sorrow thou shalt bring forth children; and thy desire shall be to thy husband, and he shall rule over thee." (Genesis 2-3)

The Christian Saint Paul wrote:

"Let the woman learn in silence with all subjection. But I suffer not a woman to teach, nor to usurp authority over the man, but to be in silence. For Adam was first formed, then Eve. And Adam was not deceived, but the woman, being deceived, was in the transgression..." (1 Timothy, 2:11-15)

The Christian Bible also declares:

"...how can he be clean that is born of a woman?" (Job 25:4)

Christianity is equaled, if not surpassed, by other religions. The male Orthodox Jew recites every morning:

"Blessed art Thou, oh Lord our God, King of the Universe, that I was not born a woman."

The Koran, The Mohammedan sacred text, says:

"Men are superior to women on account of the qualities in which God has given them pre-eminence."

The Hindu Code of Manu declared:

"In childhood a woman must be subject to her father; in youth to her husband; when her husband is dead, to her sons. A woman must never be free of subjugation."

Finally, there are the profound sayings of Confucius:

"The five worst infirmities that afflict the female are indocility, discontent, slander, jealousy, and silliness...Such is the stupidity of woman's character, that it is incumbent upon her, in every particular, to distrust her self and to obey her husband."

The new high priests of Western society—the psychiatrists—are not much subtler in their sexism... A later examination o f the mass media will show that they too perpetuate sexism.

The Women's Movement, Political, Socioeconomic, and Psychological Issues, by Barbara Deckard, pages 6 and 7).

Oppression is repulsive to the human spirit. When religious scriptures are misinterpreted or misused to justify the oppression of any group, that group will either accept oppression or reject those religious teachings. Many women who came to identify themselves as feminists saw a contradiction between traditional religious teachings and respect for womanhood. They chose to reject religious traditions they saw as degrading and oppressive. Many also chose to reject moral standards they perceived as unfair and unjust toward women. Women want the freedom of self-expression and the respect as equals that they believe is denied to them in most organized religions.

This is where the confusion begins. Women want men who are moral, decent and trustworthy. Yet, at the same time, women reject religious values that confine sexuality to marriage, perceiving such restrictions as repressive and unjust toward women. Sexuality and the ability to freely express it, for many women, are synonymous with equality and respect.

Life is a pendulum that swings back and forth. Just as the law of physics states that, "every action creates an equal and opposite reaction," the same law applies to extremes in social behavior: *Every action creates an equal and opposite reaction.* Today's

woman's rejection of any restrictions to intimate relationships before marriage or outside of marriage is a reaction to the extreme
repression of the past.

Women's Movement Redefines Sex Roles and Relationships

Sex and reproduction have become sensitive political issues
over the last several decades. The rise of the women's movement
at the beginning of the 20th century brought many challenges to the
traditional relationships between males and females.

Biologically, women tend to experience their first menstrual cycle between the ages of 9 to 14, signaling the ability to reproduce life. Sexual urges intensify during teen years, and
women's bodies reach the optimum fertility for childbearing during their early twenties. However, women want to be able to enjoy
careers and personal achievements, and many choose to delay marriage and childbirth until their thirties or forties, and instead fulfill
educational and employment goals. This decision causes women to
remain single and independent, and to seek ways of satisfying sexual desires without becoming pregnant.

In America, much of today's social attitudes evolved during World War II, when women were solicited to enter the work
force to replace the men who were serving in the U.S. armed
forces. After the war, women continued to work in factories and
offices, and the American economy prospered. Desiring even better employment opportunities, more women continued to enter college. Demands for racial equality opened doors of opportunity for
many African American women as well as white women. A thriv-
ing economy attracted many immigrants from Europe, Asia, Africa
and the Middle East, and women entered the work force in droves.

For women, the desire for marriage after high school took a
back seat to the pursuit of professional career goals. As women
delayed expectations of marriage, they demanded a change in society's attitudes toward sex outside of marriage. In pre-1960s
American culture, it was an unwritten rule that men should be
sexually active before finally "settling down." However, the

strange contradiction was that, after the man "sowed his wild oats," he was expected to find a bride who was a virgin. Women protested the inequality of society's attitude toward premarital sex, and pharmaceutical companies came to the rescue. The birth control pill granted women the freedom of sex without legal commitment, social condemnation or fear of pregnancy.

The modern woman now has the same opportunities for sexual experimentation before marriage that had always been afforded to men, without any social stigma attached.

But, even the most reliable methods of birth control can lead to an occasional accidental pregnancy. So, women worked to change social attitudes regarding the removal of unwanted life from their wombs. Court battles were waged to change the legal definition of what constitutes "life," so as not to hinder women who did not want to give birth to the human life that was growing inside of them. Legal battles continue to be waged to determine at what month of pregnancy a woman may end a child's life.

Today's American culture is a mass of contradictions, largely because of confusion about sex and the role of women. The most important role, that of wife and mother, is often dismissed as insignificant.

This is where the destruction of our society begins.

Just as the family is the backbone of the nation, a nation's decline begins with the decline of the family. Modern American culture and many other cultures around the world stress money and prestige above and beyond family stability. Children are not protected; they are exploited, brutalized, neglected and robbed of their childhood innocence. These unprotected children grow into emotionally defective adults that use drugs, alcohol, food and sex to numb the pain of their deprivation.

The mass media carries images of an opulent, sexually irresponsible, self-indulgent lifestyle to the rest of the world. As nations try to emulate this lifestyle, they begin to experience the plagues of poverty, crime, violence, alcoholism, drug abuse, divorce, suicide, child abuse, rape, and murder. These problems are not confined to any nation, race, religion, ethnic group, or economic class. They are plagues that have engulfed all of humanity. They all begin with the break down of the family.

Women across the world, regardless of race, nationality, economic status, or religion, share a common bond. All desire a peaceful existence, free from fear and repression. All desire to be respected as women.

In every form of animal life that exists on the planet (except sea horses) the female alone has the power to give birth to new life. Among sea horses, the female deposits her eggs into the male's pouch and he delivers the live sea horse babies. Still, it is the female that produces the eggs that contain their developing offspring. In every species, the female controls life.

"The hand that rocks the cradle rules the world."

This saying is more than just an old cliché. It is women who will shape the minds and hearts of the future. Motherhood is a powerful position. It is the female who, through her choices, ensures the survival of the species. She sets the standards for acceptable male behavior by selecting the males who will produce the next generation. She defines the culture by what she teaches the children. In societies where human behavior has reached a barbaric level, it is because the females in that society are not respected.

Unlike animals, whose urge to reproduce drives them to seek mates for mutual pleasure and procreation, humans have misused the sex act as a tool for subjugation, manipulation, exploitation, and aggression. Rather than a spiritual act that binds two souls, sex has become a political act that defines who holds power.

According to current statistics, one out of every three women under 30 has been the victim of some form of sexual assault. The widespread occurrence of forced sexual intercourse, known as rape, is a sign that society has become deviant. It is a sign that something has gone horribly wrong in the process of raising our male children. What kind of society produces men who use their reproductive organs as weapons of pain and degradation? Author Barbara Deckard observes:

The common view holds that rape is committed by a few sick men driven by insatiable sexual urges... Nevertheless, society's view toward the victim is at best ambivalent. It's frequently assumed that she asked for it; nice girls don't get raped. Even if the victim can show that the attack was completely unprovoked, she is stigmatized. Somehow she is to blame for having been raped...

Men often see sex as something men do to women, an act that certifies the male's superordinate position...The connection between sex and violence is not restricted to hard-core pornography...Whatever their rhetoric, many men still regard sexual relationships as conquests...

From an understanding of the sex-dominance relationship, a new analysis of rape emerged. Rape is a political, not a sexual act. It is a political act of terror against an oppressed group. According to one of the first feminist analyses of rape, "rape teaches...the objective, innate and unchanging subordination of women relative to men."...

Society's real attitude toward rape is shown by the treatment given the victim. Frequently the accused rapist is treated better than the victim. Police often refuse to believe rape took place unless the victim can show severe injuries.

The Women's Movement, Political, Socioeconomic, and Psychological Issues, by Barbara Deckard, pages 402 and 403

In such a society, sex becomes not an act of love but an act of war. No species can survive when the males and females are at war with one another.

An alarming trend is the increase in sex crimes committed by females. A shocking number of women are being convicted of child molestation. What has happened to our civilization?

Rapists. Pedophiles. Thieves. Drug addicts. Alcoholics. Murderers. These are the kinds of people that walk our streets and fill our jails. But first they come out of the homes of men and women. From innocent babies, they grow from childhood to adolescence, and somewhere along the way they become the sick, maladjusted adults that add to the dysfunction of a confused society. All of them, at some point in time, had a mother.

The intention of this book is not to lay blame on women for all of society's problems. The purpose of this book is to help women recognize that *the power to change this world is in our hands.*

The women of this present generation have made a collective mistake. As a result of our mistake, the society is in a state of chaos. We, as much as any segment of society, are suffering from the effects of crime, violence and poverty.

Many women are too angry about the history of abuse of women by religious institutions to listen to any religious-based advice. In many parts of the world, religion has become a mere political tool to maintain control over certain segments of the population. If one listened to the words from religious scriptures as interpreted by some rigid, misogynistic male scholars, one would come to the conclusion that Almighty God has a dislike for women. No wonder modern women are rejecting traditional religious beliefs. At some point in time, the scriptures of all major religions have been misinterpreted and misused to oppress women.

And yet, it is the woman who has been selected by the Creator to perform the great spiritual task of bringing forth each living soul. Inside their wombs, women mold the human beings who direct the earth's destiny. If women reject religion, how will they grasp the importance of their role in shaping each new life?

Rather than argue over theological, political or cultural concepts, let's refer to something so basic that everyone can understand it: The law of nature. One need only to study nature, with its delicately balanced interwoven systems, to realize that harmony should exist between males and females, and that children should be protected from harm so that they can reach adulthood.

Families In The Animal Kingdom Protect Offspring

Males and females in the animal kingdom instinctively form unions and develop family groups that insure the protection of their offspring. Some animal species mate for life. How do we in the human family learn to form lasting relationships and raise good children? There are certain practices that females of every species follow. If we as women observe and follow their example, perhaps we can figure out how to correct our past mistake.

At this point, many will protest, "But we're not animals! Human beings were created higher than animals! Animals act out of instinct, but we have free will and the ability to make choices! We are spiritual beings, created in God's image!" Some may refer to the Biblical scripture:

"So God created man in his own image, in the image of God created He him; male and female created He him.
The Holy Bible, Genesis, 1:27

We are, in fact, spiritual beings. We are souls inside a physical body. Our journey through life is a spiritual journey. We have the capacity to think and reason and make decisions that bring good or harm to others. We have the capacity to judge right from wrong. As human beings, our role on this planet is to maintain the balance and harmony that exists in nature. But, how can we do this if we are not in harmony ourselves?

Mate selection is perhaps the greatest spiritual decision a woman can make. A woman is choosing the being with whom she will unite to create new life. In observing the animal kingdom, one thing is clear: There is no female of any species on the planet that purposely selects the weakest male among all available males with whom to engage in the act of procreation. It is against nature's law of survival. The female has a natural instinct, not only to procreate, but also to select the most worthy male to father her offspring. This selection must be a male who has proven himself in terms of intelligence, strength, skill and endurance.

Consider the buffalo. During the mating season, the buffalo male sharpens his horns and prepares to do battle with other able bodied males, all vying for the right to mate with females of the herd. As the competing males butt heads, the females watch to see who remains standing in this test of strength and endurance. The worthy male must be one who is strong enough to fight off predators.

Consider the deer. The male must first engage in head to head combat with other likely males. Then, after the male has passed the endurance test, the female will engage him in a lively chase, in which he must run at top speed in an attempt to catch her. The worthy male must be one who is fast enough to outrun predators.

Consider the sparrow. The males of the flock compete in the building of intricately woven round nests, secured on a sturdy branch, with a hole large enough for a bird to enter, yet small enough to keep out enemies. The female inspects each nest to determine which male is deserving to be her mate. The worthy male must be one who demonstrates skill in providing a home to keep the family safe from predators.

Consider the lion. It is the lion's responsibility to protect the lion pride's territory by fighting off trespassers. In order to win the right to mate with females in the pride, the lion must be able to overpower all other males who challenge his authority. The worthy male must be brave, strong, and able to protect his family's food supply from all other predators.

There is no female of any species on the planet that selects the weakest male among all available males with whom to engage in the act of procreation. No female except the human female.

We have lost our basic instincts for survival.

Women Must Seek Spiritually Strong Men

Animals follow natural inclinations that facilitate their continued existence. Humans do likewise, but also have the capacity to make decisions based on higher moral principals. In his book, *The Philosophy and Teachings of Islam*, Hazrat Mirza Ghulam Ahmad quotes verses from the Holy Quran (often spelled "Koran" by Westerners) to explain human progression from the natural to the moral to the spiritual state:

The Holy Quran has indicated three separate sources of these three states…The first spring which is the source of all natural states is designated by the Holy Quran the "Nafse Ammarah," which means the self that incites to evil, as it says: "The mind of man is ever ready to incite to evil." (12:54) …

Thus the propensity towards evil and intemperance is a human state, which predominates over the mind of a person before he enters upon the moral state. This is man's natural state, so long as he is not guided by reason and understanding but follows his natural bent in eating, drinking, sleeping, waking, anger and provocation, like the animals.

When a person is guided by reason and understanding and brings his natural state under control and regulates it in a proper manner, that state ceases to be his natural state and is called his moral state…At this stage man ceases to resemble the animals…

The source of the moral state of man is designated by the Holy Quran "Nafse Lawwama," as it is said: I call to witness the reproving self (75:3); that is to say, I call to witness the self that reproves itself for every vice and intemperance…

The third source which should be described as the beginning of the spiritual state of man is called by the Holy Quran "Nafse Mutmainnah," that is to say, the soul at rest, as is said: O soul at rest that has found comfort in God return to thy Lord, thou well pleased with Him and He well pleased with thee. Now join My chosen servants and enter into My garden (89:28-31).

This is the stage when the soul of a person being delivered from all weaknesses is filled with spiritual powers and establishes a relationship with God Almighty without Whose support it cannot exist…That is indicated by the divine direction to the soul that has found comfort in God to return to its Lord. It undergoes a great transformation in this very life and is bestowed a paradise while still in this world.

<u>*The Philosophy and Teachings of Islam*</u>*, pages 1-3*

Whereas females in the animal kingdom must seek males with physical strength, skill and endurance, human females must seek males with spiritual strength, skill and endurance, reflecting a spiritual consciousness that raises men from the level of beasts and motivates them to act with reason and compassion.

A spiritual man will strive to develop his body. Knowing that he is responsible for the protection of his family, he will work to keep himself healthy and strong, and will not abuse his body with alcohol or drugs.

A spiritual man will strive to develop his mind. Recognizing his responsibility to provide for his family, he will work to acquire education, knowledge and skills and will continuously seek to improve himself intellectually.

A spiritual man will strive to develop his soul. He will be ever-conscious of the Power that is greater than himself, to Whom he is accountable for his actions, and this consciousness will prevent him from committing acts of cruelty or injustice against others.   If a man does not have spiritual consciousness, he cannot lead his family and community to follow the spiritual laws that create peace on earth.

We can observe females in the animal kingdom and learn great lessons about life. We who are the carriers of life must make the right choices in order to shape a future of health, happiness and security for ourselves and our families.

Each chapter in this book presents a glimpse of animal life, as a means to illustrate principles that can help human beings understand their own responsibilities in selecting mates who can help them raise good children.

Women have the power to create peaceful communities free from social ills. In order to do so, we must use our power as women to form strong, happy families and raise secure, loving children, who will create a peaceful, harmonious society. We must choose men who are fit to be the fathers of tomorrow's children. We can transform the world and make it a better place to live simply by making the right decisions today. It's that simple.

No woman can afford to be a part of the problem. Every woman, everywhere, must become a part of the female solution.

Chapter 1
The Dance of The Flamingo
Express Love As A Natural Part of Life

Bright pink feathers make a striking splash of color against the blue sea and white sand as hundreds of flamingos gather on the beach, filling the air with the sound of flapping wings and shrill bird calls. Waves pounce against shore, spraying the long necked, web footed colony with droplets of water, as each bird calls out and listens for a response from its mate. Slowly they begin to pair off, male and female, for the mating ritual.

It is a beautifully synchronized ballet. More than three hundred couples stand erect, facing each other with outstretched necks. Majestically the males march forward, lifting long legs high with each deliberate step. Next, the females march forward, gracefully striking the sand with their webbed toes and turning their heads aside in a coy gesture. The males respond by raising their heads, pointing hooked beaks toward the sky and spreading their pink feathered wings. They open their mouths to issue a beseeching call. The females then tuck their heads under their wings, preening their feathers, as if to beautify themselves for their mates.

Amidst a musical chorus of birdcalls, the males and females position themselves for the glorious odyssey of procreation, and with a joyous flapping of wings, the mating ritual is complete.

Reproduction. Sexual intercourse. Lovemaking.

This is where it all begins.

Reproduction is a spiritual act. It is the act through which every soul receives a physical body. It is the sacred bonding of male and female into a complete unit.

"Holy is He Who created all things in pairs, of what the earth grows and of themselves and of what they know not."
            The Holy Quran, Chapter 36, Yasin, Verse 37

All creatures on earth are driven to find a mate with whom to procreate and complete the cycle of life. Once they have produced offspring, animals know instinctively that they must protect their young until they reach adulthood. This is necessary in order for the species to survive. All life forms that exist on earth are an essential part of an interconnected ecosystem.

Every living creature understands that its basic objective is to continue to exist. Finding a mate, producing children and raising them to adulthood are a part of that process. Most animals perform this function easily, yet many human beings seem to have difficulty figuring out how to do it.

Human relationships are in a state of confusion. People are drawn to each other, but they don't know how to create lasting unions. People have children, but they don't know how to raise them or protect them. Where are their instincts?

Instinct: *a natural impulse or innate propensity that incites animals (including man) to actions that are essential to their existence, preservation and development; animal intuition. (Funk and Wagnalls New Comprehensive Dictionary of the English Language, 1982 edition.)*

In every species, animals prepare themselves for passage from childhood and to adulthood. Adulthood marks the time for mate selection and the excitement of romance. Even in the animal kingdom, the process of creating new life is approached with a certain amount of ceremony. Observe the dance of the flamingo.

Flamingo Courtship Provides Lessons In Love

For flamingos, courtship rituals are an important part of each couple's relationship. Singing to each other and dancing together helps the couple to create a strong bond. For many species of birds, courtship rituals are a large part in the flock's daily activities. Couples are constantly reinforcing their relationship by wooing each other with songs. Males and females that produce young together must show a lot of love for each other. This is what binds the couple together and motivates both the males and females to participate in the protection and rearing of the children.

Flamingos, like many other birds, mate for life. Human couples today can't seem to even stay together long enough to jointly raise their children. In America, 62 percent of the marriages end in divorce. Perhaps people should study birds to learn what it is they are doing right that make their unions successful.

In contrast to the constant mating rituals of birds, human couples tend to abandon all signs of courtship after marriage. Unlike the flamingo couples that woo each other daily with love songs, human couples repel each other daily with arguments.

One of the first lessons to be learned from observing birds is that one should always address ones spouse in a pleasant voice. Married couples must learn to speak lovingly to each other, even when irritated about something. In fact, it is when one is irritated that one should make the greatest effort to be pleasant. Unkind words can kill the love between a husband and wife. Too many hurtful things said in a harsh tone over a period of time will erode a relationship, until eventually a man and woman can barely stand each other.

Imagine being greeted in the morning with a beautiful song from your spouse! How could you possibly start the day in a bad mood? Imagine your spouse greeting you in the evening with an exciting dance performance. Wouldn't that make you come straight home every day, rather than finding reasons to work late or socialize with friends for hours after work?

People can learn a lot of techniques to improve their relationships by simply watching birds.

Flamingos live in large groups, called colonies. They are able to reproduce by the age of six. When they are ready to breed, birds will form pairs and engage in courtship displays. Several hundred, even several thousand flamingos are all engaging in the courtship ritual at the same time. This helps to synchronize breeding within the colony, so that most of the birds are laying eggs and raising their young at the same time.

The birds understand that by timing their mating. They are shaping their future, their children's future and the future of their community.

Flamingos seem to plan their nest building during the rainy season. Rainfall apparently affects the food supply. Flamingos and other birds hatch their eggs during the time when food is plentiful. Families raise their children together and migrate together when seasons change. Flamingo colonies sometimes number into the tens of thousands; so successful group migrations require order and harmony among parents and children.

This illustrates another point: When young couples with children live in a community with other young couples with children, they are more likely to maintain a stable marriage. Unlike single people who have no children, young couples are more likely to be going through the same phases of raising infants and toddlers, and trying to prepare their children for school. They can relate to each other's struggles and can offer each other support.

Newlyweds tend to experience problems when either the husband or the wife continues to socialize with single friends. Single adults have a totally different lifestyle and set of priorities. For one thing, they don't have to think about coming home at a certain time because a spouse is waiting. They also tend to participate in activities that will bring them in contact with other single adults, primarily because single people are still looking for a mate.

When married couples are actively involved in a community of other married couples, their social activities tend to be more family oriented. Their children make friends with other couples' children, strengthening the ties of community.

Flamingos, like other animals, find mates and have children. Human beings were told to do likewise:

"And God blessed them, and God said to them, Be fruitful and multiply, and replenish the earth, and subdue it: and have dominion over the fish of the sea, and over the fowl of the air, and over every living thing that moveth upon the earth."

The Holy Bible, Genesis 1:28

Mankind is charged with the responsibility of not only re-producing the human species, but also in replenishing the earth, so that all life continues to exist. Life forms on earth are interdependent, so it is mankind's job to maintain nature's balance. Reproduction is obedience to this Divine command.

Sexual intercourse is an act of worship. Male and female are as two pieces of an interlocking puzzle. They join together and become one soul to create another living soul.

Teaching Sex is Dirty and Sinful Creates Shame

This act is a powerful expression of physical and spiritual unity. Yet, modern culture does not address it with the respect and reverence it is due. In fact, most people in today's society are introduced to sex in a way that suggests there is something dirty about it. Some misinterpret Biblical teachings that man is "born in sin" as an indication that the act that produces life is a "sin."

Sin: *A lack of conformity to, or transgression, especially when deliberate, of law, precept or principal regarded as having divine authority. The state of having thus transgressed; wickedness.*

The Divine command is to "be fruitful and multiply." Yet, according to the misunderstanding of sexuality as sinful, sexual intercourse is an act of wickedness. So people learn to view their natural sexual desires as shameful, wicked, and dirty.

This misunderstanding is the beginning of perversion.

Twisted thinking about sexuality often starts in childhood. Parents teach children that their genitals are "nasty." To touch ones genitals is "nasty." To talk about ones genitals is "nasty." Even the words used to describe ones genitals are "nasty" words.

These same "nasty" words that are created to describe ones genitals are also used when discussing the sex act. In fact, various "nasty" words are used to refer to sexual intercourse. Engaging in sex itself is sometimes called "doing the nasty."

Talking about sex is "talking dirty." A joke about sex is a

"dirty joke." Books that describe sexual activities are "dirty books." Movies that show sexually explicit activities are "dirty movies."

Children learn early that sex is somehow connected to the "nasty" parts of their body, and people that engage in sex are "nasty" people. After this negative indoctrination to human sexuality, when children reach puberty and experience the natural emergence of a sex drive, they are somehow supposed to feel free to openly communicate with parents about their "nasty" desires.

Because of the way they have been taught to think, most children are thoroughly disgusted at the realization that their parents had sex.

Parents don't talk about sex with their children because of their own indoctrination that sex is "dirty." They leave it to the school Health and Physical Education teachers to describe the details of "how to." These teachers can only, at best, give a scientific explanation of the function of the sperm and ovaries.

So, to really learn about sexual intimacy, children have private conversations with their friends, where they can "talk dirty" and share information. They get some "dirty books" or sneak a look at a "dirty" movie. Now, with the Internet, they can go to pornographic web sites and see nudity and sex.

They become sexually aroused and want experience.

Children learn to hide their activities from their parents. They know the places to go where they won't get caught. They know whose parents aren't home or aren't paying attention. By the time parents realize their children are experimenting with sex, it's too late. Rarely do parents know how to properly handle their children's sexuality. Either they pretend it doesn't exist, or they buy them condoms and contraceptive pills and say, "Be careful. Use protection."

Unlike the flamingo birds, where lovemaking is a natural part of community life, many human families fail to introduce sex in its proper, wholesome context of marriage and family. Love is excitement, passion, and joy. It is a natural progression in ones development, an event to anticipate, an experience to prepare for.

But, because parents don't have a healthy, wholesome un-derstanding of sex themselves, they let their children learn about sex on the streets, where the words used to describe acts of inti-macy are "dirty words."

Parents who have been raised with ideas of shame associ-ated with sex pass these attitudes on to their children. They want to raise decent, moral children but they just don't know how.

So, like the misguided generation before them, they start by teaching children that there is something shameful about the pri-vate parts of their bodies. This negative indoctrination begins early, as parents teach toddlers the names for their body parts.

Parents need to know how to teach modesty to young chil-dren without making them feel like their genitals are nasty. In her article in the April 2004 edition of *Parenting Magazine* entitled "The Naked Truth: A Stay Cool Guide to Talking About Private Parts, Sex and More," author Diana Burrell explains:

Many of us are more comfortable using slang terms for pe-nises, breasts, vulvas and vaginas, but the American Academy of Pediatrics recommends that parents avoid making up names for body parts. It gives children the idea that there's something bad about their proper names.

In the rush to teach their child the names for their eyes, ears and elbows some parents never seem to get around to teach-ing the names for genitals. One study found that girls under 3 knew the word "penis" better than "vagina" or "vulva." Most of the boys were taught "penis" but were even less likely than the girls to know what to call female genitals.

Even as you're open and honest about the proper names, toddlerhood's the time to set your guidelines for modesty...You could say, "Now that you're a big girl, you should cover up. There are special parts of your body that are not for everyone to see."...

This will help you raise a child who is modest about public nudity but not uncomfortable with her body.

<u>*Parenting Magazine,*</u> *April 2004, Pages 125 & 127*

If children are raised with a wholesome understanding of their body parts and a healthy anticipation of physical intimacy within marriage, sex will not be associated with guilt and shame.

Unmarried Sexual Intimacy: Right or Wrong?

Many people never marry or even plan to marry, but they still want to experience the pleasure of sexual intimacy without being considered "sinful." But religious teachings that imply sex outside of marriage is "sinful" make it difficult for them to be religious and sexual. So, they simply abandon religion altogether and approach sex without any concept of it as a spiritual act.

Some people express desires for sexual intimacy with members of their same sex. They want society to accept their sexuality as natural. They don't want shame attached to their sexual behavior. They, too, decide to disconnect themselves from religious teachings in order to experience sexual intimacy without society's condemnation.

Without guidelines from some type of spiritual law, how can one determine under what circumstances, if any, sexual expression is wrong?

Religious leaders are not necessarily accepted as authorities on such personal matters. Across the world, people have become highly skeptical of religion. The world's major religions are based on the faith that their teachings were inspired by God or were even direct revelations from God. However, many religious leaders today are seen as representing their own personal political and economic interests rather than providing spiritual direction. And some adults have simply decided to rebel against concepts with which they disagree. Some believe that religious teachings are based more on cultural traditions than spiritual guidance.

Even people who claim to follow an organized religion rarely follow the teachings of their religion as a guide for making daily decisions. When it comes to seeking answers to complex questions regarding sexual behavior, many prefer instead to follow the latest scientific studies, believing modern science to be a more reliable source of understanding than religious traditions.

Science, unlike religion, does not require faith. It is observable and measurable. Science is mathematical calculations, statistics, facts and figures. It is a simple law of cause and effect. Scientifically, one can observe this law of cause and effect in perpetual operation throughout the earth.

This same law is also the law of nature. Those who have difficulty determining what is correct and what is incorrect need only to study animals. Most animal species are highly organized, and unless their habitat is negatively affected by human interference, they survive by living in accordance with the laws of nature.

"There is not an animal that crawls in the earth, nor a bird that flies on its two wings, but they are communities like you. We have left out nothing in the Book. Then to their Lord shall they all be gathered together."

The Holy Quran, Chapter 6, Al-An'am, Verse 39

Animals are living souls, just like human beings. They form families and communities just like people do, for the purpose of protecting and raising their children. They instinctively strive to remain alive and healthy.

The laws of nature that guide animals' instincts are the same as the spiritual laws imparted to humanity through Divine revelation. To determine whether an action is in accordance with Divine law, the rule is simple: That which promotes health and life is correct; that which causes illness and death is incorrect. The earth is designed to perpetuate life. However, even the best medicine, if misused, becomes poison. Things that are meant for health and life, if misused, will cause illness and death.

Love: The Highest Spiritual Quality

The act that consummates the relationship between a male and female is an expression of love, hence the term, "Lovemaking." Love is the highest spiritual quality. It has the power to heal the body and the soul. Love grows the more it is shared with others. It creates unselfishness, compassion, consideration, kindness and generosity. It brings peace of mind.

Before a husband and wife initiate sexual intimacy, they, like the flamingo birds, must engage in some sort of courtship display. This may take the form of soft, loving words, compliments, and gifts.

The physical expression of love is a sensuous act, and couples prepare for a pleasant sensual experience by bathing and using perfumes or oils to create a pleasant body scent, beautifying themselves and making themselves attractive to look at, dancing together to excite each other, eating pleasant tasting food and even creating a peaceful, pleasant atmosphere by playing soft music.

The bonding process begins with these courtship "rituals." They serve to stimulate sexual excitement as well as build a bond between the man and woman. The two are about to engage in an act that requires complete trust.

The man and woman are trusting each other with the most intimate parts of themselves. They must feel that what they are sharing is valued by the other. The courtship rituals are a way of affirming to each other "You are important to me. "

"And consort with them in kindness. "
<u>Holy Quran</u>, *Chapter4, Al Nisa, Verse 20*

The gentle touches and caresses that precede intercourse evoke feelings of kindness for each other. The process of love-making actually enhances spiritual qualities in the man and woman. Although men are generally sexually aroused at a faster rate than women, because of a woman's sensitivity, a man must exercise gentleness and patience. He becomes compassionate and unselfish in an effort to give pleasure to the woman. The nature of a woman is to be giving, sharing and loving. When she is touched with gentleness and kindness, these qualities are enhanced.

The bonding of a man and woman, when it is correct, is in harmony with nature. The earth is a living entity, revolving in a rhythmic motion like a pulsating heartbeat. In a burst of energy, new life explodes, like the explosion of the universe into billions of stars and planets. The man shares his essence with the woman, and a part of him will always be with her. He also absorbs some of her essence and a part of her will always be with him. They have bonded together not only psychologically, but also biochemically.

Women have often been compared to the earth, as in the term "Mother Earth." The earth gives that which sustains all life, just as a mother's milk sustains the life of her infant.

"Your wives are a sort of tilth for you, so approach your tilth when and as you like, and send ahead some good for yourselves; and fear Allah and know that you shall meet Him, and bear good tidings to those who believe."
<u>Holy Quran</u>, *Chapter 2, Al Baqara, Verse 224*

This verse actually explains the science of sexual intimacy.
Your wives are a sort of tilth for you. A "tilth," as in soil that must be tilled or cultivated before it can grow crops. Just as a farmer that tills the soil is enhancing the soil's ability to produce, with this act of intimacy, a husband is enhancing the rich potential of his wife. Like a pollinated flower, she blossoms. Her feminine qualities are heightened. Her voice becomes softer, almost musical. She moves with an extra gracefulness. Her disposition is pleasant and peaceful.

So approach your tilth when and as you like. Because human beings have the ability to feed their children all year round, they don't have to plan pregnancies in accordance with any particular' season. It becomes a matter of common sense as to when a couple is ready to conceive and care for a child.

As you like. Couples are free to explore the various creative expressions of love. Sensitive nerve endings throughout the entire body give men and women the capacity to experience intense pleasure. Sexual gratification releases endorphins into the bloodstream, producing a peaceful, calming effect and enhancing the body's immune system.

And send ahead some good for yourselves. Like seeds planted in the earth, the fluids released by the man are the seeds of his progeny. Just as the farmer's future depends on the harvest, a family's future depends on the children. In fact, the whole world's future depends on the children, because every soul that is born, and every good act to be performed by that soul depends on the seeds planted in the womb of a woman.

And fear Allah and know that you shall meet Him. Men and women are warned that they will meet their Creator in the Hereafter, and will be held accountable by God for how they treated each other in the discharging of this important task of sowing the seeds of life.

And bear good tidings to those who believe. Good tidings, as in good news. The good news is, for those who follow spiritual laws, sexual intimacy is a great reward for men and women. It produces health and creates life.

Among animals, males and females are driven to do one thing - to continue their existence. This means that that they must strive to stay alive and healthy for as long as possible, find a mate, procreate, and train their children to stay alive and healthy for as long as possible. Anything that contradicts this basic goal goes against the laws of nature.

Females of every species have been given the task of ensuring the survival of the species. The natural female instinct is to select a male whose genetic traits reflect health and strength, to ensure the health and strength of their own offspring. And depending upon the needs of the mothers before and after childbirth, they must select a male who is skilled in his role as protector or provider if this is necessary for the survival of the children.

Males of every species produce the seeds of life. The natural male instinct is to fight to preserve his own life, to find a mate and procreate, in order to continue his existence.

So what went wrong in the development of human beings that the males and females engage in sex, then destroy each other and their children?

Women give birth to the children. From the very beginning, they are specially equipped to teach values, shape behavior, and provide that essential element that is necessary for the moral and spiritual development of the child: love. If women are in fact the "tilth" or the soil that must be cultivated in order to raise good crops, i.e. children, then the children's condition is a reflection of the care and cultivation given to the soil. If the soil is neglected, abused, or poisoned, the crops that grow will be underdeveloped, sickly, or no good.

Human beings need love. Just as air, water, and food are physical needs, love is a spiritual need. And just as deprivation of air, water or food creates physical illnesses, deprivation of love creates spiritual illnesses.

The inability to show love for others is a spiritual illness. The desire to hurt others is a spiritual illness. People who commit acts of selfishness, cruelty and violence are suffering from a spiritual illness that developed sometime in their lives when they were deprived of love.

If women learn how to use the power that they have, the power of love, they can literally transform humanity.

The women of this generation have a tremendous opportunity to create a peaceful society. They only need to do one thing: Raise a better human being.

A sick society is a reflection of the state of the women. A society that abuses women destroys its future – because women give birth to the children.

The act of love that binds a male and female together is a healing act for the body and the mind, if it is done with the proper intention, under the appropriate circumstances. If not, it becomes a destructive force, producing emotional pain, physical illness, and even death.

In cultures where sexuality is approached in a wholesome manner, men and women reflect harmony and balance in their relationships and in the raising of their children. In cultures where sex is used as a tool of domination, repression, manipulation or degradation, the natural capacity for women to love and nurture their children is damaged. Poisoned soil cannot yield a good crop.

Look at the nations of the world. Those places where extreme violence and cruelty are widespread are the places where women are abused as an accepted part of the culture. Those places where people generally live in harmony are places where women are treated with respect and kindness.

When men and women understand that the sex act is a spiritual act, they approach it with reverence for the female and the profound task she must perform in the creation of life. Children who are born into such a societies reflect in their own behavior the spiritual qualities of compassion and respect for the lives of others. In his book *The Soul Of The Indian*, Charles Alexander Eastman (Ohiyesa), a mixed-blood Native American from the Sioux nation, described how, in his culture, spirituality was imparted into the child before birth.

The Indian was a religious man from his mother's womb. From the moment of her recognition of the fact of conception to the end of the second year of life, which was the ordinary duration of lactation, it was supposed by us that the mother's spiritual influence counted for most. Her attitude and secret meditations must be such as to instill into the receptive soul of the unborn child the love of the "Great Mystery" and a sense of brotherhood with all creation...

And when the day of days in her life dawns—the day in which there is to be a new life, the miracle of whose making has been entrusted to her, she seeks no human aid. She has been trained and prepared in body and mind for this her holiest duty, every since she can remember.

She meets the ordeal of childbirth alone, where no curious or pitying eyes might embarrass her; where all nature says to her spirit: "It is love! It is love! The fulfilling of life!"

When, at last, a sacred voice comes to her out of the silence, and a pair of eyes open upon her in the wilderness, she knows with joy that she has borne well her part in the great song of creation!

<u>The Soul of the Indian</u>, *pages 28, 29 and 30.*

A woman who has ambivalent or hostile feelings toward the child she is carrying because she did not intend to get pregnant in the first place, will be unable to transmit positive feelings of love to the soul of her unborn child. A child who feels rejection from the mother is already spiritually wounded before birth.

We Are All Connected

We are all connected. This is the first lesson we should learn as children. It is an unchanging law of nature, and it defines our ultimate destiny. The sacredness of creation can only be understood if one understands that ones own life is part of a greater interdependent system.

Living beings must procreate in order to maintain the earth's life cycle. Everything within the earth's atmosphere is a part of an ongoing recycling system. There can never be a food shortage, because plants and animals are all made up of the earth's matter, just rearranged and recycled. Life and death coexist, because the death of one entity facilitates the life of another.

"When we die, we become grass and the antelope eat the grass. Look around you. Everything, from the crawling ant to the leaping antelope, all are a part of a delicate balance... We are all a part of the great circle of life."
Mufasa, The Lion King, *Walt Disney Pictures*

We are biologically connected to the earth and to each other. We inhale oxygen and exhale carbon dioxide. Plants absorb carbon dioxide and release oxygen. Earth's atmosphere is 21% oxygen. Any serious reduction in plant life would eventually diminish animal and human life. Similarly, any serious reduction in animal life would cause plant life to suffer from the lack of carbon dioxide. In his book *Planet Earth*, author Jonathan Weiner observes the delicate balance created by the interdependence of plant and animal life:

With no oxygen, for instance, there would be no respira-
tion. With just a little more oxygen, on the other hand – even 25
percent instead of 21 – the whole living world would burst sponta-
neously into flames. Earth's air holds just the optimum amount.
Similarly, without carbon dioxide, photosynthesis would fail,
plants would die and life would vanish from the earth. With more
carbon dioxide, however, so much heat would be trapped in the air
and sea by the greenhouse effect that the planet would descend
into hell.

By consuming and inhaling these gases, the animal, plant
and microscopic kingdoms help to keep them in equilibrium. The
biosphere also produces many millions of tons a year of methane
and nitrous oxide. These gases combine quickly with oxygen and
thus keep its level from climbing. Thus, even termite mounds,
stagnant swamps and ruminating cows may help to keep the planet
alive.

Planet Earth, by Jonathan Weiner, page 327

The human body is, by weight, 70 percent water, and each of us consumes about five pounds of water daily, in one form or another. Similarly, the earth's surface is about 70 percent water. However, most of the water on the planet is in the form of salt water from the oceans. Humans and animals consume fresh water, which is only 3 percent of the earth's global supply. The sun evaporates a trillion tons of water each day. It is stored in the clouds, and released as fresh water in the form of rain, sleet and snow. Some of this water is soaked up and stored in the leaves and roots of plants, and some gathers in lakes, ponds, streams and rivers, where animals and humans can consume it. The water eventually flows back into the ocean, and the whole cycle begins again.

Water is the element that cleanses and purifies all things, from the earth's surface to the skin's surface, from the food we wash with water and eat, to the impurities in our bodies we cleanse away with water we drink.

Just as human beings need the earth's elements for continuous biological rejuvenation, they also need elements from each other for continuous biological rejuvenation. We are chemical beings. Scientists have discovered that human beings are drawn to each other based on body chemistry.

Recent studies have revealed that the sense of smell is connected to the body's immune system. Each person has a personal scent. Males and females are attracted to each other's scents, and studies show that men and women are attracted to members of the opposite sex whose immunities are different from their own. Apparently, nature has designed this natural attraction so that the offspring between the two people would have the combined immunities of both parents, thereby expanding the immune system of the next generation.

The Importance of Positive Imprinting

Sexual reproduction is a delicate affair. If the psyche has been damaged, the person may not be able to perform this process properly.

Scientists have observed that when a baby duck hatches from its egg, it attaches itself to the first being it sees, usually its mother, in a process called "imprinting." It is as if the mother has stamped her own imprint on her child, and it will follow her and imitate her from then on. Interestingly, even if something other than the duckling's mother – a dog, a chicken, or even a human being – were to hatch the egg, the imprinting process would still occur. The duckling would waddle around, trying to follow the dog, the chicken or the human being.

In many ways, the same thing happens with human sexual development. The first experience leaves an imprint, shaping future attitudes and behaviors. When ones first sexual experience is with ones own spouse, if it is a pleasant encounter, it serves to create a lasting bond between the two people.

In ancient Mayan culture, steps were taken to insure that a young couple's wedding night was successful in order that the marriage would be built on a harmonious foundation. Two elderly women locked themselves in the room with the newlywed couple and step by step instructed them in the arts of sexual intimacy. The result was that both the husband and the wife had an enjoyable first experience. As embarrassing as this method may have been, history records that the Mayans had very few divorces.

One is most easily permanently attached to ones "first love." It is like sticking a piece of tape to a surface. It will stay stuck unless you pull up the tape to stick it to another surface. Then the tape does not stick as well as it did the first time. There are usually still pieces of the first surface stuck to the tape, making it difficult for the tape to stick properly the second time. Similarly, when you detach from your first love, it may be more difficult to reattach to someone else. The new bond may not be as strong because of emotional remnants from the previous relationship.

By nature's design, the sex act prepares the body and mind for a permanent union with another being. When men and women choose to become sexually intimate on the grounds of superficial physical attraction, the results are often disastrous for both of them. In the rush to experience sexual fulfillment, men and women become physically involved, then later find themselves emotionally attached yet hopelessly incompatible.

In an article published in *Psychology Today* magazine entitled "The Damaging Relationship: Getting Unstuck," author Hara Marano points out that the bond created by sexual intimacy can blind women to obvious signs of incompatibility. She states that in many of the letters she receives from readers, women say they are in love, but are miserable and depressed. She observes:

Most have fallen into relationships with men who are egregiously unsuitable partners. Not men who changed and became difficult, but men whose behavior from the beginning was a blinking neon sign warning Bad Mate Material. These men had had affairs, sometimes with other men; they were drinkers or drug users; they had personality problems; they lied about themselves; they couldn't hold a job. That kind of thing. Serious stuff...

And often enough, no matter how loutish or just plain inappropriate the partner, leaving isn't an easy option. Sometimes they're still struggling to make the guy pay attention to them. Or they don't have the financial independence to break away. Or there are children they need help with. Or the depression is so severe they can't see out...

A good friend of mine, a well-known mental health profes-sional, a social and political liberal, voiced an observation to me that makes her sound, to an outsider, like a screaming put-the-genie-back-in-the-bottle conservative. No, she wouldn't reverse the sexual revolution. But she did confide that she wished women wouldn't jump into bed too fast.

My friend wasn't spouting politics. She was talking biology. Biochemistry inclines women to emotionally bond to the men they have sex with. In other words, women often get attached before their cognitive machinery is up and running at full throttle.

By Hara Marano, <u>Psychology Today</u>, May 21, 2003

Incest: A Natural Taboo

The drive to procreate coincides with the body's maturation process. Children of 11 and 12 years old suddenly become acutely aware of their own sexuality and often desire to explore the bodies of the opposite sex. Yet humans, like many animals, have a built in aversion to incestuous relationships. It is known to be biologi-cally unhealthy. While siblings may have the physical capacity for sexual intimacy with each other, any offspring they produced would likely be sickly or malformed. In ancient times, when "royal" families practiced inbreeding as a way to keep power within the family, children from such unions were often born with physical deformities.

Most human communities today have natural taboos against incest. Even within the animal kingdom, most animal communities follow patterns of behavior that prevent inbreeding. When animals reach adulthood, they only seek out other adults and do not try to mate with children. In species where this produces unhealthy offspring, brothers and sisters do not mate with each other. They instinctively form relationships outside of the family.

What animals follow instinctively in accordance with the laws of nature, human beings have had to be taught. Scriptures from the various religions reiterate the idea that mankind has a direct connection with the Creator of the universe. The instructions on how human beings should behave are relayed through an individual, identified in most cultures as a prophet, spiritual teacher, or messenger. These teachings, when not corrupted by the politics of the time, are always in accordance with nature's laws, laws that are designed to enhance health and produce life.

Humans, like other animals, are sensual beings. We are guided by the senses of hearing, smell, sight, touch and taste. The human body's nerve endings are located on the surface of the skin, making the skin the most sensitive part of the body. The sensual pleasure that comes from being touched can have a soothing, healing effect. It can also have a sexually arousing effect.

The sight of an unclothed body also can trigger sexual arousal. Psychological studies have shown that both males and females are aroused at the sight of a naked female body. A naked male body may elicit interest from females, but for greater arousal in females the other senses are required – touch, hearing and smell.

Sexual arousal is easily activated, therefore human beings, like animals, must follow nature's guidelines when it comes to preventing inappropriate sexual contact between individuals. The problem for humans is that they cannot agree on what is inappropriate sexual contact.

In the Bible, the 18th Chapter of Leviticus spells out the prohibited sexual relationships. The chapter quotes God as commanding Moses to instruct the children of Israel to follow these specific guidelines:

"None of you shall approach to any that is near of kin to him, to uncover their nakedness: I am the Lord. The nakedness of thy father, or the nakedness of thy mother shalt thou not uncover: she is thy mother; thou shalt not uncover her nakedness.

The nakedness of thy father's wife shalt thou not uncover: it is thy father's nakedness. The nakedness of thy sister, the daughter of thy father, or daughter of thy mother, whether she be born at home, or born abroad, even their nakedness thou shalt not uncover.

"The nakedness of thy son's daughter, or of thy daughter's daughter, even their nakedness thou shalt not uncover: for theirs is thine own nakedness. The nakedness of thy father's wife's daughter, begotten of thy father, she is thy sister, thou shalt not uncover her nakedness. Thou shalt not uncover the nakedness of thy father's sister: she is thy father's near kinswoman. Thou shalt not uncover the nakedness of thy mother's sister: for she is thy mother's near kinswoman.

"Thou shalt not uncover the nakedness of thy father's brother, thou shalt not approach to his wife: she is thine aunt. Thou shalt not uncover the nakedness of thy daughter in law: she is thy son's wife; thou shalt not uncover her nakedness. Thou shalt not uncover the nakedness of thy brother's wife: it is thy brother's nakedness.

"Thou shalt not uncover the nakedness of a woman and her daughter, neither shalt thou take her son's daughter or her daughter's daughter, to uncover her nakedness; for they are her near kinswomen: it is wickedness. Neither shalt thou take a wife to her sister, to vex her, to uncover her nakedness, beside the other in her life time."

Leviticus 18: 6-18.

These regulations served several purposes: they established the appropriate level of respect for personal privacy; they disallowed sexual intimacy between close family members – fathers, mothers, sisters, brothers, aunts, and uncles; and they also prohibited sexual molestation of children, which would include sons and daughters as well as nieces and nephews.

The Physical Effects of Homosexuality

Regarding other kinds of sexual relationships, the command continues:

*"Thou shalt not lie with mankind, as with womankind: it is
abomination. Neither shalt thou lie with any beast to defile thyself
therewith: neither shall any woman stand before a beast to lie
down thereto: it is confusion.*

Leviticus 18:22-23

Every species is created in pairs that chemically complement each other. The exchange of body fluids between a male and
female during sexual intercourse creates a change in body chemistry that enhances health, strengthens the immune system, and provides natural opiates that generate feelings of peace and well being. This exchange of fluids enhances the masculinity of the male
and the femininity of the female, and increases their desire for each
other. In his book *Thus Speaks Zarathustra*, Dr. Behrooz Bassim,
MD, explains how biochemical changes affect behavior:

*The difference between masculine and feminine behaviors
is due to the chemical differences in men and women. That is, homosexuality is a behavior dictated in part by one's hormonal complex. These are partly genetic and partly acquired.*

*One's mix of natural hormones and enzymes drive one's
behavior as do alcohol and the street drugs. This is so because behavior is a chemical reaction. In fact, an electro-chemical reaction. One neuron drops some molecules on another causing a response (chemical reaction) which travels along its axon (electrical
reaction) to activate a cell or another neuron.*

*Even one's "free will" can easily change by changing one's
body chemistry as one would behave differently under the influence of alcohol or a different set of hormones, enzymes, and other
consumed chemicals...homosexuality is not a disease but a variant
of biochemistry in one's blood resulted from one or more causes:
genetic variance, mind/body connection, cultural gender-typing,
induced biochemical changes, etc.*

Article from <u>*Thus Speaks Zathustra*</u>*, dated October 9, 2000
Copyright 2000 by Behrooz Bassim, MD*

Homosexual contact involving an exchange of body fluids is an induced biochemical change. Like heterosexual contact, this also influences behavior.

When a male absorbs body fluids from another male during a sex act, his body chemistry is altered to make him more like a female. He will exhibit female traits and mannerisms and will develop an increased sexual desire for males.

Similarly, when a female absorbs fluids from another female during a sex act, her body chemistry is altered to make her more like a male. She will exhibit male traits and mannerisms and will develop an increased sexual desire for females.

The rapid spread of Acquired Immune Deficiency Syndrome (AIDS) among males that engage in sex with other males demonstrates that people of the same sex do not have complementary body chemistry. Rather than strengthening the immune system, sexual relations between people of the same sex does not enhance health, but can actually lead to sickness and death.

Syphilis, a venereal disease that can lead to blindness, strokes, and heart attacks, was caused by human sexual intercourse with sheep. The book of Leviticus warned against human sexual contact with animals. One need not adhere to any particular religion to understand nature's basic law: that which is correct enhances health and life; that which is incorrect causes sickness and death.

One of the most controversial arguments today involves the development of sexual identity and sexual orientation. Many who practice homosexuality vehemently insist that they were born that way. Some research suggests that genetic factors may influence sexual identity. However, the idea that homosexuality is a genetic trait presents a contradiction, as Dr. Behrooz Bassim observes:

If homosexuality was purely innate or genetic, it would not have become prevalent, and this due to homosexuals' failure to reproduce. Its genetic code should become extinct every time it would appear.

One might argue that homosexuality did not become extinct because its taboo forced the homosexuals to get married, not counting those who took refuge in religion as priests, nuns, or monks. However, now after two generations of openness, there should have been a gradual reduction in their numbers with each succeeding generation...

Sexual drive is largely due to testosterone in both sexes. Yet, men's sexual drive is stronger because they have more of it. The sexual attraction is due to a combination of hormones and environmental influences.

Certain normal hormones may be inadequate or excessive. The ratio between male and female hormones in a person may be disproportionate. Or, a hormone may be defective.

Article from <u>Thus Speaks Zathustra</u>, dated October 9, 2000
Copyright 2000 by Behrooz Bassim, MD

Some state that they have always felt as though they were born in the wrong body. Many women express the feelings that they always wanted to be boys rather than girls when they were growing up, and many men reveal that as children, they identified more with the girls than the boys.

During her appearance on the Oprah Winfrey show, clinical psychotherapist Jana Ekdahl explained why a five-year-old boy on the show named Dylan might have been insisting that he really is a girl. She stated that sexual identity actually develops during pregnancy:

"It does occur in the womb. The research so far shows that it occurs in the first trimester. Something happens, whereas the brain develops in one direction and the body develops in another. For instance, for Dylan, it might be that his body was developing as a boy, whereas his brain was developing as a girl. Then he comes out, and he looks like a boy."

Jana Ekdahl, <u>The Oprah Winfrey Show</u>, May 12, 2004

Even with modern ultrasound technology and knowledge of prenatal care, in many ways the development of a child within the womb is still a mystery. Nature has its own way of removing its mistakes, such as the spontaneous miscarriage of a malformed fetus. However, when children are born with contradicting traits, such as the case of hermaphrodites who have both male and female genitals, society must respond with compassion. These are individuals who must figure out a complicated dilemma. How does one decide how to function sexually when one does not have a clear sexual identity? In many such situations, the decision to adopt a male or female identity cannot be made until after puberty.

In the case of the "transgendered" – those whose brains may have developed a different sexual identity than the body - medical professionals are still not certain whether the answer is a sex change operation or psychotherapy.

As for those who believe that they were born homosexual, and cannot function in a heterosexual capacity, they too face a serious dilemma. The purpose for each living being is to live, grow, and reproduce. Two males cannot reproduce, nor can two females. Those who do not reproduce have in fact terminated their own genetic line, unless they choose to engage in a heterosexual relationship just to produce children.

Simply dismissing homosexuals as "sinful" does not allow society to explore and understand biochemical factors or even societal factors that influence the shaping of sexual identity.

Religious teachings that condemn all sexual activities as "sinful" create confusion in the minds of children. The recent exposure of widespread sexual molestation of children in the Catholic church raises the question: if we teach our children that heterosexual intimacy, even between husbands and wives, is sinful, can an adult pedophile take advantage of our children by telling them that homosexual intimacy isn't really sex, and therefore isn't sinful? Parents must explain sexuality properly, so that children know what is appropriate and inappropriate contact.

John J. Dreese, a Catholic Priest in Columbus, Ohio, states that he feels a deep sense of shame because of what priests have done to children. In the book *At Issue*, in the chapter entitled "Priest Child Molesters Disgrace The Catholic Priesthood," he writes:

Now we find among us a growing number of priests who have betrayed the confidence and trust that other priests have won for them. They have misused their positions of respect to defile, abuse and steal the innocence of children and young people...

Mixed with the feelings of shame and embarrassment there is great anger. I am angry at the priest-pederasts and abusers. Why did they do what they did? They knew the meaning of celibacy, of chastity, of continence. They knew the importance of innocence in the young and the scars of scandal to the community. Ignorance is not an alibi if they attended any kind of theological school. And they all did!

If they knew what they were doing but could not control a compulsion to act out, they were clearly sick. At this point they had two choices: to get professional help or to get out of the priesthood. Professional help would have avoided further pain for all who eventually became involved. Getting out of the priesthood would have taken away the possibility of scandal to the church. But it appears that the priest-offenders were not thinking of anyone but themselves.

<u>At Issue</u> *"Priest Child Molesters Disgrace*
Catholic Priesthood," page 69

Often, when a child's introduction to sex is through a homosexual experience, this becomes the imprint that shapes future behavior. It sets in motion a change in body chemistry that increases desire for sexual intimacy with a person of the same sex.

When a child's introduction to sex is through a negative heterosexual experience, this also becomes the imprint that influences future behavior. Sometimes a child's ability to bond intimately with the opposite sex has been destroyed because of an early negative sexual experience, such as rape or molestation.

Adult survivors of childhood sexual abuse tend to experience profound psychological trauma, manifested in any number of problems: alcoholism, drug addiction, promiscuity, depression shame, guilt, embarrassment, thoughts of suicide, and inability to form intimate relationships with the opposite sex.

Physical Love, Physical Health

When adults are confused in their thinking about sex, they pervert the natural development of children. Children need physical affection in order to develop the capacity to express physical affection. As children grow into adolescence, this expression of physical affection naturally develops into a desire for sexual intimacy. This desire, rather than being condemned or exploited, should be guided toward a wholesome anticipation of a very special, exclusive relationship. When sexual intimacy is presented as a natural consequence of reaching adulthood, finding a mate and getting married, there is no shame, guilt or disgust attached to it.

Parents are responsible for protecting the delicate psyche of a child from an improper introduction to sexuality. They are responsible for making sure a child knows that ones private parts are not to be touched by other people. Parents are responsible for introducing a wholesome, age appropriate understanding of the intimate relationship shared by husbands and wives.

Men and women need love from each other to enhance their physical health and emotional well being. They need love from each other in order to have inner peace and tranquility. Love stimulates the body's natural opiates. Life is stressful, and without love's soothing effect, the body develops stress related illnesses that can lead to sickness and early death. Studies show that married men live longer, healthier lives than single men, and married women experience less stress related illnesses than single women.

People overindulge in physical pleasures to compensate for the lack of love. Such artificially induced pleasure tends to destroy ones health. Overindulgence in drugs causes physical and psychological addiction and impairs judgment, often motivating the drug user to commit theft to obtain money to buy drugs. Overindulgence in alcohol creates drunkenness, cirrhosis of the liver and loss of brain cells. Overindulgence in food leads to obesity, which leads to other illnesses such as heart attacks, high blood pressure, diabetes, and strokes. Overindulgence in sex with different partners leads to sexually transmitted diseases, some of which can be fatal.

Overindulgence in drugs, alcohol, food and sex are all symptoms of the same emotional deficiency caused by the deprivation of love.

People who are depressed from loneliness and a lack of companionship experience more physical illnesses. Do you find yourself overindulging drugs, alcohol, food or sex as a means to combat stress and depression? Have you turned to drugs, food, alcohol, or sex as a means of comfort after a broken relationship?

In addition to a rise in drug abuse, alcoholism, and sexual promiscuity, health care professionals have noted a dangerous rise in obesity. Food is a common source of comfort for many who are deprived of loving relationships. When intimate relationships fall apart, men and women turn to food to overcome loneliness. Despite widely available information on proper nutrition and healthy eating habits, obesity continues to increase, particularly among women. Sadness and depression often causes people to eat while watching television, listening to music or other sedentary activities. This increases the likelihood that ongoing overindulgence in food will lead to excessive weight gain.

Studies show that when people are "in love" they experience improved physical health. They feel periodic euphoria, they have increased energy, they laugh more. Laughter itself is a natural healer, producing chemicals that strengthen the body's immune system. People need love to stay healthy.

The physical expression of love between a husband and wife is a spiritual act that binds them to each other and to their Creator, Who, through them, brings forth new life. Love is a gift that should be shared between two people who are united in spirit. It is a Divine command. It is positive energy, the natural healer for sadness and distress. It is an enchanting experience that joins two souls. Love should be celebrated with happiness and delight.

So, like the flamingo birds, freely express love with your mate. Sing! Dance! Enjoy!

Approaching Intimacy With A Wholesome Attitude

In healthy families, children learn about intimacy in a way that is connected to positive cultural values of marriage and family. Parents who don't know how to approach discussions of sexual intimacy in a way that is wholesome are uncomfortable about discussing sex with children. They often prefer to leave this important task to school teachers.

When children are introduced to sexual intimacy at an improper age or in an inappropriate manner, they may have difficulties establishing healthy relationships in adulthood.

Please review the following questions and select the answer that best reflects your own beliefs and personal experiences, then read the analysis.

1. How old were you when you learned the details about sexual intimacy?

___a) I never have
___b) 2-4 years old
___c) 5-7 years old
___d) 8-10 years old
___e) 11-13 years old
___f) 14-16 years old
___g) 17-18 years old
___h) Over 18 years old

2. Where did you first see the complete anatomy of a member of the opposite sex?

___a) I never have
___b) In a textbook
___c) In a pornographic magazine
___d) In a movie or video
___e) On the Internet
___f) In person – someone in my family
___g) In person – someone not in my family

3. Who first explained sexual intercourse to you?

___a) No one ever did

___b) My mother or female guardian

___c) My father or male guardian

___d) My Biology/Health/Phys. Ed. Teacher

___e) An older adult friend or relative

___f) A religious leader or teacher

___g) A doctor

___h) A friend or relative near my age

4. Who do you talk to when you have questions about sex?

___a) No one

___b) My mother or female guardian

___c) My father or male guardian

___d) My Biology/Health/Phys. Ed. Teacher

___e) An older adult friend or relative

___f) A religious leader or teacher

___g) A doctor

___h) A friend or relative near my age

5. When should a woman become sexually active?

___a) When she is married

___b) When she is mature

___c) When she is truly in love

___d) When she uses some protection

___e) When she has finished high school

___f) When she has a job and her own apartment

6. When should a man become sexually active?

___a) When he is married

___b) When he is mature

___c) When he is truly in love

___d) When he uses some protection

___e) When he has finished high school

___f) When he has a job and his own apartment

Analysis:

At what age are children old enough to learn about sex and reproduction? When they are old enough to ask. Use simple language, do not imply that it is anything dirty or disgusting, but do emphasize that it is a private act between two married people. Failure to put sex in the proper cultural context of marriage makes children vulnerable for exploitation or molestation by older children or adults.

Don't make your child wait until a Junior High School biology teacher explains the facts of life. Parents should explain basic body functions to a child at a pre-school age, when the parent is still helping the child bathe.

Sexuality should be explained to children in a way that is age appropriate and does not generate fear or disgust. Do not expose small children to pornographic images or sexually explicit language in music or literature. This will impede the development of a wholesome attitude when the child reaches puberty.

Do not respond with shock, anger, or disgust when children ask questions or even express opinions about sexuality. Listen patiently, provide correct information and never make your children feel ashamed of their feelings or curiosity. They must be able to talk to you, otherwise they will turn to someone else who may not have their best interest at heart.

Be clear about when sexual intimacy is appropriate, in order to give clear guidance to children. When parents are vague or inconsistent, they cannot prevent children from making bad decisions. Parents need to teach the same high moral standards for male children that they teach for female children. Both boys and girls should be instilled with a healthy respect for intimacy. They should not use vulgar or degrading terms to refer to themselves, their anatomy or each other.

Good marital relationships begin with proper attitudes towards intimacy. As adults, we have to analyze the influences in our own lives. Our own experiences may have been inappropriate. Sometimes it is necessary for us to erase negative memories in order to enjoy a sacred union with another human being.

Chapter 2
Social Order in the Wolf Pack
Teach Children Respect for Elders

The bright full moon slowly peeked out from behind wispy white clouds as they floated across the midnight sky.   A shining white light illuminated the rocky hills below like a midnight sun, where a large four-footed figure emerged from the shadows and stealthily climbed to the top of a hill.   He stood still for a moment as a brisk wind rippled through his silvery fur. Slowly he pointed his long gray nose toward the sky. A slight mist appeared as his hot breath hit the cold air.

"Owooooooh! Owoooooh! Wooh wooh woooooh!" The howl of the wolf echoed throughout the valley. In answer to his call, gleaming eyes emerge from the darkness of the caverns inside the hills where the eleven members of his pack made their homes.

One by one, the wolves approach their leader, displaying the appropriate posture of respect - head tucked down, ears drawn back, tail hanging low – and extend the proper greeting, licks on the side of the face. The leader stands erect as each member of the pack steps forth to greet him.   A mother and her four large cubs leave their den and climb the rocky moonlit hill. The cubs stand back to observe from a respectful distance. After the rest of the adults have exchanged greetings, the cubs too approach the leader, heads down, ears back and tails tucked underneath as a sign of submission.

It is the wolf pack's nightly ritual before the hunt. Members of the pack greet each other with a series of sniffs and licks. They point long gray noses toward the sky and begin a chorus of howls, until finally it is time to go forth into the night. The wolves set out together to track down their prey – perhaps an aged or wounded antelope, or an inexperienced buffalo calf. They would encircle their victim and bring it down, working together to kill an animal large enough to feed the entire pack.

The wolf pack demonstrates an important principle in the wild: the family that preys together stays together. Animals that depend on each other in order to obtain food must develop the skills of co-operation. They realize that their collective survival depends on being able to get along without fighting.

Wolves uphold a very distinct social order that is essential to maintaining peace. It is regularly reinforced with ritual behaviors that confirm respect for leadership and acknowledgement of kinship as members of the pack. There is very little infighting in a wolf pack. Once the leader has fought to establish his dominance, the others submit to his authority. Selecting leadership in a wolf pack is not a complicated political decision. It comes down to the biggest, strongest, and most experienced wolf that has the courage to stand up against rival predators and the wisdom to avoid deadly enemies. The leader must be one whose hunting knowledge and skills benefits the group. Cubs learn from observing the adults that as members in a community of wolves, they must show proper respect for their leaders and must always submit to the authority of their elders.

Among human families today, children talk back to their parents, use profanity in the presence of elders, call their school teachers insulting names, and express total disregard for rules of polite social conduct. Some children have lost all respect for parents; the only authorities they recognize are armed police officers that can arrest them, throw them in jail or shoot them to death. The real reason for the rise in crime and violence is not poverty, lack of police protection, violence on TV, or the availability of drugs, but the loss of respect for parents.

When young people respect their parents, that respect is translated to the way they treat other adults. They are polite and well mannered in the presence of elders, because they know that their behavior is a direct reflection on the parents who raised them. When children are raised properly, they respect their own parents too much to bring shame upon their families by committing criminal acts.

> *"It takes a village to raise a child."*
> *Old West African Proverb*

A community is safe when people can trust each other not to commit any actions that cause harm. The reason why it takes a village to raise a child is because in order to learn proper social conduct the children need to observe how adults interact with each other. So what have our children learned from us? How to insult others, steal from others, physically assault others, sexually abuse others, even kill others. Everyone wants to point fingers of blame at someone but the responsibility for the mess we have made is on all of us. We, the adults, are the village that raised these children.

We have the power to change the future by changing the way we raise our children. We can create peace and harmony in the neighborhoods where we live. We can enjoy a society when there is respect for elders and those in authority.

Men and women who wish to transform crime-ridden communities into safe places to live can learn a few lessons by observing the social order in the wolf pack.

Learning the Family Business

A wolf pack is actually a family group, made up of wolves that are connected by kinship – fathers, mothers, sisters, brothers, aunts, uncles – along with a few outsiders to remove the possibility of inbreeding. In the pack there is a dominant male and a dominant female. Scientists who observe animal behavior label them the Alpha male and the Alpha female. This is the only couple that mates and produces offspring. It is the pack's way of making sure only the strongest genes reproduce.

Although the children belong to only one pair of adults, all of the adults help to raise the cubs. When a mother wolf has just given birth, she cannot leave her cubs alone. Her mate brings food back for her from the kill. Weeks later, after the cubs are old enough for her to leave for a few hours, she joins the hunt. Another adult, usually an uncle or an aunt to the cubs, will watch the cubs in her absence. Adult wolves take turns watching the children while the others go on the hunt. The mother and father will carry food in their stomachs back to the den, which they regurgitate for the cubs to eat.

Wolf cubs grow up watching the nightly ritual of the family gathering together for the hunt. They spend time with the adults who watch them while the rest of the pack is away. The adult wolf who baby sits plays with the cubs and watches them play together. He or she keeps a wary eye out and barks out an urgent command for the cubs to return to the den at the first sign of danger. There is a bonding, a sense of family that the cubs experience. They grow up together, play together, fight together and are reprimanded by the adults in the pack when their behavior is incorrect. When they finally get old enough to accompany the family on a hunt, it is a lesson in cooperation. At first they are allowed to come just as observers from a safe distance. They see how the pack works as a team to capture its dinner, so that everyone may eat. Eventually, once the wolf cubs are old enough, they will hunt with the pack. By that time, they have learned that in unity there is strength. They know how to work together for the good of the family.

It's like bringing up children in a family business. First your children see you leaving the house and coming back home with money. Then they come to your shop and watch you handle customers. They watch and observe all aspects of your work. Eventually, they learn how to operate the business, handle the customers, and make money for the family.

Before children can learn how to function in a society, they first must learn how to function in a family. The society is simply a larger extension of the family. Our society is dysfunctional because the families are dysfunctional.

Teaching Disrespect By Example

Children respect adults when they observe adults respecting each other. In the heat of an argument, parents often ridicule and insult each other in the presence of their children. They'll even try to get the children to take sides, engaging in vicious backbiting while their spouse is absent in order to prove to the children that the absent spouse is the one in the wrong.

This is a deadly mistake. When you undermine the authority of an adult, you're teaching your children to disrespect all adults. In a community where all adults are respected as an ingrained part of the culture, you don't hear children saying nasty things to teachers like, "You can't tell me what to do! You're not my mother!"

This attitude is a reflection of what is happening in the home. Often, when parents are in the midst of a conflict leading to divorce, the children hear the most intimate details of the couple's conflict. Charges of incompetence, accusations of infidelity, threats of physical violence – the children hear it all. They are literally destroyed on the inside. In divorce, as in war, both sides are losers. Both parents lose the confidence of their children that they can provide a stable, secure, loving, two-parent family. Both parents lose credibility in the eyes of their children.

When women get divorced and become single parents, they often feel compelled to prove to the children that their father was really no good. This is another deadly mistake. If you divorced a man because he treated you badly, regardless of how no-good the man is, he is still your children's father, the other half of who they are, so therefore they are half of whatever he is. You can't raise children to have healthy self-esteem if you pound the idea into them that their other half is rotten. If their father was that bad, and you chose him to father your children anyway, what does that say about your judgment?

In a wolf pack, every adult member of the pack does not produce children, only the dominant male and female. While human society doesn't practice birth control to this extent, it is a fact that all adults are not ready to be parents. If men and women have children before they have reached a certain level of maturity, they create problems not only for themselves, but also for their families, and ultimately for the society in which they live. Children represent the future of the family, not just the mother, or just the mother and father, but all of the ancestors of the both of them. Children are connected to all of the grandmothers, grandfathers, uncles, aunts, nieces, nephews, cousins and siblings on both sides. When children are raised as part of an extended family, they realize that their actions affect more than just themselves.

"O ye people! Fear your Lord who created you from a single soul and of its kind created its mate, and from them twain spread many men and women; and fear Allah, in Whose name you appeal to one another, and fear him particularly respecting ties of kinship. Verily, Allah watches over you."
<u>The Holy Quran</u> *(Chapter 4, Al Nisa, Verse 2)*

Just as the wolf pack gathers each evening to share in the capture of their daily meal, when human families sit down together at mealtimes, they reinforce the special bond that ties them together. Every family gathering is a reminder to the children that they have a special place in the world, they belong to people who care about them, their lives have a purpose, and the good that they do brings pride to the entire family.

When a family breaks apart, the connections with relatives are often severed. Children experience the pain of divorce when traditional family gatherings no longer include certain relatives. Parents, in their anger and bitterness, may cut all ties with former in-laws. Children are disconnected from aunts, uncles and cousins, the people who helped to give them a sense of belonging to a greater family.

Adult children of divorced parents suffer as well. When divorced parents are hostile towards each other, their adult children often find themselves forced to take sides when it comes to issues such as where to spend holidays and who to invite to family celebrations.

Parenthood is not for the selfish and immature. Men and women must have the capacity to give love, first to each other, then to the children that they reproduce. In a wolf pack, the Alpha male and the Alpha female have demonstrated their skill in providing for the family. They become the core that holds the pack together. Their siblings help to raise the couple's children, reinforcing family ties that keep the children safe.

There is no divorce in the wolf pack. Wolves mate for life. They don't even take on another mate when one mate dies. Among humans, however, although many couples repeat marriage vows that proclaim, "Til death do us part," in American society, 62% of the married couples end up divorced. They rip apart their family ties, leaving children to conclude that marriage is only a temporary living arrangement.

Daily Affection Increases Self Esteem

Children learn how to treat others by experiencing the way parents treat them and observing the way parents treat each other. In a home where parents show a lot of love and affection toward the children and toward each other, children develop a healthy sense of self-esteem and self worth. Just as the wolves in a pack have daily greeting rituals that show respect and affection toward each other, human families must also reinforce their love and respect for each other on a daily basis.

When children are raised in families where physical affection is absent, they are deprived of an element that is essential for their physical and emotional health. All living beings give off rays of energy, imperceptible to the human eye, but felt nevertheless. Some people have called these rays of energy "vibrations" or "vibes."

Recent advances in photography have enabled this energy to be captured on film. It appears as various colored rays of light, called an "aura." When a person is giving off positive energy, the aura is bright. If the mood of the person is negative, creating negative energy, the aura is dim. It has been noted that people who are skilled at growing plants emit a very bright light. Human energy has an effect on plant life. As botanists have observed, plants grow well when they are talked to and cared for lovingly. The same goes for human beings. When human beings are in the same room, they can actually feel each other's energy. If a person wishes you harm, you can feel the negative energy, or "vibes" being emitted. If they wish you well, you can feel their positive vibes.

When people touch each other, they are giving and receiving energy. Living beings have energy receptors that are affected by the presence of others. Just as when you connect battery cables to two car batteries, the positive to the positive and the negative to the negative, the positive charge will transfer energy from one car to the other, giving energy to the car whose battery is low. If you connect the cables the wrong way, attaching the positive to the negative and the negative to the positive, the negative charge will drain the other car battery of all its energy. Living beings affect each other the same way every time they interact.

Touch receptors for humans are mostly in the skin. Scientists have discovered that touch is therapeutic. In one experiment, scientists observed that newborn infants that were massaged three times a day grew at a faster rate than newborn infants that were not massaged at all.

Newborn animals are stimulated by the mother's tongue. It has the same effect as a massage for humans. The mother licks the baby to stimulate blood circulation, which is necessary for brain activity, breathing, and a strong heart beat. Newborn baby animals left alone for a long period of time soon die.

Babies need love. They need love like they need air, water, and food. They need a loving touch and a soothing voice. They need the positive vibrations of people who want the best for them.

Giving your children things is not the same as giving them love. Buying your children lots of toys, games and clothes, then showering them with verbal abuse is not love. Giving them excessive amounts of money to spend, but having no time to spend with them is not love.

Love is personal contact, verbal and physical, reassuring them that their lives are important to you. When parents lament that they gave their children "everything" and still the children turned out bad, this indicates that the parents did not know how to give their children love.

Love is guidance and direction. This means that you don't allow the streets to introduce the most intimate details of life to your children through pornography and common vulgarity. You guide their understanding of intimacy in a wholesome direction.

Love is protection and provision. This means that you provide a safe place for them to live and provide responsible supervision for them when you are absent. You don't leave them in the care of friends or relatives who engage in inappropriate behavior, teaching your child bad language, bad habits, and bad attitudes.

Love is encouragement and comfort. Many parents who don't understand what it takes to strengthen a child emotionally will criticize everything a child does, falsely believing that this will motivate the child to strive harder. It doesn't. It destroys a child's self esteem and self-confidence, making the child see himself or herself as a failure, and ultimately becoming one. Or the child will become so needy for approval, he or she will grow into an emotionally imbalanced adult, willing to endure abusive treatment from friends, spouses, and employers, just to gain acceptance.

Children Deprived of Love Become Angry and Destructive

Many parents, rather than offering words of comfort, will ridicule a child who openly expresses hurt feelings or pain, saying they don't want the child to be a "cry- baby." This doesn't help the child learn to handle difficult situations in a mature manner. Instead, it makes the child feel hurt and angry at what appears to be the parents' lack of concern and sympathy. It causes the child to grow into an even more needy adult, craving for attention and sometimes doing self-destructive things to get it.

Chicago actor, playwright and hip-hop artist Kevin Mines recalls his emotional struggle as the neglected youngest boy in a family of six sisters and five brothers.

"My parents drank and partied all the time. They never paid any attention to me. I could come home at 11 or 12 o'clock at

night when I was eleven years old, they didn't care. I had a key. They didn't care what I did or where I was.

"I didn't really have any parents. I raised myself. They stayed drunk all the time. I've been independent since I was ten years old. I made my own money with a paper route. I remember sometimes coming home and my mother would be laid out drunk on the steps. I had to try to drag her up the stairs. My brothers and sisters, they didn't care. They would let her just lay there.

"My parents never encouraged me to do anything. They never said anything positive to me.

"I used to feel like I was a mistake. I remember at one point I was suicidal. I decided I was going to go into the closet and hang myself. I remember…I was in the closet, I had the rope tied around the rod and I was about to put it around my neck when the doorbell rang. I went downstairs to answer the door.

"It was these Jehovah's Witnesses. They said to me, 'Whatever you're going through, just pray, God will help you.' That's what saved me. I went back upstairs and into the closet and prayed. I decided not to kill myself. I prayed so much in that closet. I had to learn how to feed my own soul.

"I have children of my own now – four boys and two girls. I try to be very supportive of my children.

"It's hard for me to trust women, though. I'm very hard on women. When I was growing up, our lives were so unstable. All of my brothers and sisters have problems today. They're in and out of jail, on drugs. I think it's because of the way we grew up.

"I see a lot of anger and aggression in men today who had no good upbringing. I try to tell them to grab on to something, study something or somebody that can be a good example."

Kevin noted that although he belongs to no particular religious denomination, he believes that prayer is the necessary healing force for a person whose sense of self worth has been destroyed by parental neglect.

People who have been deprived of love often live with an inner resentment that easily explodes into rage. When this happens, it becomes easy for them to hit, stab, or shoot another person. The prisons are filled with people who, at some critical point in their lives, were deprived of love.

The character of a child is shaped in the home, by members of the family. Among wolves, cubs display definable personality traits early in life. Some appear to show more aggression than others. Cubs may be playful, curious, short tempered, impatient, and every other personality trait observable in human children. The cubs establish their own hierarchy, based on their own personalities and experiences together. They engage in play-fighting to establish who is the strongest, bravest and most aggressive between them. The adult wolves let them play and explore, only intervening to protect them from harm when enemies are near. But in the wolf pack, the adults do not show favoritism of one cub over another. The cubs must establish their own position in the pack, a position they may maintain until adulthood, when one of them becomes the pack's leader.

In many human families, parents are unable to hide their preference of one child over another. They may openly praise one child while condemning another. If one child gets better grades in school, or one child might be considered more attractive, or if a boy child is preferred over the girl or the girl over the boy, the praise that the parents give one child creates resentment in the other child. Children often grow up seeing themselves as rivals for their parent's love and affection.

Do your children engage in a lot of bickering and tattling? This may be a sign that they feel insecure, and believe they need to compete with each other for your acceptance. The way the adults in the family respond to bickering children is critical. Adults must teach children the skills of cooperation and mutual respect. A family, just like a wolf pack, must see itself as a team, in which all members are valued for whatever they contribute to the whole. Children should be praised for working together to solve problems, not rewarded for tattling on each other over petty things.

The events that take place in the home are important in the shaping of each child's ability to give positive contributions to the greater society. Children learn meanness and selfishness in the home, in an atmosphere where parents either ignore them or show clear favoritism towards a sibling, encouraging rivalry between them. The same mean, selfish child becomes the mean, selfish adult who lacks compassion for other people.

Raising The Children: A Collective Responsibility

Being in a family means being a part of a whole. It means responsibility to a group. Adult wolves take turns watching the cubs, each reinforcing the idea of family unity. Although the uncles and aunts guarding the cubs are not their parents, these cubs still represent the continuation of the family blood line, and the survival of the pack. The adult wolf given the responsibility of watching the cubs knows that they are protecting their own future. In many human families, however, when siblings have been raised as rivals and enemies, they are unable to bond with each other's children in this manner. They are unable to form the kind of extended family group in which the children are always supervised by a caring adult family member rather than a stranger.

The disconnectedness of families is what has given rise to so many childcare facilities. Couples are unable to rely upon their own parents and siblings to share in the responsibilities of raising the children. With the western concept of the "nuclear family" men and women tend to isolate themselves as a separate and independent unit. If the marriage breaks up, the custodial parent, usually the mother, is often struggling to raise children alone. The grandparents, aunts and uncles may respond with resentment at being asked to assist in the regular supervision of children that are not their own.

In order for children to maintain the bonds of family into their own adulthood, they have to be raised as a close-knit family unit. This is difficult if the parents have not created an atmosphere of family harmony in the home.

The mother is the one who creates the atmosphere inside the home. She is the homemaker. This has nothing to do with whether a woman has a job outside of the home. This is her natural role as a female. Home is where your mother is – whether that home is a round nest of grass and twigs in a tree, or a dark den in the side of a hill. Home is where a mother feeds her newborn children and keeps them warm and safe.

The home is a reflection of whatever state of mind the mother is in – it reflects her upbringing, her skills, her moods, and her choice of a spouse. It is the mother's responsibility to create an environment in the home where children can receive the care they need to grow into physically and emotionally healthy adults.

Home is a place of peace and comfort – not a place of anxiety, where children hear parents' hostile arguments, insults, accusations and threats of divorce.

Home is a place of order and structure – not a place of confusion, where children don't know when a mother may stumble into a disheveled house after a drugged out night of partying and remember that there is no food for them to eat.

Home is a place of safety and security – not a place of fear, where children have to worry about whether a father will burst in the door in a drunken rage and terrorize the family with threats of violence.

Home is a place where the family gathers together and celebrates the joyful presence of children. It is the existence of children that reminds a family that their past is connected to a future.

For the wolf pack, raising the children and preparing them for adulthood is everybody's responsibility. When her cubs have reached a certain age, a mother wolf will leave her den to go and hunt with the pack. This is just like a woman who has to return to a job or run an errand in which she cannot take along an infant. In the wolf pack, an uncle, aunt, or even older sibling or pack member is given the responsibility of watching the cubs in the mother's absence. It's what they learn to do as part of the family.

In too many human families, however, it is the older sibling, cousin, aunt or uncle left in charge who mistreats a child in the absence of the mother. Something went wrong in the home when those who should be responsible for the safety of a child are in fact the culprits who cause harm.

Behavior, good and bad, is learned in the home. Parents whose children are often fighting or engaging in some other anti-social behavior seek to place blame on some outside entity: "The shows on television are too violent...this music the kids listen to nowadays is a bad influence...these athletes and entertainers need to be better role models..."

Rarely will parents admit that it is they who are the role models their children emulate. If a parent is present in the home and is behaving badly, it has a negative influence on the child. If the parent is absent from the home, it has a negative influence on the child. In either case, the parents are the people who have shaped the child.

Children are born pure. They inherit physical traits from the genes of their parents. They develop behavior from the actions of their parents. Children mimic what they see. This is how they learn. In today's society, adults blame children for defiant, disre-spectful, disobedient, destructive behavior. The children's behav-ior is simply a reflection of the parenting skills, or lack thereof, of the adults who raised them.

Children Reflect Their Home Environment

Children are influenced by everything the parents allow to come into the home. This includes television shows, video games, books, magazines, pictures, music, and even conversation. A child absorbs it all, even as a growing fetus in the womb. The first sense that develops is the sense of hearing. The voices of people around the pregnant mother create positive or negative impressions for the child before birth. The child is either absorbing the positive vibra-tions of a loving home, or the negative vibrations of a hostile home.

The personality and attitude of the child is shaped during the first two years of life, even before the child begins to speak. During a discussion about family life, Rev. Willie T. Barrow, author of the book *How to Get Married and Stay Married*, observed,

> *"Training starts in the home. The child starts training for nine months in the womb. After the baby comes, for two and a half years, that baby does nothing but listen. If you are arguing and fussing and cussing and using profanity, that baby is listening. So when he starts to talk, he brings back all that memory. So at an early age, he starts cussing."*

Visual images create lasting memories for a child. Adults will sit in front of a television set and watch movies with graphic violence and explicit sexual content, totally oblivious to the presence of children in the room. It's as if they think the children are blind and deaf.

They aren't. Their brains are recording every image and every word.

"Adult" magazines lie around the house, sometimes carelessly mixed in with other papers and magazines, other times hidden away on shelves or in drawers, but always accessible to children. Today, with the Internet, cable and satellite TV, children often learn at an early age how to get access to graphic sexual images. Many children are introduced to sex through pornography in the home. This has a profound impact on the behavior of children as they approach puberty, and sometimes even before that. Older children, left alone to baby sit younger siblings, cousins, nieces or nephews, use this as an opportunity to explore the bodies of those who are too young to know how to protest. While "playing doctor" has always been a common childhood game to examine human anatomy, children who are exposed to sexually explicit images start out by experimenting with various sexual acts.

In the book, *At Issue*, edited by Paul A. Winters, in the chapter entitled "Child Molestation Committed by Other Children," the author observes:

> *The national debate over how to deal with adult sex offenders continues to rage: Should they be punished or treated? Should*

they be locked up permanently or paroled?   And even after New Jersey passed Megan's Law, requiring police to notify community members when released offenders move into their town, the controversy over the usefulness and constitutionality of this approach remains heated.   Confronting the problem of children who are child molesters is even more confounding.   And making the issue more pressing are new findings that show that more than 50 percent of the adults arrested for sex crimes began their aberrant behavior as juveniles...

Around the country, police, prosecutors and social–service workers are struggling to deal with the rise in the number of juvenile sex offenders.   Much of the increase is due to the higher visibility of the problem and, therefore, better reporting of abuse, but experts won't rule out a bona fide increase.

"In the past, people frequently wrote off everything as 'sexually exploratory behavior.'   But I can say, anecdotally, that there's much more physical aggression and violence shown by today's children," says Judith Becker, Ph.D., a professor of psychology and psychiatry at the University of Arizona.   "I've gotten referrals for seven- and eight-year-olds who have serious sexual behavior problems."

According to researchers' most conservative approximations, juveniles now commit one third of all the sexual abuse reported every year.

<u>*At Issue*</u>*, pages 52 and 53*

Invasion of privacy by another's unwanted touching of is a violation of the soul. Not only is the child's innocence destroyed; the feeling of personal defilement creates an emotional scar that affects all personal relationships. The ability to trust is destroyed. Sexuality becomes associated with feelings of shame; the victim tries to block out all memories of the abuse; but in order to emotionally remove oneself from the experience, one ultimately removes oneself from any feelings connected with intimacy.

In his book *If Men Could Talk*, marital therapist Dr. Alan Gratch discusses the emotional struggle of one of his patients,

John. A victim of childhood molestation, John realized that he did not have the ability to form close emotional attachments. He was seeking to overcome his feelings of aloofness in order to form a more loving relationship with his girlfriend. During a therapy session, Dr. Gratch discovered his patient's underlying problem:

> *From about age five to eleven John was periodically molested by his older sister's boyfriend (and later husband). When he finally told me about it, even after he acknowledged "irrational feelings of shame," John refused to describe it as abuse. And when I made the mistake of using that word he corrected and admonished me. This was not only because John liked to think of himself as an independent thinker, but also because his memories of the "so-called abuse" – we finally settled on that term – were not unpleasant...*
>
> *While sometimes, as in the case of rape or other violent abuse, the child's experience is that of sheer horror, in most cases the emotional picture is more complex. The child might be very attached to the abusive adult and he might get pleasure – if not sexually, emotionally – from some aspect of the interaction. When that is the case, the child invariably says to himself, "It's not that bad," or "At least I'm getting something out of it," or "Maybe I made it all up."*
>
> *With these notions, the child intuitively seeks to protect the adult in order to preserve the possibility of love and coherence in his world. But try as he may, he cannot shake the knowledge that it's all wrong; that he is being used and manipulated, that he is made to feel shameful and guilty, that the secret relationship is alienating him from his family and friends, that it makes him question his masculinity and sexuality, and that he is becoming fearful or sickly. And even when this knowledge is repressed or ejected out of consciousness ("dissociated"), which is often the case, the child is no longer able to trust love or the rules of reality. He adopts a skeptical, icy disposition and rejects emotional attachments.*
>
> *If Men Could Talk*, by Dr. Alan Gratch, pages 66 and 67

Sex crimes are committed by people who were improperly introduced to sex themselves, often by a caretaker or person in authority who subjected them to abuse. Many times the abuser was prompted by exposure to pornography.

Pornography becomes prevalent when the adults in a society have not yet evolved to a level of spiritual maturity regarding their sexuality. They remain on the level of a small school child, secretly scribbling crude words and pictures of human genitalia on a bathroom wall. Producers of pornography take the beauty of creation and transform it into demeaning and degrading images that generate both arousal and disgust.

Pornographic material is often found in the possession of people who commit crimes of sexual assault. When sex is coupled with violence or degradation, as is often the case in pornography, those who are exposed to such images learn to associate sex with violence and degradation.

Sexual abuse has a domino affect. The abused often becomes the abuser. It is like a contagious disease that spreads throughout society, killing the innocence of children and destroying future relationships.

When harmful materials are brought into the home and defined as "adult" this sends confusing signals to children. Children instinctively imitate adult behavior. It is their job; they are striving to become adults. When adults consume alcoholic beverages, they tell the children that only "adults " are allowed to drink So, what do children do when their parents are away and they want to be "adult?" They get out the whiskey and try to drink it! They're not bad – they're doing what children are supposed to do: imitate adult behavior. Sometimes children will play games in which they pretend to be a drunk adult. It would be comical if it wasn't so tragic.

When people are intoxicated by alcohol, judgment is impaired and inhibitions disappear. Speech becomes lewd and vulgar. Many times it is in this altered state of mind that adults commit acts of sexual molestation against children.

In healthy families, harmful things are not brought into the home – not alcohol, not drugs, not pornography. Some parents will make excuses: "We lock things away so that the children can't find them."

The problem is not the children – what about the affects of these things on adults? An adult who is drunk or high and lewd and crude loses the children's respect and will never gain it back.

Companies that sell alcoholic beverages warn consumers to "drink responsibly." But consuming anything that impairs ones judgment, even slightly, is in and of itself irresponsible.

There is no right way to commit a wrong act.

Our children are angry. They feel betrayed. Homes that were supposed to be safe havens where they could grow and develop have become dwellings of dysfunction and distress. Parents are fighting, siblings are fighting, and peace and comfort are nowhere to be found. Children come to school, full of frustration and hostility. They ridicule and bully other children, pick fights, challenge the authority of the teachers, use profanity, and create general disorder. They are bringing the disorder from their homes into the school, and too often the teachers are blamed and accused of not having "classroom management skills." How can a teacher, who is not a therapist, manage thirty children suffering from the emotional distress created by their dysfunctional parents? Talk to most chronically misbehaving students, and you'll find that they are struggling with anger over conflicts between parents, divorce of parents, the absence of a parent, neglect by parents, remarriage of a parent, conflicts with a step parent, conflicts with a sibling who appears to be favored by parents or abuse by parents or another adult caretaker.

The Root of Crime: Disrespect For Parents

The social order of the wolf pack demands that those who become leaders must earn the position of respect. They must be bold, brave, cunning, and strong; they must have the social skills to keep the pack together, working together as a unit to insure that all are well fed. The Alpha male and the Alpha female must be stable and mature, because they are the nucleus of the pack. If the core of the family disintegrates, what happens to the rest of the members? If they scatter and lived separately, many would not live long. A lone wolf, trying to survive on a scarce supply of rabbits, rodents, and other scraps of meat, can starve out in the cold winter plains. But a strong pack can hunt down the big buffalo for a hearty meal.

When men and women have children before they are mature enough to be good parents, they create conditions that cause children to disrespect them. Young teen mothers, pregnant and barely out of high school, are forced to live in their parents' homes while they try to raise their children. The children don't see their mother as the wise woman of the house who nurtures and protects them; often, what they see is an immature child like themselves, still being reprimanded for irresponsible behavior. Grandparents become the parents and the mother becomes like a sibling. Children grow up seeing their mother being fussed at for not doing chores, not doing homework, coming in too late from parties, and hanging around questionable characters. Biologically she is their mother, but emotionally she can never command their respect. Disrespect for the laws of decent conduct in society begins with disrespect for ones own mother.

"If you're calling your Grandmama 'Mama' and you're calling your Mama 'Pam', you're going to jail."
Chris Rock, Comedian

In one of his popular comedy routines, comedian Chris Rock points out that children who are raised by their grandmothers often end up treating their own mothers as one of their peers rather than a mother. He derides careless young mothers who leave their children at home while they go dancing at the nightclubs in the middle of the week. Irresponsibility such as this breeds children that develop total disdain for parents, and consequently, all authority figures. Children who have lost respect for adults because of what they have experienced at home soon head down the path of rebellion. They stumble along, tripping and falling, trying to find their way to adulthood. Instead, they often find their way to jail.

In today's world, wealth, not age and wisdom, determines the level of respect a person receives. Children raised in an environment where age does not translate into wisdom and respect perceive that the goal in life is to obtain wealth by any means necessary. In this entertainment driven society, wealth often goes to those who can sing, dance, act, or excel in sports. Since music and sports are dominated by youth, many young millionaires are created whose only claim to fame is that they have musical talent or a physical skill.

There have been few demands made upon sports figures or entertainers to acquire morals, ethics, social skills, a cohesive family, or a sense of responsibility to the community. They have money, but unless they had strong guidance from wise parents, they often live disastrous lives, using money for drugs, illicit sex, and any other vice they can afford. These wealthy but misguided entertainers and athletes become role models for frustrated children who lack a clear direction and purpose for their lives.

If children have not been raised with a sense of responsibility to a family unit, they will not feel any compulsion to help family members when they reach adulthood. No matter how much financial success a family member may acquire, it will not benefit the rest family unless the family philosophy was one of unity and sharing for the good of the whole.

Sharing is learned in the home, and so is selfishness. When parents argue over material possessions in the presence of children, they are teaching selfishness. "This is *my* house...*my* car...*my* furniture!" Couples often break up over financial disputes. Even though they got married, they never really understood the concept of "ours." Some married couples operate as merely two single people occupying the same living space and benefiting from each other's possessions. Then one person gets angry and, like a disgruntled child losing a game, says "I quit! Give me back my stuff!"

Parents have to teach children how to share food, clothing and attention. Rather than to over-indulge every child with an excessive amount of toys, parents should buy games that require the children to play together. If they can't play together as children, they won't be able to work together as adults. When it comes to critical cooperative activities that could assist in the family's overall progress, such as purchasing family property or running a family business, they won't be able to work collectively if they have not been taught how to do it.

A family is just one unit in an entire community. A community is made up of families. When families are stable, they can form close-knit communities. Just as flocks of thousands of flamingo birds migrate, build nests, and hatch eggs together each year, a healthy community is one that lives in harmony. Happy couples raise their children together.

When communities are fragmented, crime ridden and poverty stricken, it is because the families are divided. People are vulnerable for exploitation and oppression when they cannot form strong and lasting family ties, in which members of the family interact to help each other. When people work together, they can exchange talents, skills and resources, so that not just one family, but all families in the community prosper. But when children are raised in broken homes, with an individualistic outlook on life, even if a few children from the community achieve financial success, the community in which those children were raised will not change. Cooperation among families must become a way of life in order to change a condition of poverty and desolation.

Values that prompt successful adults to reinvest in their own communities are taught in the home. Children from broken, dysfunction families may learn to perceive themselves, their parents, and their communities as defective. A sense of personal inferiority sets in and wealth becomes a means to buy an escape from what is perceived as a shameful heritage, rather than a means to change conditions for ones family and community.

Sociologists have often examined why, despite the growing numbers of wealthy African Americans, many black communities continue to suffer devastating poverty. In his book *Black Men: Single, Obsolete, Dangerous?* author Haki R. Madhubuti states:

However, it is sad to say there are tens of thousands of Black people in the United States with serious money, skills and talent who do nothing except talk bad about their own people and compete in the Western race for conspicuous consumption champions.

The real dilemma among most Blacks with money is that of values. Really, how many houses does one need; how many cars can one drive; how many vacations to Europe and the Caribbean in a year are needed; how many closets of clothes can one wear; how much money must one accumulate to be successful or prove a point; and how much jewelry is necessary to make a statement of wealth? The Black poor and middle class, by comparison, give more to the less fortunate of our people than the Black rich. Many will observe, "that's why they are rich." Don't buy into that answer. The Black rich and the white rich are different and respond differently to their respective communities. The two groups also view their responsibilities to their people differently.

The white rich start foundations, build art centers, finance new wings for museums and libraries, endow university chairs and create scholarships for the less fortunate of their people and others. The white rich finance all types of summer camps, help keep white businesses viable, start independent think tanks, support their writers, artists and musicians and buy sports franchises.

<u>Black Men: Single, Obsolete, Dangerous</u>, *page 20*

Respect for community, life, law, property, and authority all begin with respect for parents. We can change the future if we change the way we raise our children. We can transform low achieving schools into institutions of academic excellence. We can create secure and loving homes where children feel safe and protected. We can form extended family groups in which all adults take responsibility for the upbringing of the children. And above all, we, the parents, can treat each other with respect, and conduct ourselves in a manner that will gain and maintain the respect of our children. When we are able do this, we will transform crime-infested neighborhoods into the peaceful communities we desire.

Who Is Your Extended Family?

An extended family is necessary for support. People often become homeless because they are disconnected from family and close friends who could offer assistance. Are you dangerously isolated from other people? Consider the following situations. What family members or close friends can you call for help?

1.   Your house caught on fire, and everything you own was destroyed. You have no place to live and not enough money in the bank to rent a hotel room for any extended period of time. Name three people that you know you can count on to help you out with living arrangements for the next several months to a year.

2.   You have been diagnosed with a serious illness and will be bedridden for perhaps a year. You will need someone to take care of you around the clock until you recover. Name three people that you know you can count on to help take care of you for the next several months to a year.

3.   You traveled across the country to a city where you know no one. While walking down the street, you were mugged. Your wallet, identification, credit cards, and cash were all stolen. You filled out a police report, but there is nothing else they can do for you. Name three people you can call to send money to get you home.

4.   You are driving along the highway in the middle of a cold, cold winter night. Suddenly, your car skids on ice and you crash into a light pole, smashing your car. You call for a tow truck, but because of the weather and so many other demands, it will take a few hours for it to arrive. Your car heater won't work and you are freezing. Name three people you can call who will come out and get you.

Chapter 3
The Skill of the Sparrow
Provide a safe, secure home for your family

The early morning springtime air is filled with the twitter-tweet of sparrows as this 100-plus member flock settles into its selected nesting place amid the thick bushy maple trees. Mating calls ring out as each male announces to his intended loved one that her new home – a round nest of intricately woven twigs securely affixed to a sturdy branch – is now ready for inspection.

The males of the flock have been working diligently to woo a new bride. Each female is looking for a mate who can provide just the right house for her and their future children.

Three males have all spotted a perky little female sparrow. They each call out to her, urgently persuading her to come and inspect their handiwork. She lands on a nearby branch and glances at each nest. The male on the highest branch beckons to her in his most melodious voice. She flutters over to him and peeks inside the nest he has constructed. Her head darts up and down, back and forth, as she inspects the sturdiness of the knots of twigs holding the nest secure on the branch. They don't seem to be tied tight enough. A nest full of eggs could weigh it down, sending both nest and eggs crashing to the ground. Disappointed, she moves on to inspect the next nest.

The male on the branch below frantically summons her and she lands beside his nest to examine his home building skills. The knots are sturdy, the nest is secure on the branch, but the small hole that serves as the entrance to the nest is way too big. Another predator could fit inside, injure her and steal the eggs. Disappointed again, she flutters away.

The third male beckons her with a crooning voice. She flies over to inspect his carefully constructed nest. It is tightly secured on a sturdy branch. The twigs are weaved together, along with pieces of string and wisps of grass for added strength and rein-

forcement. The tiny entrance is just big enough for her to fit through but not big enough for an enemy to reach inside. She enters the nest and peeks out from inside. It is secure, comfortable and safe. She is pleased. She stays. The third male twitters in delight. He has won his bride.

Being a woman is a tremendous responsibility. It requires clear judgment and practical thinking. Wrong decisions can jeopardize the lives of children and destroy a family's future. When choosing a mate, a woman has to at least have the sense of a sparrow.

Female sparrows realize that choosing a mate means choosing someone who can build a safe, comfortable home for their family. That means that mating must be more than a passing act of pleasure. It is a commitment to a lifelong union and raising children together. Sparrows, like many other birds, mate for life.

In the early spring the female lays her eggs in the round nest built by her mate, made of twigs and grass, tied securely to a sturdy branch, far up in a tree away from predators. The male goes out and brings back food for her – worms, bugs and other nutritious insects – while she stays inside the nest to incubate their eggs. She must sit on them for nearly three weeks until they hatch. The male must be committed to taking care of her during this process or she and her chicks will not survive.

The female sparrow understands that before she lays eggs, she must select a mate who has prepared himself to handle the task of providing for a family. Her life and the life of her children depend on her making a good choice.

Sex Education or Mis-education?

Centuries ago, sex was not openly discussed in school, but was instead whispered about in private conversations, with much misinformation spread about by young people who knew much too little to be experimenting with sex. However, today's society has become very public about human sexuality. In fact, with mandatory sex education in schools, combined with sexually explicit material in movies, magazines, and even on the Internet, it is practically impossible for a pubescent youth not to be able to find detailed information on "how to." The problem is that rarely are young people today given specific guidelines on "when to."

In a survey of 200 high school students, 100 males and 100 females, the question was asked, "When should a woman become sexually active?" The following choices were given:

a)   When she is married
b)   When she is mature
c)   When she is truly in love
d)   When she uses some protection
e)   When she has finished high school
f)   When she has a job and her own apartment

A total of 32% said, "When she uses some protection," while 18% said, "When she is mature," 16% said "When she has finished high school," and 12% said "When she has a job and her own apartment." A total of 8% said "When she is truly in love." Only 14% of the 200 youth surveyed said "When she is married."

Adults have done a great job in driving home the message about using contraception and condoms to prevent pregnancy. But what have we taught our children about marriage and commitment to family? Obviously, very little. That same group of 200 youth was asked the question, "When should a man become sexually active?" They selected their answers from the same following choices:

a)   When he is married
b)   When he is mature
c)   When he is truly in love
d)   When he uses some protection
e)   When he has finished high school
f)   When he has a job and his own apartment

A total of 44% said, "When he uses some protection," while 16% said "When he is mature." Although 12% said "When he has a job and his own apartment, only 8% said "When he has finished high school." Likewise, only 8% said, "When he is truly in love." Only 12% of this group of 200 youth aged 14 to 18 said "When he is married."

Children reflect the values taught to them by their parents and the society in which they live. Women are responsible for selecting men that uphold the values that encourage respect for them and their children.

When the male sparrow builds a nest and calls out to the female sparrow, he is declaring that he is a mature adult male and is ready for a mate. He is telling the female sparrow that he can take care of her and their future children in the home he has prepared for her. He is proposing a lifetime commitment.

What is it called in human society when a male proposes a lifetime commitment to a female, declaring his willingness and ability to provide a home for her and their future children?

Marriage.

When should a young man and woman become sexually active? When they are married.

The female sparrows heard birdcalls from many anxious males advertising their interest. None of the females flew over to males who had not built a nest. Why mate with someone who hadn't even prepared a place to lay eggs? A male who had not built a nest was clearly not ready for a family.

The female who had her choice of three anxious males didn't select the ones whose nests were poorly designed and unsafe. She knew her decision would affect not only herself but her future children. She selected the male that was most prepared to take good care of a family.

The Need for Teamwork

Right about now, a lot of women are defensively saying, "Sex isn't always about having children. That's what contraception is for. A woman has a right to enjoy a healthy sex life without planning to get pregnant."

This is the error in modern thinking that has created the

mess we have made with our families. It is this type of thinking that has contributed to the 62% divorce rate and the 53% of children born out of wedlock.

If you keep doing what you're doing, you'll keep getting what you've got.

Old American Proverb

In order for women to make correct decisions, they first have to understand the female's role in the process of evolution. Each generation is supposed to advance higher than the previous generation in terms of strength and intelligence. The female's choice of a mate determines whether the next generation gets stronger and smarter or weaker and dumber.

Nature's law of "survival of the fittest" demands that children learn from the trials and errors of their parents in order not to commit the same mistakes. Those that fail to learn from the past will eventually die out.

The female's job is to choose a mate who will enable her to do her best for her children. She must teach her children the collective wisdom from previous generations. An intelligent female will select a male with survival skills who will strive to insure that his progeny live to carry on his genetic line.

The female sparrow knows that a male that has taken the time to perfect his skills at nest building is also mature enough to perform the essential duty of bringing food to her while she sits on her eggs and waits for them to hatch. A male who has prepared a good home for his mate understands the connection between sexual pleasure and taking care of a family.

Now, some women may be stubbornly saying, "But why does the female sparrow have to wait on a male to build her nest? She can build her own nest and take care of her eggs by herself!"

Okay, let's say the female builds the nest. She then selects a mate she likes and they copulate. He flies on about his business while she lays eggs in the nest she built herself. She can't leave to get food for herself, or her eggs would get cold and never hatch, or worse, they'll get eaten by predators. If she stays and sits on them until they hatch, she'll starve to death.

The male's act of building a good, sturdy nest is the sign that he is mature enough to handle the responsibilities that come as a natural consequence of mating. Raising children requires mutual commitment and teamwork. Birds understand this.

Raising human children also requires mutual commitment and teamwork. A woman must be free to nurture and protect her newborn babies while her physical needs are being taken care of by her husband. Couples must work in harmony so that infants remain safe and healthy. So, then, in view of this reality, why are there so many single mothers struggling alone with small children?

The rising phenomenon of single parent homes has escalated in the last three decades. Unlike the male sparrow, who knows he must be able to build a secure nest and find worms and bugs for his mate, too many human males don't seem to know what to do to take care of a family.

Something has gone terribly wrong with our culture. Men are no longer being raised to fulfill the role of husband and household breadwinner. The Woman's Movement brought a demand for economic equality, a demand prompted by the fact that many women were working the same jobs as men, but were given less pay. Simultaneously, African Americans, Hispanics, and other groups that had suffered long time economic discrimination demanded that the government force corporate America to institute fair hiring practices. In her book *Whatever Happened to Daddy's Little Girl?* author Jonetta Rose Barras examines the social and economic impact of Affirmative Action and racial quotas:

> *Corporations and other employers received special benefits for giving preferences to African Americans and for hiring women and other "minorities." Black women became known as twofers. That is, an employer received double credit for hiring a person who was not only a racial minority but also a "gender" minority. As a result, sweeping and unprecedented opportunities became available for black women. They had greater access to jobs, job*

training and education. The gap that appeared between them and black males widened further.

Simultaneously, the country shifted from an industrial economy to a service economy. Where once black men could always find jobs working with their hands, fewer and fewer of those jobs were available upon the altered landscape. Further, wages that came with those positions were not keeping pace with the cost of living...black men were not desirable employees for corporations looking to score points with the federal government and the market. Literally and figuratively, the African American men were placed on or kicked to the curbside, like old refrigerators or cans of rubbish...The tensions between black men and black women heightened, giving the feminist movement sufficient footing for buttressing their own platform.

<u>*Whatever Happened to Daddy's Little Girl?*</u> *pages 42, 43*

As employment among young men between the ages of twenty-five and thirty-four declined, the number of father-absent families increased, particularly in high-poverty neighborhoods, according to a 1994 report by the Annie E. Casey Foundation. By 1990, almost 5 million children were growing up in neighborhoods where a majority of working age men had been unemployed during the previous year. In these same neighborhoods, more than 45 percent of all families were headed by women – almost twice the national average. Jonetta Rose Barras observes.

Without work – a means of caring for a family – many African American men couldn't or wouldn't get married. Consequently, women who engaged in romantic relationships with these men ultimately married the government, which, until recently, proved to be a jealous lover, refusing to permit men to remain in the home with the children they had fathered, said Washington Post columnist William Raspberry.

"Young men stopped being valued as they might be [because they couldn't earn a living]. They became at first useless and then positively dangerous," says Raspberry.

The result was a "convenient rationalization, shared and reinforced by other men in similar situations, rationalizations that reject the institution of marriage," says William Julius Wilson of Harvard's John F. Kennedy School of Government.
            <u>*Whatever Happened to Daddy's Little Girl?*</u> *pages 43, 44*

Women either became the family wage earners, or they were supported by government welfare. Either way, the presence of an unemployed man in the home became unwanted. The role of husband, for many families, never existed. Many men and women grew up in families where "Daddy" was someone who came around sometimes and brought a little money – never enough – or perhaps left a few gifts. Marriage didn't exist, so fatherhood was undefined. The only thing children learned was that when they got old enough, it was time to start having sex.

A father's absence makes a big difference in a child's development. When a working single mother can't take the time to teach and train her young children, the children suffer. Basic language skills may be slow to develop, as well as knowledge of the alphabet and recognition of numbers. When children start out academically behind as early as kindergarten, they may never catch up. Seventy-one percent of all high school dropouts come from fatherless homes.

Sex Too Soon Equals Arrested Development

The period between puberty and adulthood is a time when male hormones are raging. The high levels of testosterone create bursts of aggression that must be channeled toward the development of physical and mental agility. If young men are allowed to remain idle, their aggression will become destructive.

Emotional maturity comes with age, instruction, and experience. A man is ready to take on a wife and start a family after attaining a certain level of emotional maturity. The strong sex drive in pubescent boys is meant to be the driving force that propels a boy to strive to meet the demands of manhood, in order to obtain the object of greatest pleasure: sexual union with a female. In communities where marriage is the culturally accepted prerequisite for sex, boys strive to prepare themselves for marriage.

Among many people in today's modern culture, however, a lot of boys experience their first sexual encounter at age 12 or 13. Sex isn't connected to marriage or preparation for family. Instead, sex follows puberty and the emergence of a sex drive.

Inattentive parents have made it easy for youth to experiment with sex. In an article written for the Associated Press, author Laura Meckler points out that lack of proper adult supervision enables many teenagers to engage in sex right in their parents' homes, almost literally under their noses:

WASHINGTON (Sept. 26) – Parents wondering if their teenagers are having sex might look upstairs or down the hall. New research finds most sexually active teens first had sex in their parents' homes, typically late at night...

"Kids no longer need to drive to lookout point to have sex," said Sarah Brown, director of the National Campaign to Prevent Teen Pregnancy. "The data suggests the adults may be in the house."

By the time students are in the ninth grade, 34 percent have had sexual intercourse. That rises to 60 percent by 12th grade.

The report, by researchers at Child Trends, is based on a national teen survey that has been tracking about 8,000 teens since 1997. The ages of the teens ranged from 12-15 when the survey began, and researchers have interviewed the same group every year since then. This report looks specifically at the 664 teens who reported having sex for the first time between 1999 and 2000.

Of those surveyed in 2000, 56 percent said they first had sex at their family's home or at the home of their partner's family.

Another 12 percent had their first sex at a friend's house; 9 percent at a teen's own home; 4 percent in a truck or car; 3 percent at a park or other outdoor place and 3 percent at a hotel or motel. Ten percent said someplace else.

Associated Press, September 26, 2002

In a culture where teenage sex has become the norm, the idea of preparing boys to grow up and get married before having sex is an alien concept. Every instinct tells a pubescent youth that he must strive to fulfill his sexual desires. There is very little encouragement of males to practice abstinence until marriage. So, what happens when a young teenage boy has sex?

Arrested development.

He no longer has an inner drive to reach a standard of manhood in order to obtain a wife and enjoy a complete physical and spiritual union. The young man's only drive from that point is to obtain more sexual pleasure. The act is not connected with anything related to marriage, children, or providing for a family. It is a selfish act, seeking pleasure for the self, to satisfy the self's own urges. Whatever it took to experience this pleasure is what the male will strive to master in order to repeat the experience. What did he have to do – buy a girl dinner? Give her a ride in his car? Take her to a show? Tell her she is pretty? Buy her an expensive gift? Tell her he loves her? He'll learn how to perfect whatever technique he used to obtain the object of his pleasure.

When a woman has sex with a man who has not married her, she destroys his instinct to strive for excellence in order to be worthy of her. She removes nature's natural incentive for him to prepare for his progeny. She robs him of his manhood.

Males of every species have a natural drive to reproduce life. Males throughout the animal kingdom instinctively form family groups and protect their children. This instinct is also present in men – unless women kill it with premature sex. When that happens, the man often remains in a state of adolescent immaturity, selfishly living to fulfill his own needs and desires, unwilling to use his skill and energy for the provision and care of a woman or his own children.

Do you know of grown men who are sexually active, and have children, but are still living single? Why do you think that happened?

The mark of a mature male is the ability to take care of himself, protect his mate and provide for his offspring. Observe this standard at work among the beaver colony of southern Florida.

Beavers are some of the hardest working animals one could ever see. A male beaver single handedly builds a home for his family, using his long, sharp front teeth. Beavers create dams made of trees, straw, mud and stone. These dams block the flow of water from rivers and streams, creating a place where the beaver's family can be protected from alligators, crocodiles, and other predators.

First the male beaver will cut down trees with his large two front teeth. He can cut down a tree that is more than two feet in diameter. He places them side by side against the current. He constructs a large part of the dam under water, holding his breath for up to 15 minutes while building first the foundation then the walls of the dam. He methodically seals the logs together with mud, straw and stone. When he is finished, his mate joins him behind the walls of the dam and there they conceive and raise their children.

Beavers live in colonies. Young beavers learn how to build from watching their parents and other adults. When males reach the age where they are ready to mate, they know that they must prepare a safe place for the female beaver and their children. What would happen if a young female decided to just copulate with any young beaver she found attractive, a beaver with no dam building skills and no interest in taking care of a family? Her babies would fall prey to foxes, wolves, hyenas, alligators, crocodiles, and every other carnivorous predator.

In a beaver colony, young male beavers learn that their role is to build a dam to provide security for their family. In a community of people, young men have to be taught that their *role,* the reason for their gaining an education and acquiring skills, is to take care of a family. When they come into puberty, their energy has to be directed towards improving their knowledge, so that they can excel in life and earn a living. Whatever profession they choose, whether they plan to get a job in a field requiring a college degree or other technical training, or they plan to own a business, they must aggressively pursue their profession so that they can master the necessary skills to get paid for their work. As they approach adulthood, they must be taught how to acquire independent living space, furnish it and keep it clean. They must be taught how to manage money responsibly, pay debts on time, and live within a budget.

A young man's sex drive may tell him to seek satisfaction with a woman, but proper upbringing will tell him that if he's still unemployed and living in his parents' home, he needs to wait. He has not reached the level of mature manhood. His physical and emotional need for a woman must be the driving force that makes him complete his education and seek employment or a means of earning an independent income, so that he can pay for adequate living space that can one day be shared by a mate.

Women also have a sex drive. But it is the female who is responsible for choosing when this sexual union will occur and with whom. Women have to seek men with the skills and re-sources to take care of themselves, men who have the means and the intention to provide for a family.

Marriage, Not Sex For Money

Some women will misread into this, "Look for a man with a lot of money." The point isn't whether he has a lot of money. The point is, *is he ready to share it with you?* A man has reached mature manhood when he is prepared to share what he has earned within a committed marital relationship. This involves much more than finding somebody with money who buys you expensive gifts and takes you to expensive places before you have sex with him. This means raising the standard of manhood to mean someone who is emotionally ready to share his life, time, and material resources with a woman on a permanent basis.

In her book *10 Bad Choices That Ruin Black Women's Lives*, psychologist Dr. Grace Cornish warns women, "If you treat a man as a money object, don't be offended if he treats you as a sex object." She tells the story of a 29 year-old part-time model named Petal who became enamored with a handsome and successful 36 year-old national public speaker, Ronald. Ignoring a three-year steady relationship with her less financially successful boy-friend Semore, she decided to use her feminine charms to capture Ronald:

Petal told Ronald that she was interested in becoming a spokesmodel and asked if he would be able to give her some guidance. He said he'd be delighted. He invited her for coffee and she accepted. They exchanged phone numbers.

Ronald's career always had him on the road. He would come to Petal's city about twice a month and they would see each other. They developed a sexual relationship. Ronald would take Petal on shopping sprees and bring her gifts. During this time Petal was still involved with Semour, who thought they had a monogamous relationship...Petal was enjoying the attention—she had not considered Semour's feelings at all. She just loved being spoiled with Ronald's gifts...

Ronald had promised to buy her an apartment and told her that someday maybe they would get married. She broke off her relationship with Semour. Ronald went overseas to give a speech in Nigeria, and when he returned, he brought back three beautiful traditional African dresses in different colors. He showed her all three and told her she could choose only one.

"What do you mean, one?" she asked.

"One's for you. You get first choice; the other two are for two other friends."

"Friends? What kind of friends? Are you sleeping with other women?"

"Well, you didn't think you were the only one, did you?"

"Of course I did! That's why I broke it off with Semour. Because you were talking about marriage and buying me my own apartment."

"I said I was only thinking of it. Baby, be real; after the way you treated that brother...I could never trust that you wouldn't do the same to me."

Petal became angry. Ronald stood his ground. They ar-

gued. He left...

Sisters like Petal are motivated by greed. They become weakened by money. They'll quickly trade sex in hopes of having their bills paid. A woman like this will use her body to entrap a man in exchange for money. As time goes on, she may come to believe she is falling in love with him. Then, when the brother does not return the emotional feelings she expects, she is devastated!

10 Bad Choices That Ruin Black Women's Lives, pages 47, 48.

When a man has sex with a woman whom he has not married he is saying, "I want sex, but I am not ready to take responsibility for any emotional attachment that you may experience as a result of our physical union. I want sex, but I am not ready to take responsibility for any chemical changes that may occur inside of your body as a result of our physical union. I want sex, but I am not ready to take responsibility for any life that may be conceived as a result of our physical union. I want sex, but I don't want to make a permanent commitment to you, just in case I find somebody I like better."

A woman gets pregnant. She approaches the man and asks him what he plans to do about it. Of course he is unprepared. He's angry and feeling trapped. He's resenting the fact that an act of pleasure is going to cost him some money, one way or another. He may urge the mother to go ahead and kill the child before it is born, rather than deal with the responsibility of raising a child he didn't intend to have.

Some women are hurt and angry when a man responds with hostility, or worse, indifference at the news of an unplanned pregnancy. Sometimes a woman expects that the reality of a child on the way will increase a man's love for her and motivate him to make a commitment to a permanent relationship. She is often sorely disappointed when her pregnancy actually drives him further away. Many men will deny paternity rather than be forced into a role of father they are not ready to fill.

Do you know of a man who had sex with a woman and when the woman later told him she was pregnant, he denied being the father of the child? The man wanted sex, not fatherhood. He wanted pleasure, not commitment.

Do you know of a woman who had to file a paternity suit against the father of her child, forcing him to take a blood test to prove that he was in fact her baby's father? Do you know of a woman who had to take the father of her child to court to make him pay child support? Often, such men don't even see the children for whom they are paying money. The court extracts a portion of the father's paycheck and mails it to the mother.

For such a man, fatherhood is a burden, not a joy. The child sometimes becomes a mere bargaining chip for the mother to receive more money. Women feel outrage and demand stiffer penalties for men who are negligent or fall behind in child support payments. Women often complain about men who show no sense of responsibility for their children, while men feel resentment that they are being forced to pay for the maintenance of children even though their relationship with the mother has been severed.

When a man does not marry a woman before having sex with her, he is declaring that he is immature, irresponsible, and unreliable. Why is she surprised that after she becomes pregnant he is immature, irresponsible and unreliable? It is the woman's responsibility to only have sex with men who have attained mature manhood.

Rule Number 1: Real Men Marry

Many women, after examining the pregnant woman's dilemma, will still insist, "The problem isn't sex before marriage. She should have used birth control. She should have made him wear a condom."

The issue isn't birth control. It's *development into mature manhood.*

Men aren't naturally aloof, selfish, immature, lazy and irresponsible. They only become that way when their natural development toward manhood is disrupted by sex too soon. In a healthy community, men organize to protect the women and children from harm. They direct neighborhood programs, sports teams and other activities that help in the development of children.

Marriage and responsible fatherhood is what creates community stability, because the children are connected to men who act in the capacity of protectors and providers for the woman and children. The family is the smallest unit in a community and a broken family creates a weak link in the community. When a child is born to a mother whose father is not involved in the child's upbringing, the child will grow up disconnected from the father.

When fathers are not attached to their children, they also tend not to have the same sense of responsibility to the community. Single, unattached men are less likely to get involved as coaches or scout leaders as are men whose sons and daughters are involved in these activities.

Young men reaching puberty need the father figures in the community whom they respect to help them channel their aggression toward positive activities. When a young man grows up disconnected from his father, unless he has formed a strong bond with another respected father figure in the community, he will become disconnected from the community. His testosterone-induced aggression will not be used to protect the weak in the community, but to prey upon them.

Do you know of a community where young males commit crimes against the women, children, and elderly? Do you know of a community where young men go on the prowl at night, robbing homes and places of business? When such young men are caught, where are the fathers who step forward to say, "That's my son – I'll take him home and discipline him so that this never happens again"?

Seventy percent of juveniles in state operated institutions come from fatherless homes. Eighty-five percent of all youths sitting in prisons grew up in fatherless homes.

In healthy communities, the parents are the authority figures who lay down the law and establish codes of acceptable conduct. Children obey the rules, not because they fear the police, but because they fear the disapproval and disciplinary actions of their parents. When young men have no involved fathers, mothers have no backup to enforce the rules in the home or in the community. Young men obey because they respect the authority of the older men in the community. The older men receive that respect because they are the fathers of the young men. They are the fathers who loved and nurtured their children from infancy and have therefore earned their respect. They are the fathers who, by their own example, guided their sons to serve the community. An absent father cannot earn the respect of his children, nor teach his children respect for the community in which they live.

When too many young men in the community are disconnected from their fathers, the community becomes a dangerous place to live.

Young men who are raised without the influence of sensitive, caring fathers are more apt to be influenced by negative definitions of manhood. They do destructive things, trying to appear "macho" and not be perceived as weak by other men. They fail to develop the emotional capacity to express deep feelings and to fully trust another human being, both necessary skills to have if one is to become a good spouse and a good parent. Dr. Kenneth Nave, in his book *A Season of Afflictions*, explains why some men fail to reach this critical level of emotional maturity:

Society, especially the subgroup of black America, gives many subtle but profound messages to little black boys that often begin to misshape and destroy the area of a man's soul where emotions reside. "Don't cry; only sissies cry. Don't show your love, or a woman will think you're weak. Don't let others know you're afraid, or they'll try to punk you." And the lies gain momentum and begin to perpetuate themselves as the false facades of manhood that many brothers hide behind. Most of us are so busy trying to project the images of men we think our subgroup of society desires us to be that we never get to discover just who we really are.

As young men, we begin to seek out and establish behaviors that repress those natural emotions that are inferred as being "unmanly" by the subjective social norms of black urban America.

We play vigorously; sports, rough housing, and games. We love haphazardly: womanizing, closet homosexuality, and masturbation. We perpetuate the bad-boy social image: gang banging, drug dealing, and domestic violence. But mostly we indulge in suppression by self-medication: marijuana, cocaine, alcohol and other narcotics.

A Season of Afflictions, page 118

The emotional pain of fatherlessness prompts many to seek to "self-medicate" themselves with drugs or alcohol, in attempts to drown out feelings of depression, rejection, and low self-esteem. Men that hide emotional pain by indulging in mood altering drugs or intoxicating drinks place an impenetrable barrier between themselves and a potential spouse. Fearing the vulnerability of revealing their emotions, they are unable to openly express love to women or children.

In too many communities across the country, single motherhood has become the norm and a father in the home has become the abnorm. Boys are learning from the irresponsible older men in their communities that 'real men" know how to use women without getting "caught."

When a woman has sex with a man before the man has matured and is ready to become a responsible father, it delays the development of the man's paternal instincts. Rather than having sex to produce children, he is having sex hoping *not* to produce children, and is often regretting any children that happen to be conceived. This goes against the laws of nature. It is a natural instinct for mature males to strive to reproduce. In many animal communities, fathers make great sacrifices for their children. Just observe the close-knit community of the Emperor Penguins of Antarctica.

Mating season occurs in the bitter cold arctic snow. After both the male and female have gorged themselves on fish to produce enough body fat to keep them warm, the couples gather by the thousands near the frosty shores of the Antarctic Ocean. Each couple stakes out its own little patch of ice. This will be home for a new baby penguin in just a few months.

The mother lays a single precious egg. The father tucks the egg under his skin, in the folds under his belly, making a nest for the egg out of his two feet. All of the mothers then head out to sea, while all of the males, their round bellies stuffed full of fish, huddle together to keep warm. Each male patiently waits for his own offspring to hatch.

Male penguins demonstrate dedication to family at its best. For the next two months, the fathers huddle together, eggs resting on their feet under the folds of their bellies, with only their body fat to keep them warm. The fathers eat nothing for an entire two months, living off of their stored up fat. When the eggs finally hatch, the chicks inside live off of a fatty substance emitted from the father's esophagus. It is thick and white, like milk, designed to create enough body fat to keep the baby penguin warm.

In two months, the mother returns, with a belly full of fish. She is huge, while her mate has grown skinny from the loss of body fat. She regurgitates fish for her young child to eat, then the couples change places. The females stay with the newborn penguins and the males all head out to sea to once again gorge themselves with fish, making up for a two-month long fast.

This is a community in harmony. The females bond together, the males bond together, and the parents bond with their children.

In a healthy community, all mature males are committed to their families. Consider how much trust there has to be between a male and female penguin. She lays an egg and leaves for two months. He's waiting with nothing but his fat and the body heat of his companions to keep him alive. How does he know she'll come back?

What would happen if some young single penguin male decided to go sneaking off after the females when they went out to sea? What if a few female penguins swam off with him and never returned to their dedicated mates and their newly hatched babies? This would disrupt the entire social order of the penguin flock, and might even affect the whole Alaskan ecosystem.

Even the Emperor Penguin knows that commitment comes

before sex and childbirth. Otherwise, there can be no trust.

Just as the males in the Antarctic penguin colony feel the safety, trust and camaraderie of a collective commitment to family and community, human males can feel that same sense of safety and trust – if all other males have been socialized properly.

Rule Number 2 – Smart Women Wait For Real Men

Some women may still be protesting, "But, just because you have sex before you get married doesn't mean the man is immature, or that he won't marry you! Some couples had sex before marriage, and still have good marriages!"

The problem isn't just the occasional unplanned pregnancy in which the father refuses to take care of his child or pay child support. In every community, it is the women who set the standards for manhood. The problem is the low standard of manhood that women have set that allows men to do absolutely nothing to demonstrate maturity and yet still engage in sex with women. Because women set such a low standard, many men remain immature well into adulthood. At the age of 30, 40 and 50 years old, they are still refusing to make a commitment to marriage and family, even though they are sexually active, and many are producing children. This non-committal relationship with women and children is what keeps communities in a state of instability, because young men have no examples of how to grow into mature men and get married. For most men, even if they do eventually marry, the sex act carries with it very little sense of an exclusive commitment.

Many men and women started having sex in their teen years. A few waited until their twenties. By the time they finally met someone with whom they felt they had developed a loving relationship and would like to marry, they had experienced a number of sexual unions already. For them, sex became merely an intimate, pleasurable act, not a permanent bond that unites two souls for life. It became just as easy to share this pleasurable experience outside of marriage as within marriage. Today, neither men nor women are socialized to understand sex as a permanent commitment.

At puberty, young men are experiencing a physical transformation which is necessary for their ability to produce offspring.
They may find themselves suddenly obsessed with sex. Their bodies are highly sensitive to the touch. Their minds are highly sus-
ceptible to suggestion. Any physical display of female nudity often leads to immediate sexual arousal.

In his book *If Men Could Talk...*, therapist Dr. Alon Gratch
points out that in the minds of many men, the need for love and the
desire for sex become intertwined. He notes that men tend to use
sex to satisfy other emotional needs, including the need for attention, control, or power. Sometimes sex becomes simply an opiate
to cope with stress, as in the case of one of Dr. Gratch's patients,
who confessed that since his lonely childhood days, he was often
sexually aroused and had desperate desires for someone to touch
him. He spent much time alone with his private fantasies, then
eventually sought out sexual stimulation from strangers. He regularly sought out casual sexual relationships with women, but was
unable to form a healthy emotional relationship with any of them.

Boys are as easily excited by mental images of naked
women as they are by the actual sight of them. In this manner,
boys and girls are different, as Dr. Gratch explains:

*Biologically, there are generally well known hormonal dif-
ferences, as well as important genital differences. For example,
men usually need a shorter period of time and less direct stimulation to become sexually aroused. This, by the way, is particularly
true at a younger age and with less experience, which is when and
how men, or really boys, develop the "skill" of sexualizing mental
contents. In other words, the simplicity of boys' sexual responses
– on top of weighty evolutionary, cultural and hormonal pressures
– makes it more likely that they will seek the powerful reward of
arousal and orgasm to escape, or cope with, emotional conflicts.*

*A simple example is one patient who grew up in a home
with physically abusive, emotionally erratic, and periodically, altogether absent parents...*

This sexualization of his starvation for love had set the patient on a course shared by many men with depressive tendencies. Confusing sex with Prozac, as a grown man, he would lose himself in the warm, sensual bodies of pretty women, using them much as an antidepressant.

If Men Could Talk... , pages 252 and 253

When young men are raised in a healthy, nurturing environment, they are less likely to misuse sexual intimacy to compensate for feelings of depression and low self-esteem.

If parents properly prepared their children for marriage, young people would not experience such a long delay between their physical maturation and their emotional maturation. One of society's problems is that sex has been made easy, but marriage has been made difficult. The fragmenting of families into smaller isolated units has made marriage at a younger age extremely challenging. Whereas in the past, families lived in closer proximity and even shared living space and financial resources, today every individual couple is expected to be able to survive on their own. Young couples just out of high school often find that even their combined wages are not enough to provide the kind of lifestyle they may have grown accustomed to while living with parents.

High Economic Expectations Discourage Marriage

Young couples may be emotionally ready to commit to each other, but financially unable to afford independent living space. Unlike previous years when couples tended to marry while in their twenties, many couples are delaying marriage until their thirties and even forties. The irony is, men and women are performing all of the actions of a married couple without any of the legal benefits: they live together, engage in physical intimacy, and have children together but will not make a legal commitment because they say they can't afford it yet. Supposedly, the tax laws are designed to provide an incentive for marriage. So, why are many couples choosing to stay single and simply cohabitate?

In the October 20, 2003 edition of *Business Week* Magazine, Michelle Conlin examines current marriage trends in her article entitled "Unmarried America."

The U. S. Census Bureau's newest numbers show that married-couple households--the dominant cohort since the country's founding—have slipped from nearly 80% in the 1950s to just 50.7% today. That means that the U.S.'s 86 million single adults could soon define the new majority. Already, unmarrieds make up 42% of the workforce, 40% of home buyers, 35% of voters, and one of the most potent—if pluralistic—consumer groups on record...

Indeed, we are delaying marriage longer than ever, cohabiting in greater numbers, forming more same-sex partnerships, living far longer, and remarrying less after we split up...

Married couples with kids, which made up nearly every residence a century ago, now total just 25%--with the number projected to drop to 20% by 2010, says the Census Bureau. By then, nearly 30% of homes will be inhabited by someone who lives alone...

Fully 54% of female high school seniors say they believe that having a child outside of marriage is a worthwhile lifestyle, up from 33% in 1980, according to the University of Michigan Survey Research Center. And 40% of female twentysomethings would consider having a baby on their own if they reached their mid-30s and hadn't found the right man to marry...

There is also a creeping disconnect between marriage and child-rearing, with an 850% increase since 1960 in the number of unmarried couples living with kids. As for children, 40% of them will live with their mom and her boyfriend before they turn 16, according to the National Institute of Child Health & Human Development.

<u>*Business Week*</u>*, October 20, 2003, Pages 106, 108, and 114.*

Some say that it is better for couples to wait until they are more mature before they get married. But because so many couples never marry, even though they have children together, it would appear that pre-marital sex is actually causing adults to take longer to mature. Some adults never reach the point where they are willing to make a legal lifetime commitment.

In his book, *A Season of Afflictions*, Dr. Kenneth Nave discusses a condition he calls "commitaphobia."

Phobia is defined as "an irrational, excessive and persistent fear of some particular thing or event." A commitaphobic, then is a man or woman who has an abnormal fear of commitment. Comitaphobia is a term usually applied to men who resist the challenge of commitment. Such men run when the crossroads of a long-term relationship come into view. They either run off, ahead of their lover, taking the low road of relationship dissolution (i.e. divorce, break-up, abandonment) or they U-turn, disappearing back over the horizon of broken promises.

A Season of Afflictions, pages 118 and 119

By the time men and women have reached the emotional maturity to share their time, skills, and living space with a spouse and children, many have already had children in a pre-marital relationship that didn't work out. Or they have had intimate relationships that left emotional scars that they carry into the marriage. At any rate, the residual affects of past relationships are often the cause of marital breakups, whether they consist of children from former relationships, lovers from former relationships, or bad memories from former relationships.

The Emperor Penguins live as long as 20 years. Every year, the female lays her egg and swims out to sea, while the male patiently waits until the egg hatches. Two months later, the female returns and the male swims out to sea. In two months he returns and, if their child has survived the winter, they raise it together.

Currently, 53 percent of American children are being raised in single parent homes. Couples cannot stay married long enough to raise their children together. There is something that the penguins are doing right that we have not yet learned how to do.

Prepare Children to be Spouses

In a community where children are raised within families, they learn by watching their own parents and the parents of their friends how to perform the roles of husband and wife. Stable marriages set the example for the creation of more stable marriages. Simply marrying someone before having sex does not insure that the marriage will work. Marriage is more than a civil union between two people to legitimize their sexual activities. Marriage is the foundation of the family. The family is the foundation of the community. A community is stable when the families are stable.

Many men and women want to enjoy intimacy, but have been content to delay marriage until they are well into adulthood, hoping to learn, through trial and error, how to find a compatible mate and establish a good relationship. How can we trust something as important as marriage to trial and error?

Consider this:

You have a fourteen-year-old child. In two years, by the age of sixteen, your child will be old enough to receive a driver's license. Currently, your child doesn't know anything about how to drive. In fact, even after halfway paying attention to you as you start up the engine and shift gears, the only thing your child really knows how to do is turn the key in the ignition to be able to listen to the radio, a cassette tape or a CD.

But you know that in two years, your child will be able to get a driver's license. So you go out and buy a brand new car, and come home with the keys and hand them to your child. Cheerfully you say, "This is your car. Figure out yourself how to drive it. You have two years to learn. After that, you can get your license."

Over the next two years your child crashes and smashes up and down the street, figuring out how to shift into drive, neutral, and reverse and learning how to put on the brakes. After numerous accidents and extensive damage to the bodies of both the car and the child, finally your child has mastered the art of driving. At the age of sixteen, after healing from all the stitches and castes, your child is able to pass the driving exam.

Surely there is a better way to qualify for a driver's license. Wouldn't careful, patient instruction and preparation be a less painful method of learning?

But this same "figure it out yourself" method is what we offer our children when it comes to preparing them for marriage. They enter their teen years and we tell them they are old enough to start "dating." The relationships they form are like the new cars they crash and smash, damaging the minds, bodies and souls of other innocent young people as they try to figure out how to form loving relationships.

A successful marriage requires that two people have patience, generosity, trust, kindness, truthfulness, forgiveness and affection. These are qualities that need to be taught in childhood, not eventually learned through the trial and error of numerous failed relationships. Each failure, though it may provide valuable lessons, also causes disappointment and distrust, feelings that can prevent a person from forming any future intimate relationships.

When teen sex leads to teen pregnancy, rarely are young people emotionally mature enough to form a stable union. Often neither the father of the child nor the child's mother is ready to commit to an exclusive sexual relationship. In many cases, young fathers have little or no contact with their own children. They are emotionally incapable of performing the role of father.

In her book *Where's Daddy? How to Provide What's Missing When Dad is Missing,* in the chapter entitled "Uncommitted Fathers and Unwed Mothers," author Claudette Wassil examines the different ways teens handle early parenthood:

> *Many factors affect the likelihood of teenage fathers remaining in contact with the mother of their child. Were the mother and father each other's exclusive sexual partner before the pregnancy? Have either of them, even now, reached a stage where they are ready to be sexually faithful to one person? How committed were the mother and father to each other prior to the pregnancy? How does each family feel about the other mate? How long the couple dated or were sexually active with one another will influ-*

ence the father's degree of attachment and sense of responsibility as well as the mother's willingness to let him remain involved with her and their child.

At one end of the scale we have the teenage father who has been having intercourse exclusively with the teenage mother to whom he has felt very committed. Whether or not they marry is then influenced by how each of the couple's parents feel about early unions...

At the other end of the scale there is the promiscuous male who has no interest in becoming a husband, let alone a father. Developmentally, he is obviously at a very self-centered stage and is not much use to anyone until he has completed this stage. Though he can be held financially liable for a child he fathers, if he earns no money he can hardly pay child support, and he is likely to see the threat of having to share money he earns as all the more reason not to start earning money.

<u>Where's Daddy</u>, *pages72 and 73.*

Parents have a responsibility to prepare their children for a mature adulthood, in which they are able to take on the roles of husbands, wives, and parents.   Boys must be allowed to mature into manhood before engaging in sex. They must be motivated to achieve the necessary education and skills to take care of themselves, a spouse and children.

When a man and woman's first sexual relationship is within the security and trust of a committed marriage, a marriage for which they have been well prepared with careful, patient instruction by their parents, there are no residual effects from previous sexual relationships to create complications leading to divorce.

According to recent statistics, 53% of America's children were born out of wedlock. Many single young men have fathered children, but still have no clue as to how to perform the role of husband.   They are only periodic visitors in the lives of their children, uninvolved in the day to day decision-making process. They are conspicuously absent, leaving young, inexperienced mothers to handle the job of actually raising the child.

Marriage is a necessary institution, because it civilizes men. In his book *Fatherless America*, author David Blankenhorn observes:

Indeed, political philosophers, no less than anthropologists, have clearly recognized the socialization of males in to the fatherhood role as a precondition for the rise of successful human societies...To lose fatherhood would be to regress to the state of nature...For men, marriage is the precondition, the enabling context for fatherhood as a social role. Why? Because marriage fosters paternal certainty thus permitting the emergence of what anthropologists call the legitimacy principal. This is my child, not another man's child. In turn, paternal certainty permits and encourages paternal investment: the commitment of the father to the well-being of the child.

By contrast, in mere nature where there are no matrimonial laws, males simply impregnate females and then move on. All responsibility for children is on the mother... Paternity is absent in the state of nature. Fatherhood is a defining characteristic of a civil society. The emergence of fatherhood as a social role for men signifies the transition from barbarism to society.

<u>Fatherless America</u>, pages 180, 181

The safety of a community is not determined by the size of the police force, but by the involvement of the men of the community. Men who are in the home helping to raise the children are less likely to commit crimes against their neighbors.

Boys who respect their fathers will also respect their mothers and other women in the community. They will grow up to follow rules of good conduct based on obedience to parents, not fear of law enforcement officers. If women want to live in safe, secure communities, they must have children who are connected to mature, responsible fathers.

If you want men to be mature and responsible, you must use the same good judgment as the female sparrow: Before you engage in sex, choose only a mate who has proposed a lifetime commitment and is prepared to take care of a family.

The Courage To Make A Commitment

Men and women hesitate to make permanent commitments in relationships because of fear and lack of trust. When adults don't have good models of successful marriages in their own lives to emulate, they simply don't know what to look for in a potential lifetime partner.

A person who has the courage to make a commitment has thought about his or her desires and is willing to discuss them. Following is a list of points for men and women to discuss early in the relationship to determine whether marriage is even possible.

1. Do you envision yourself getting married one day?
2. Can we talk about your ideas about marriage?
3. What kind of qualities would you like to see in a person you would consider marrying?
4. What personal goals would you like to reach before you decide to get married?
5. How do you think your marriage would be different from your parents' relationship?
6. How do you think your marriage would be the same as your parents' relationship?
7. What faults or weaknesses would you want to correct in yourself before getting married?
8. What faults or weaknesses would you consider absolutely intolerable in someone that you married?
9. Do you think it's possible to marry someone before having a sexually intimate experience together?
10. Do you think its possible to stay married to someone for the rest of your life?

Red Flags *(Signals that this relationship is going nowhere)*:
1. A "No" answer to questions 1, 2, 9 or 10.
2. An "I don't know" answer to questions 3, 4, 5, 6, 7, or 8.

Chapter 4
Contest of the Caribou
The power of the male ego

A colorful shower of red, yellow, green and orange leaves rain gently from the trees, trickling down in a slow motion dance through the air and touching softy upon the grounds of this sparsely wooded area. Brown coated deer leap gracefully between the trees, their nimble hooves prancing lightly upon the dried, crinkling autumn leaves. The splash of rushing water from a nearby stream is punctuated by the crash of deer antlers. It is the fall of the year, and among this lively herd of caribou, it is the rutting season. The females are in estrus, meaning they are fertile and ready to mate. The babies they conceive, called fawns, will be born in the spring of the year.

The scent of fertile females incites the males to engage in vigorous combat. The female caribou watch with interest as various challengers square off. Big, muscular caribou bucks with sharpened antlers lower their heads to do battle. The winners get to mate with their share of females. The losers get nothing.

A group of females prick up their ears as a dark brown caribou male approaches. He lifts his head to display a beautiful set of large, shapely antlers. His flaring nostrils blow hot breaths into the crisp fall air. As if on cue, the females move in his direction. He stands protectively beside them and surveys the other bucks in the forest. The proud tilt of his head and firm glare in his eyes sends a clear signal that these females belong to him and no one will get near them without a fight.

Suddenly, a loud, bellow rings out in the distance. Across the field, a large, heavily muscled dark gray figure is poised for a confrontation. The massive antlers on his head are sharpened to a point. He bellows his challenge again. The females hear the deep booming sound of his voice, indicating a broad chest, a sign of strength and power. They see his sharp antlers jutting forth from a proud, erect head. He struts forward, muscles rippling under a smooth, dark gray coat. The dark brown buck stands firmly, his eyes meeting the eyes of his challenger without a blink. He bellows in return. The two size each other up – muscle mass, antler size, voice tone. The challenger then lowers his antlers and charges at the dark brown buck. Two sculls crash together, and the bucks lock horns in combat. They tussle, twisting and turning, each trying to make the other lose his footing. The objective is to disable the competition and emerge the clear victor.

Each rears back and smashes into his opponent again, sending a thick spray of dust and leaves into the air, while nearby females observe the fight. Although the caribou seldom battle to the death, puncture wounds from sharp antlers can inflict serious damage. A badly wounded caribou is a good target for predators.

The dark brown buck wrestles his determined challenger to the ground, twisting his opponent's head in a neck-wrenching move. The tip of his antler has pierced the challenger's side. The overpowered gray buck concedes defeat, staggering away dejectedly to privately nurse his wounds.

Again, as if on cue, the females move towards their hero. The dark brown buck lifts his head victoriously, his pointed antlers sitting atop his head like a crown. He has successfully defended his position as the strongest, most worthy male. The proud champion receives his reward immediately-- an excited female, ready to mate.

Autumn is the mating season for many herd animals, in which males compete for females in violent contests of butting heads and locking horns. Whose genetic line will control the future? Each wrestling match determines who is the strongest and most worthy male to sire the next generation.

Among the herds of animals that are hunted by many predators, females know that their job is to is to make sure the children they conceive are given the best possible opportunities to live long, healthy lives. They instinctively seek out strong, aggressive males that can complement them in this task.

Females know they must bear strong children who are able to get up and run just a few hours after birth. When it comes to mate selection, animals seem to instinctively understand genetics: A strong father will likely produce strong children. A weak father will likely produce weak children. Females are attracted to strength and power. Therefore, the males in the herd strive to demonstrate to the females that they are the strongest and the most powerful, so that the females will select them for mating.

Despite the trappings of modern civilization, most human behavior is also motivated by these same basic animal instincts. Once women recognize this, they will have a better understanding of how they influence the social dynamics in today's society. Men are motivated by the admiration of women. They strive to acquire the things that will attract women.

Women have the power to create a society of responsible, hard working, honest men. Just as the caribou females collectively respond to the male that has exhibited the greatest strength, women must collectively respond to men that exhibit qualities essential to human survival – qualities such as hard work, decency, integrity, honesty and respect. It is the women's responsibility to encourage these qualities in men.

Men need love. They need love like they need air, water, and food. The love of a woman is a powerful influence in the shaping of a man's character. Some of the world's most popular literary tales are of men who performed great feats of bravery in order to win the love of a woman. The need for love creates a drive that can bring out the best qualities in a man – compassion, tenderness, unselfishness, and courage.

Women are attracted to strength, power, intelligence, and skill. When in the presence of women, men will compete with other men in striving to project these qualities. Praise and admiration from women motivates men to strive to prove themselves superior.

The competition among the caribou males is healthy, in that it motivates them to strive to be their absolute best. The females choose the best males to father their children. Then, once the rutting season is over and the females have been impregnated, the herds continue their peaceful migration in search of fertile grasslands. The old, sickly, and wounded may fall prey to wolves or other predators along the way. The rest continue their annual cross-country journey, concentrating on fattening themselves up before the cold winter sets in. The males have until the next season to build up their strength, sharpen their antlers, and prepare themselves to again battle for the right to mate. Until then, there is peace in the caribou community.

When Competition Becomes Destructive

A competitive male spirit is a positive thing. Among human beings, it can motivate men to strive for, in addition to physical prowess, great achievements in science, art, literature, music and other intellectual pursuits.

However, too often men compete for dominance in a manner that leads to war and death. Rather than temporary struggles followed by peaceful resolution, men's conflicts lead to violent wars that destroy the earth and kill vast portions of the human population. This is why a female influence is necessary, in order to create a balanced society. Competition must be for the purpose of encouraging the best traits among men. Women define what is desirable male behavior, by the way they react to men.

The human family has divided itself into hostile camps based upon national, racial, ethnic and religious differences, although human beings are all part of the same species. The males in each group are in a never ending battle for dominance over the other. Like bucks in a herd of deer, when men gather together they size each other up and challenge each other to determine who will be the dominant male.

Most nations of the world today are engaged in a perpetual power struggle between races and classes of people. The reason for this struggle is not much different than the motivation behind the clashing sculls and locked horns of the caribou males. Whose genetic line will control the future?

This is the underlying cause of most human conflict that leads to war. Women's responses to the behavior of men have had a major impact on the shaping of history in this regard.

Among herd animals, females set the balance between the male's competitive drive and the herd's need to coexist. The family structure in most herds is matrilineal in nature, with related females forming the core of the family and outside males earning the right to sire their children and perform the role of protector. In his book *Demonic Males*, zoologist Richard Wrangham observes that among animal species where the family structure is patrilineal, there is much more violence and aggression:

Very few animals live in patrilineal, male-bonded communities wherein females routinely reduce the risks of inbreeding by moving to neighboring groups to mate. And only two animal species are known to do so with a system of intense, male-initiated territorial aggression, including lethal raiding into neighboring communities in search of vulnerable enemies to attack and kill. Out of four thousand mammals and ten million or more other animal species, this suite of behaviors is known only among chimpanzees and humans.

<u>Demonic Males</u>, Page 24

Human history is a long chronicle of migrations, as people from different lands traveled and discovered different looking people in other parts of the world. Periodic migration is necessary to prevent inbreeding. When there is mutual respect, migration is a positive thing. It helps people from other cultures share and exchange knowledge. The natural attraction between men and women leads to intermarriage and is often a means of preserving peace. Through marriage, men and women join families, clans, tribes and even nations in a bond of kinship.

Marriage is a sign of mutual respect between men. When a man consents to give his daughter in marriage to another man, he is declaring that man to be worthy to join his family and produce the next generation.

A female influence is necessary for a cultural balance between competitive striving for advancement and cooperative sharing of resources. When a society becomes imbalanced by the lack of a positive female influence, male aggression and conflicts over control of territory escalate into war.

Wars are especially perilous for women. During wartimes, all rules for civilized conduct are abandoned. The most destructive aspect of male aggression is unleashed, and women become the targets of attack. Men at war will brutalize and degrade women as a sign of conquest. By force, seeds are planted in the wombs of women. The children that are born from these wartime acts of rape carry the genes of the conqueror.

In her book *Against Our Will, Men Women and Rape*, author Susan Brownmiller explains the twisted psychology that encourages men to engage in rape during war:

The sickness of warfare feeds on itself. A certain number of soldiers must prove their newly won superiority – prove it to a woman, to themselves, to other men. In the name of victory and the power of the gun, war provides men with the tacit license to rape.

Among the ancient Greeks, rape was also socially acceptable behavior well within the rules of warfare, an act without stigma for warriors who viewed the women they conquered as legitimate booty, useful as wives, concubines, slave labor or battle camp trophy.

A simple rule of thumb in war is that the winning side is the side that does the raping ... Rape is considered by the people of a defeated nation to be part of the enemy's conscious effort to destroy them. In fact, by tradition, men appropriate the rape of "their women" as part of their own male anguish of defeat ...

Apart from genuine human concern for wives and daughters near and dear to them, rape by a conqueror is compelling evidence of the conquered's status of masculine impotence."

Against our Will, by Susan Brownmiller, pages 24, 25, and 27

In healthy communities, men value the dignity of women and strive to protect them from harm. They strive for excellence in order to be worthy of marriage to them. Therefore, women have the power to inspire men to demonstrate their strength as men, not through acts of violence, greed and oppression, but through acts of intelligence and compassion.

A Violent Clash of Cultures

America was founded in a violent clash of cultures. Many immigrants left Europe to escape economic, social and religious oppression. They came from an oppressive society in which families claiming "royal" heritage controlled the land and the government and forced men and women to farm the land and pay taxes. Poor farmers who could not afford to pay taxes were sometimes thrown into prison. Those who held religious beliefs contrary to the ruling class were also sometimes thrown into prison. Prisoners were often brutally tortured.

When prisons became too overcrowded, some inmates were given the option to remain in jail or be deported to the "New World." Europeans arrived on the shores of what became known as America, and found a colorful people who maintained a spiritual reverence for nature. The men were strong and demonstrated great skill in hunting. Women worked in harmony to provide a peaceful home life for children.

The native philosophy was one of hospitality to strangers, and as long as the Europeans did not appear to have harmful intentions, they were treated as visitors and guests. Most encounters between early European immigrants were peaceful. In fact, as American school children are taught, native Americans helped the white immigrants survive the first harsh winters by showing them how to grow corn and hunt for meat. American children learn the story of Thanksgiving, the first winter in which a feast was shared by the European immigrants and the Native Americans. Whites, though lacking in survival skills, were treated with human kindness during the earlier years of European immigration.

However, as the white population grew, the social dynamics between the European immigrants and the natives changed. Europeans used armed violence to take over the land inhabited by the native people and tried to impose the same sort of caste-based feudal system they had left behind in Europe.

In her book, *The Women's Movement, Political Socioeconomic and Psychological Issues*, Barbara Deckard observes that European cultural attitudes evolved out of ancient Greek society, where women had no rights. This contrasted with Native American communities, such as the Navaho and the Hopi, where clans were matrilineal, women had leadership status, and the land was owned collectively by the entire clan. There was no privileged class. In ancient Greece, however, people were either of the ruling class or they were slaves that worked in the fields:

Later, in Athenian Greece, 80 percent of all women were slave women, that is property. The slave owner's wife was to be seen, not heard. She was well off materially but, even in so-called democratic fifth-century Athens, she was not to leave the house...

Women's place was in the home with children. Demosthenes said: "Mistresses we keep for our pleasure, concubines for daily attendance upon our person, wives to bear us legitimate children and be our faithful housekeepers."...

The husband owned all the property and slaves, and his sons inherited most of it. Ruling-class women usually learned to read and write, but higher education was reserved for boys. Slaves were never educated, except where their job necessitated it.

In Western Europe, slavery was followed by feudalism. Under feudalism, human beings were no longer owned by other human beings; rather, serfdom prevailed. Serfs were slightly better off than slaves in that they were not owned, but merely bound to the landlord's land. Serf men and women had to labor a certain number of days a year for the landlord; in return, he was supposed to "protect" them...

Although the Church stated clearly that women were the weaker and inferior sex, that did not stop either secular or reli-

gious landlords from working their serf women in the field the same as the men.
The Women's Movement, pages 191, 192 and 193

Whites left Europe with the desire to be free of feudal society, yet, they knew nothing else. As white settlers continued to move westward to claim territory in the Americas, they engaged in violent confrontations with the natives.

Oppression breeds oppression. Those who had been oppressed farmers in Europe came to the new world to create the same oppressive, exploitive system in order to become wealthy landowners themselves. They killed entire communities in an effort to take over the land, and produce crops for the European market. There was a violent clash of cultures. Most native societies were founded on the principals that land and the animals that inhabit it all belong to the Creator and, just like air, they cannot be privately owned but must be shared. However, Europeans arrived and began the business of fencing off the land and claiming private ownership. Soon the native people and their philosophy were nearly exterminated.

From Prison Labor to Forced Imported Labor

The pursuit of wealth by any means necessary became the cornerstone of American law. Following a system used by the ruling class in England, white landowners used the prison industry to obtain workers. Poor men and women who were convicted of crimes could work off their sentence by serving for seven years as "indentured servants."

This drive for wealth is what eventually prompted the forced importation of Africans. When white indentured servants finished their seven-year sentence, landowners still wanted free labor. As the nations of Africa waged war with each other, American landowners discovered that by buying those prisoners of war, they could launch a rapid growth of the farming industry. These African people were strong men and women who had agricultural skills and experience. Colonial governments created laws so that Africans could be imported and become servants for life.

White men marketed black men as big, mindless brutes who could be taught to perform fieldwork and basic labor. The black females were marketed as fieldworkers, house servants and child breeders. Slave traders, in their advertisements of the sale of human cargo, tried to project the image of these people as some sort of sub-human species. Those who purchased Africans to use as slaves argued that these were inferior human beings, capable of only the most basic training, better off under the supervision of the more intelligent whites. This was so as not to offend sensitive whites that might be repulsed at the idea of human beings being sold at auction right along with cattle and sheep.

Europeans discovered that Africans had great strength and endurance for heavy outdoor labor. Agriculture was a way of life in many parts of Africa. Africans had produced crops such as cotton and rice for centuries, developing systems of planting and harvesting which were unknown to Europeans.

Many Africans, having come from the advanced kingdoms of West Africa, also had architectural and building expertise and possessed skills in smelting iron that were unknown to Europeans. They built the houses and the roads, creating the unique architecture that defined Colonial America.

Forced to work at gunpoint, and lashed at intervals with whips, they labored under the hot sun, singing musical chants in harmony so as to make the work go faster, synchronize movements, and increase work efficiency. This was the way farming was done in many of the West African rural communities. Like many Native American societies, Africans had also formed clans in which property was owned and farmed communally.

Music not only helped create a rhythm for the planting and harvesting of crops, but also became a means of secret communication through hidden messages in the songs. Music restored the souls of those who had lost hope of ever seeing freedom. These were a people who could not be broken. They were beaten down, and yet they sang.

This gave rise to the common stereotype of the happy black slave, singing and dancing in the fields. This was the image that slaveholders sold to anti-slavery skeptics who heard horrendous stories of torture inflicted daily upon those held in captivity.

Soon, an entire industry was created around the importation of Africans to serve as permanent laborers in North America, Central America, and up until the late 1700s, some parts of Europe. Prisoners of war were joined by thousands of kidnapped men and women from across the continent of Africa. All were tightly packed as cargo and sent overseas in specially designed slave ships. This enterprise, financed by wealthy businessmen and backed by the participating governments, became the means whereby America gained its wealth and international influence. The formation of Wall Street and the New York Stock Exchange was based on the international slave trading business and the goods that slaves produced.

Legalized Rape and Adultery

This is the skeleton in America's closet. Unknown to many recent immigrants to America, the social and economic system of slavery created at America's inception is the driving force behind all current U.S. social, political and economic policies. At the root of American culture is an underlying power struggle between black and white men.

Under slavery, white men raped black women and tortured and killed black men that resisted capture and confinement. Laws in the slaveholding states protected slave owners from being prosecuted for the horrendous acts they committed.

The ability to enforce respect for ones woman is a sign of power. The rule is simple: *I am powerful. You will not touch my woman. You are weak. I can use your woman for sex.*

This is a universally understood principle among men. It was expressed vividly during the slave era and for many decades thereafter. While many white men desired black women, they did not afford them the respected status of wife. They openly violated their own marriage vows, flaunting black concubines and out-of-wedlock children under their wives' noses.

As slave owners, white men could openly practice adultery under the protection of laws that defined enslaved black female concubines as mere "property." Intimacy with ones black slave did not carry the same social stigma as relations outside of marriage with a white woman.

Many prominent white slave owners had black female concubines. President Thomas Jefferson, and Benjamin Franklin are just two of America's founding fathers that were widely known to have had black mistresses. They fathered numerous children by black women, as did many wealthy landowners during America's inception. In his book, *Sex and Race in the New World*, author J.A. Rogers states:

Men were much less careful of concealing their morals than now. Having a Negro concubine or two was the fashion, even as now in middle class Southern society a white father will sometimes refer with pride to his son's "yellow gal." As for having mulatto children, it was thought so little of that as one writer (cited by Calhoun) said, "Men of worth, politeness, and humanity could listen with composure to their dinner-guests tracing the paternal features of the slave sons waiting at the table."

Benjamin Franklin, who used to turn a thrifty penny along with his printing business, by dealing in slaves, was accused of having sexual relations with Negro women. Thomas Jefferson seems to have had a particular fondness for dark feminine flesh. He was openly attacked by the politicians of his time for his relations with "Black Sal" Hemming or Hemmings.

"Or seek in a dark and dirty alley
A Mr. Jefferson's Miss Sally."
reads a political pamphlet of the times. Visitors to America openly commented on Jefferson's mulatto offspring...

Patrick Henry, governor of Virginia, of "Give me liberty or give me death" had a Negro son, named Melancthon. Patrick Henry seems to have left him well provided for. The great Colonel

Schuyler, aristocrat, who stood "foremost" in upper New York, had a son by "a favorite Negro woman to the great offense and scandal" of his family, says Anne Grant...

As regards George Washington, E.B. Reuter says he is among those mentioned as having Negro mistresses, but the written evidence is hazy...

An undeniable instance, however, is that of Colonel Richard M. Johnson, ninth vice-president of the United States, 1837-41, who was very much in love with his mulatto concubine, Julia Chinn, and had two daughters by her, whom he both had married to white men in elaborate ceremonies.

Among others named as having mulatto children are Jefferson Davis, Henry Clay, John Tyler, and Zachary Taylor, presidents of the United States.

<u>*Sex and Race in the New World*</u> *by J. A. Rogers, page 222*

When exploitation becomes profitable, immorality becomes acceptable. Slavery developed into more than just a means to reduce the cost of farming crops. The slaves themselves became the product that farmers bred and sold on the market. They and their white hired hands made a business out of impregnating female slaves to produce children for sale.

The offspring of a white man and a black woman was a child of lighter skin. Mixed race slaves often sold at a higher price. Slave auctions were shocking events where men, women and children were stripped of their clothing and made to stand naked before gawking crowds while an auctioneer called out prices and potential buyers made bids.

Sex and Race: The Roots of America's Conflict

Slavery became socially and politically acceptable for another reason. Many early European settlers in America were heavily influenced by the sexually repressive culture of England's puritanical society. The enslavement of African people gave white men an opportunity to act out their repressed fantasies. In the book

Long Memory, The Black Experience in America, authors Mary
Frances Berry and John W. Blassingame observe:

> *Until the last decades of the twentieth century white men, of-*
> *ten suffering from puritanical and psychological inhibitions and*
> *taught that sex was somehow sinful and unnatural, put up many*
> *barriers to interracial sexual contacts.   Yet, blacks fascinated*
> *them.*
>
> *Many of the white man's sexual fantasies, dreams and de-*
> *sires that he considered sinful were projected onto blacks.   The*
> *fantasies appeared most clearly in the myths about black women.*
> *The image of the white woman was just the opposite. By creating a*
> *mythological black Venus and a white Virgin Mary, the white man*
> *dehumanized them both.   In myth, considered frail, cold and con-*
> *cerned only with the ennobling aspects of life, the white woman*
> *was not expected to show passion or erotic interests.*
>
> *In effect, as the sociologist John Dollard observed in Caste*
> *and Class in Southern Town in 1949, "the idealization of the white*
> *woman...especially in the South...made her untouchable." But not*
> *the black woman. Obviously, if the black Venus was as passionate*
> *as the white man's image of her suggested, then she had to be ex-*
> *ploited for the sexual pleasure of the white man. Similarly, if the*
> *black male was the Apollo white men said that he was, white*
> *women might be seduced by him. To prevent this from happening*
> *the middle- and upper-class white man cloistered his women, shel-*
> *tering them from contact with black men.*
>
> <u>*Long Memory, The Black Experience in America*</u>
> *pages 115 and 116*

Just as white men were fascinated by black people, so were
white women. But for white men, the unwritten rules of sex and
power demanded that black men be prevented from establishing
intimate relationships with white women.

White men often called black men apes, gorillas and brutes,
conjuring up the most distasteful image they could create, hoping
to make black men repulsive in the eyes of white women, and

thereby prevent white women from becoming attracted to them.

It didn't work. Black men were tall and powerfully built, with well-developed muscles from heavy labor, while white men grew fat and pudgy from a life of ease and indulgence in liquor. Black men's rich, dark, sun-bathed skin was quite a contrast to the pale flesh of white male aristocracy. Black men's deep voices re-sounded across the fields as they moved with strength and agility in performing their daily work. White women saw them and found them beautiful. As J. A. Rogers notes in his book, *Sex and Race in the New World* white women sought black men out and wanted to marry them:

In colonial days, the newly-arrived Englishwoman or Irishwoman not only had no color prejudice but felt positive at-traction toward the blacks. There was not only the sexual novelty but the black man, from very early times, had rightly or wrongly, the reputation of being a better lover than the Caucasian. I have already given elsewhere abundant evidence of this from Oriental and European literature where even queens and noblewomen pre-ferred Negro slaves...

But whatever the cause there was much association be-tween Negroes and white women, or one had better say between white women and Negroes because in the early colonial days it was the white women who at first took the initiative.

<u>*Sex and Race in the New World*</u>, *by J.A. Rogers, page 232.*

Seeing white women's strong attraction to black men, white men became frightened. Many Southern states enacted laws making marriage between a black man and white women a crimi-nal offense. In a number of cases during the 1700s, free white women who chose black male slaves as mates were themselves sold at public auction. Laws were enacted that declared that any white woman who married a slave would herself become a slave.

Ministers were fined for marrying black men and white women, such as Rev. John Cotton in North Carolina in 1725, ac-cording to court records. White women were publicly whipped for bearing children by black men, as in the case of Hannah Bonny, a free white woman whipped for having an illegitimate child by a black man.

Much of American culture is still based on this unspoken, hostile and sometimes violent struggle for supremacy between black men and white men. By nature, every male strives to reproduce himself. A male's seed represents his immortality. The man that fathers a woman's children controls her family's future. Repressive laws during slavery and the decades following abolition reflected white men's fears of black men marrying white women.

Responsible Men Prepare a Way For Their Sons

Many in the feminist movement have mistakenly identified the struggle as that of men against women, when in fact, men and women were designed to perform complementary roles in the forming of families. Rather than to be adversaries, they are designed to be a source of mutual support and encouragement. Women have to recognize that if a man is psychologically beat down and made to feel inferior, he will not have the necessary drive to compete with other men. Women want to be respected as equals to men, but at the same time, they expect men to remain strong and confident. This requires encouragement and support.

The male ego is a necessary motivator, in that it reflects a man's sense of pride and self esteem. A man must believe himself to be worthy of respect in order to strive to obtain it. The system of slavery in America was designed to destroy the black man's ego, the sense of self worth that makes a man resist domination by another man. Slavery was designed to destroy the natural instinct to protect and provide for ones children, by eliminating the institution of marriage between enslaved African Americans. Black women were forced to be mere breeders of children for sale on the market. Black men were encouraged to impregnate women, but were not allowed to be fathers who could protect or provide for their children. They were separated from their children and sent on to impregnate other women. After a few generations of enslavement, they no longer knew how to be husbands and fathers. Many had lost the natural drive to protect their own sons and daughters.

Responsible men, knowing that men are expected to be able to function as heads of households, prepare a way for their own sons to succeed. When a man does not provide a means for his sons to excel, his sons will be subjugated by other men. A subjugated man is not attractive to women, because women want strong men who can enforce respect for them and their daughters. Strong men make sure other men respect their daughters through marriage and will not permit out-of-wedlock childbirths.

Responsible men who have obtained economic prosperity or political influence want to pass it on to their own children. Men establish schools so that their own children may excel in knowledge. Men establish businesses so that their own children may become prosperous. Men establish governments so that their own children may rule nations.

The social problems that exist in present day American society are rooted in the slave experience. Although marriage between black people is no longer illegal, African Americans still engage in self-destructive behaviors that lead to out-of-wedlock pregnancies. Men are not in the home. They are not establishing businesses to employ their families. They are not establishing schools to educate their children. They are instead expecting those who practice racial discrimination to suddenly have a change of heart and become more fair-minded in hiring and education.

People who are struggling against discrimination must recognize this fact: *No men who are in a dominant position are going to establish a system to enable men from another group to excel above them.* In every multi-racial or multi-ethnic community, whether it is within a city, a nation or an organization, systematic discrimination exists. Discrimination is never accidental. It is designed to maintain positions of power for those who have them.

"Power concedes nothing without a demand. It never has and it never will."

Frederick Douglas

The only way any group can excel in society is by striving to develop superior intelligence, strength and skill. The people must organize among themselves to establish schools so that their children excel in knowledge, businesses so that their children prosper and governments so that their children can govern.

Jealousy Triggers Racism

The end of the Civil War in 1865 marked a new chapter in American history in which men and women of African descent were no longer bound by State law to be servants and slaves to whites.

The end of slavery meant the beginning of opportunities for blacks to make up for generations of deprivation and lack of access to education, economic development and political empowerment. Given opportunities to excel, blacks made amazing strides in just a few decades following the end of the Civil War. Schools were founded, communities were organized, and businesses were developed. The formerly enslaved African Americans struggled to regain their dignity. They married and raised families, they sacrificed to send children to school. By the turn of the century, some blacks had risen to economic prominence.

This period following the Civil War, known as Reconstruction, was a dangerous time for blacks and a frightening time for whites. Over a period of a few centuries, whites had developed a race-based caste system that placed them at the top of the social, political and economic ladders of society. Like the old feudal system did for the ruling class in Europe, this caste system gave whites an artificial sense of superiority over all other groups designated as part of a lower caste - Natives, Africans, Asians, and all other non-white immigrants. It falsely inflated the white male ego, creating arrogance and bigotry.

White men could only maintain their false sense of superiority if other men were projected as inferior. Whites used literature, the arts, and every means of communication to portray themselves as more intelligent than other men.

Women are attracted to powerful men. Power means the ability to think, make decisions, make things happen, and lead others. Black men rose from slavery to become educators, inventors, doctors, businessmen, writers, musicians, and even elected officials. Given the opportunities to develop their skills, black men proved that their abilities were equal, and even superior to the white men that once held them in captivity. This created anger, resentment, and jealousy in white men. In order to keep up their pretense of racial superiority, white males desperately needed to make black males appear weak and stupid.

To prevent black men from winning the admiration of white women, white men created social customs requiring blacks to pretend to be inferior, in an attempt to reinforce impressions of black male powerlessness. Any black male who failed to display the appropriate posture of submission – head bowed, eyes down – when approaching a white person could be lynched.

Lynching – the murder of a person by a mob of people – was often the punishment for blacks who were "uppity" that is, blacks who refused to pretend to be weak, stupid and otherwise inferior to whites. Such public, mob directed murders involved everything from hanging to dismemberment to being burned alive.

A black man who did not speak in the broken English of a slave, but instead used correct grammar and sounded "educated" might easily become the victim of angry white mob violence. A back man who dared to start his own business and become affluent… tried to vote or run for public office… tried to organize his community to get better service from the government… asked for a much deserved raise or promotion on a job… sent his children to a top school…or dared to date a white woman…any such offense could get a black man killed.

A black man's supposed involvement with a white woman was a common rallying point for a mob of angry white men. Just as they were during slavery, white men were obsessed with fear that black men would attract and marry white women. The usual excuse for mob violence was the accusation of "rape" of a white woman by a black man. Lynching was meant to instill such terror in black men that they would never dare to approach white women.

Newspaper publisher and activist Ida B. Wells implored the government to enact anti-lynching legislation to make such mob action illegal. The all-white male federal government refused. Lynching escalated in the early 1900s and continued well into the late 20th century. The lynching of 12-year-old Emmett Till in Mississippi in 1955 is said to be the catalyst for the Civil Rights Movement. Emmett Till's case made national headlines when white men kidnapped him from a relative's home in the middle of the night and beat him beyond recognition for supposedly "whistling at a white woman."

The recent apology from the government for this shocking period in American history comes much too late, according to a June 5, 2005 *Chicago Sun-Times* newspaper editorial:

So, 105 years after an anti-lynching bill was proposed and 50 years after Emmett Till was dragged from his uncle's home and killed, the U.S. Senate has officially apologized for its refusal to enact the legislation – without which an estimated 4,750 people, mostly blacks, were murdered by lynch mobs between 1882 and 1968.

To some, the apology, as welcome as it is, seems little more than a symbolic gesture...But in conjunction with various recent efforts to keep America from sweeping lynching under the rug of its collective memory...the Senate action promises to make a significant difference in how this chapter of history is treated.

<u>Chicago Sun Times</u>, Commentary, June 5, 2005, page 75

The White Male Inferiority Complex

Despite the passage of time and a supposedly changed social environment, the same underlying emotions of the past continue to trigger racially motivated violence today.

Every year, blacks conduct sociological studies, hold conferences and conduct endless debates on how to deal with racial injustice. The presumption is that whites practice racial discrimination because they erroneously believe that blacks are intellectually inferior, and that all blacks have to do is prove themselves intelligent and whites will treat them better.

That's not it.

White racism is a really a reflection of a white inferiority complex, a fear that blacks, if given equal opportunities, would excel over whites. Whenever people insist upon having an unfair advantage in any competition, it is because they don't believe they can win any other way.

Consider this:

You decide to try out for the school track team. You arrive at the tryouts and the Coach informs you that there are only three spots on the team left. You and seven others must race each other for the three positions. The Coach says he will have all eight of you run a hundred meter dash, and the fastest three will make the team.

Just as you step up to the starting line with your opponents, the other seven suddenly protest your presence. They say that you should not be allowed to run, you're just in the way, you'll only slow them down. They urge the Coach not to allow you to try out. As a compromise, the Coach asks you to step back, so that you're starting out ten meters behind the other runners. This way, he says, you'll be out of their way. Grudgingly, they agree to this arrangement. The Coach prepares to start the race.

"On your mark...get set..." Bang! The starting gun goes off and you take off like lightening, passing first one, then two, then three, then four, then five of the other runners. At the end of the race, you cross the finish line in third place. You have earned a spot on the team.

The other five runners that you beat are protesting loudly, claiming it wasn't fair, saying that you still shouldn't be allowed on the team because, after all, they say, you only came in third place, proving you're still probably too slow.

When people refuse to allow you a fair opportunity to compete with them, it's not because they think you are inferior; it is because they think *they* are. They are afraid that, in an honest competition, you will win.

When people deny you access to education, it is because they fear you are more intelligent than they are. The greater the discrimination, the greater the feelings of inferiority in the one who discriminates.

Education remains a battleground for blacks seeking opportunities for self-improvement. Inadequate funding for predominately black schools force black youth to strive twice as hard to keep up with the achievements in well financed white schools. Black students attending understaffed, ramshackle schools must overcome broken computers, not enough books, poor lighting, and inadequate supplies to compete with newly remodeled white schools that offer the latest modern technology. When black students score lower than white students on standardized achievement tests, whites can compare the scores and again pretend to be intellectually superior.

Young black men today face extreme obstacles, such as racial prejudice, economic neglect and negative peer pressure. They are systematically forced out of educational institutions and discouraged from attending college, sometimes by teachers who make them feel intellectually inadequate. In many cases, outstanding athletic talent provides their only hope for access to higher education.

For decades white men resisted allowing talented black athletes to attend college, fearing that they would mix socially with whites. Integrated college campuses today reflect many white men's greatest fears: their daughters are overwhelmingly attracted to young black men. In fact, many predominately white college campuses have become social battlegrounds for black women and white women as they fight over the highly prized black athletes.

Black men, demoralized from years of ridicule aimed at them by a hostile white society, often enter higher education emotionally wounded and suffering from low self-esteem. Black women, conditioned by white racism to see black men as weak, ugly, and inferior, continue to dismiss black men as if they are not worthy of respect. They destroy black men's egos, diminishing black men's feelings of self-pride.

Men are drawn to women who admire them, confirming their worth as men. Men avoid women who treat them with disdain, making them feel worthless.

White women, intrigued by black men's style, fascinated by black men's appearance and excited by black men's physical prowess, express open admiration and interest. After years of being ridiculed and called ugly by black women, many dark skinned black men discover that white women consider them quite handsome. Black men are drawn to white women because they supply what black men need to rebuild their shattered self esteem: praise and admiration.

This is the social dynamics occurring on many integrated college campuses. Black women bemoan the fact that many of the most popular black athletes select white women over them. They forget the fact that they initially rejected some of these same men, whom they derisively described as "ugly" or "too black", reflecting their own self-loathing.

Racism in the professional athletic industry further exposes the white male inferiority complex. Physical prowess is a sign of power. Power itself is a bit of an aphrodisiac for women. Just as young bucks butting heads excite female deer, men engaging in physical combat generate sexual excitement in women. Contact sports like football are actually simulations of men in battle. This and other sports allow men to demonstrate superior skill, strength and speed. Women are attracted to athletes because physical ability tends to be associated with virility, as well as the ability to protect and defend.

Black men that broke through color barriers and excelled in sports were met with white male hostility. From Olympic gold medal winning track star Jesse Owens to baseball's Jackie Robinson, each black athlete encountered threats of violence because their outstanding performances refuted false notions of white male superiority. Heavyweight boxing champion Jack Johnson enraged white men precisely because he openly flaunted his white wife and white girl friends in public.

Intelligence, and the ability to verbally express it, is also attractive to women. Men who demonstrate superior wit and oratorical skills sometimes generate as much excitement in women as the well-built, agile athlete.

Today, some of the greatest targets of white male wrath are black leaders with powerful speaking abilities. Such men generate enthusiasm in audiences and inspire masses of people to follow them. Women will follow and support such men with their time, organizational skills and financial resources. Charismatic black leaders, despite harsh criticism from prominent white men, become more powerful and influential, largely because of the enthusiastic support of women. Like the female deer that gather around the strongest caribou buck, women will rally around a strong man.

The real reason for white men's scurrilous attacks on aggressive black leaders is simple: Jealousy. Women of many races admire these black men for their intelligence, a quality that sharply contradicts the image of the ignorant black brute that white males strive to promote through literature and films.

The film industry helps to reinforce images of black men as either ignorant, degenerate criminals, or docile flunkies of white men. These are the images that receive accolades and awards from the white male controlled Motion Picture Academy.

A common TV and movie image today is the black male homosexual, projected on screen not so much to symbolize the social acceptance of homosexuals, but more as a means to neutralize the image of a strong, virile black man. Meanwhile, the white male character, no matter if he is overweight and balding, will always be portrayed as the romantic lead who attracts the beautiful women. The first films that featured black men and white women in interracial relationships ignited protests among audiences. White producers still hesitate to cast black men in romantic lead roles.

Another cinematic tactic to reinforce the idea of black male powerlessness is to have the strong black male character tragically die at the end of the movie. A dead man poses no threat.

The Criminal Black Male Stereotype

The news media often serves to reinforce negative movie stereotypes of the criminal black man who must be restrained, controlled, or killed. Daily news reports, describing robberies, assaults and gang violence, often show black men being led away in handcuffs by police. These images have influenced public opinion around the world, creating fear of black men in the minds of many immigrants before they even arrive in America.

The international drug business, which makes a large share of its profits by drug trafficking in the inner cities, leads to a degenerate culture of violence and illicit sex evolving from widespread drug addiction. Those who control the international drug business target urban areas where strong fathers are absent and children are left to fend for themselves. The absence of viable businesses, schools, and community institutions leaves many young people vulnerable to the lure of the profitable yet deadly drug trafficking business.

Now that the mass media has helped to firmly ingrain the criminal black male stereotype in the American psyche, random stops, harassment and arrests by police are common experiences for black males of all ages.

According to Amnesty International's current statistics, although African Americans make up just 12% of the U.S. population, they make up 42% of the prison population. Young black males are frequent targets of the criminal justice system, with high rates of arrest and conviction, many simply for the lack of good legal representation to prove their innocence. Young, strong black men are being removed from the general population and rendered incapable of establishing families or providing for children. This is no accident. Just like the caribou bucks during rutting season, the intent of men in power is *to disable the competition.* As long as they prevent other males from gaining economic prosperity or political influence, they can maintain the dominant male position.

Understanding this reality can help those who fight against injustice to develop a better strategy to overcome it.

The Politics of Beauty

Physical features – height, weight, body shape, head shape, nose shape, lip size, eye color, skin color, hair texture – identify a person's ancestry and parentage. Clans, tribes, races and ethnic groups identify themselves by the subtle differences in physical features.

The powerful male is the male who can continue his genetic line. Children who look like him are evidence of his dominant influence. This is the rule in the animal kingdom as well as throughout the human community.

Every ethnic and racial group has its own standard of beauty, based on the common physical features of the people. Beauty is simply a reflection of a people's natural genetic traits. In healthy societies, people like the way they look. However, when different family groups intermingle and men fight for genetic domination, female beauty becomes the political standard that determines who is the superior male.

Again, the rule is simple; I *am powerful; my woman is beautiful. You are weak; your woman is ugly.*

During the slave era, this notion was deeply engrained in the American psyche. Slave auctions reinforced the notion that human value increased with the percentage of white ancestry. Light skinned women with straighter hair, obviously the daughters of white men, brought high prices as potential concubines. Through their liaisons with black women, white men fashioned a class of women who reflected a white woman's beauty standard but a black woman's slave status – meaning she could be used for sex. The life of the white man's mistress, though degrading on the one hand, had its practical benefits on the other. The light-skinned concubines wore better clothing, ate better food, and enjoyed more privileges than their darker skinned, field-working sisters.

White men committed adultery with black women as a regular part of Southern culture. Just like the Greek Demosthenes expressed in his day, "Mistresses we keep for our pleasure, concubines for daily attendance upon our person, wives to bear us legitimate children and be our faithful housekeepers." For some women, their light skin was a ticket to higher social and economic status – if they were willing to pay the price.

Sadly, more than a century after Emancipation, the politics of beauty in America remains the same. Women with light skin and Caucasian physical features are profiled in magazines, billboards, television ads, and movies as representative of black beauty. The politics of beauty is solidly backed by economics. Women who possess Caucasian physical features are often afforded lucrative careers in modeling, acting, singing, and dancing and other career opportunities over and above their darker sisters. This economic reality prompts many dark skinned women with crinkly hair to lighten their skin with make up and straighten and dye their hair with chemicals to achieve, as much as possible, the preferred Caucasian look.

Asian women who get eye surgery to remove the ethnic-identifying folds in their eyelids, dark haired Hispanic and Middle Eastern women who dye their hair blond, all reinforce the white male's dominant position.

When men have a healthy sense of self-esteem, they appreciate images of beauty that reflect their own genetic traits. In communities where men are independent, self reliant, self-sufficient and in control, women express their own unique styles of beauty and do not try to imitate the women of a dominant culture.

Political revolutions are often marked by a change in the appearance of the women, who may have previously been influenced by the culture of a colonial power. After a revolution, women consciously select clothing, hairstyles, and other physical enhancements that highlight their own cultural traditions and natural physical features. The decision to look like oneself is a declaration of power. The powerful man is the man whose woman is respected. Her dignity is a reflection of his status. As the carrier of his seed, she represents the future of his progeny.

The demeaning media images of black women are designed to confirm the weakness of black men. Again, this very political decision is solidly backed by economics. Film and video producers that portray black women as low and immoral receive plenty of encouragement and financial backing. Actresses that portray such roles in television and movies are handsomely rewarded with top honors from the entertainment industry, encouraging other women to emulate them. Through the degradation of black women, white men maintain a dominant social position over black men.

In her book, *The Isis Papers*, Dr. Francis Cress Welsing, states that white racism is prompted by white males' fear of genetic extinction if black men marry white women. Blacks have the dominant genes – i.e. dark skin, hair and eyes – and whites have the recessive genes - light skin, hair and eyes. Dr. Welsing asserts:

> *The global white male collective understands the priority of white male domination. They fully understand, consciously or unconsciously, the threat that Black men represent to them...*
>
> *The more the Black male strives to stand, the weaker the white male feels by comparison, and the greater the white male's thrust to effeminize the Black male – to weaken the Black male's psychological potential for aggressive and assertive challenge...*
>
> *This challenge has assumed various subtle and overt forms during recent decades. For example, in the U.S., heavyweight boxing, basketball, baseball and football have all been taken away from white males (by Black males) as symbolic expressions of white male virility and manhood.*
>
> *As mothers, wives and sisters of white males, white females consciously or unconsciously always have understood white males' envy of Black males, even though the envy was expressed in terms of white male hysteria over white women being "raped" by Black males...Thus, it is not surprising that there is increased white female/Black male activity (initiated in most instances by white females who have signaled to Black males that they are available)...*
>
> *These dynamics are at the root of the fear of all true competition white males feel towards Black males, thus preventing true competition in all areas of people activity; economics, education, entertainment, labor, law, politics, religion, sex and war...*
>
> <u>The Isis Papers</u>, pages 84, 85, 98 and 99.

Slavery's Aftermath: Cruel, Perverted Men

White women who championed the cause of white racism erroneously believed that this race-based caste system gave them a greater status and access to more wealth. Racism appealed to their vanity: The least attractive white woman could console herself with the idea that her whiteness made her more desirable than the most beautiful black woman. The notion of white superiority appealed to white women's egos: No matter how much they were lacking in wealth, education, or social status, white women could always tell themselves that they were better than black women. Many white women believed that slavery was a good thing – it brought them a life of ease, luxury and higher social status.

In actuality, just like slavery in ancient Greece, American slavery created an environment where all women were treated like property, even wealthy white women. The same philosophers that declared blacks as intellectually inferior also declared all women, white women included, to be intellectually inferior. Despite the flowery language of the Declaration of Independence, America's first government officials sought to restrict education and property rights to white males only.

Slavery was an institution that degraded all women. It brought out the worst traits in men - brutality, cowardice, sexual abuse and disregard for human life.

Slavery had a damaging psychological effect on black men, but it also had a damaging psychological effect on white men. It produced a sick mentality, creating an appetite for the sadistic and the perverse. What happens to men that have been allowed to buy and sell women as property? What happens to young boys who have seen their fathers stripping women naked, tying them up and whipping them bloody? What happens to young men who, in their teen years, are given girls to use as sex objects in any way they choose, girls who must call them "master?" This was the degradation of slavery. Can such men ever form healthy relationships with any women after that? Consider the widespread incidences of domestic violence and child molestation among whites today.

Slavery condoned the importation of women from Africa to use as concubines. How can a government founded on legalized rape and adultery claim to stand for moral values? White women lived with constant humiliation: Here were these black women, having intimate relations with their husbands and bearing children by their husbands, all under the legal protection of the government.

After abolition, those men who had become accustomed to having women they could degrade and abuse at whim did not want to end the privilege. The rape of black women became something of a sport among white men in the South. For decades, it was nearly impossible for a white man to be tried in court for the rape of a black woman. Today the practice of rape and exploitation has spread to include all women. Current statistics state that *one out of every four women in America has been raped or sexually molested.*

The slave industry conditioned generations of men to abuse women. Sex crimes become prevalent in a society when respect for women is absent. Despite the influence of the Women's Movement, the culture of America remains one of exploitation of women, and degradation of black women in particular. Generations of black women have been conditioned to accept degradation and generations of black men have been conditioned observe their degradation without protest.

Couples Confirm Each Other's Self Worth

Women, regardless of race or nationality, want men whom they respect and who will treat them well. Given a wide range of choices, women sometimes choose men outside of their race.

Interracial relationships happen because we are all one human family, and modern means of travel and communication have removed the physical barriers between us. People now have a wider selection of mates to choose from. Left alone, many people would choose someone who may be outside of their racial or ethnic group, simply because people find themselves compatible in terms of personality traits and shared interests. Most people select mates that fulfill a need that they have, a need for love and confirmation of self worth. Some people select mates for good reasons, some for bad reasons.

The ugly social remnants of American slavery, the racial politics of beauty and the unspoken power struggle between men of different races sometimes influence the process of men and women choosing mates.

Some men choose women of other races or nationalities because they believe that these women will be more docile and submissive than women of their own race or nationality.

Some women choose men of other races or nationalities because they believe these men will be more responsible and hard working than men of their own race or nationality.

Some black men and men of other races men have been conditioned to view white women as status symbols, symbols of white male power. They consciously select white women to symbolize that they have finally achieved equal status with white men.

Some black women choose white men because of economic stability, a choice that may be interpreted by black men as a confirmation of black male powerlessness. However, black women often discover that white men are intrigued by their style and find them beautiful, intelligent, charming, and exciting, while black men may have dismissed them as undesirable.

Sometimes individuals just make choices based on mutual attraction. People are attracted to people who value them for who they are. In healthy relationships, couples confirm each other's self- worth and boost each other's self-esteem.

May The Best Men Win

When women realize the strong influence they have in shaping male behavior, they will be more conscious of how they choose the men in their lives. The role of the female is to set a high standard for males to strive for and to insure that only the best males are allowed to reproduce life. This is nature's way of continually evolving and improving the species. The females' selection of the best males insures that each generation produces stronger, more intelligent offspring. Men should compete with each other in the best manner to demonstrate their superior intelligence, strength and skills.

When women select men who use their abilities to improve the world and uplift humanity, women are setting the standard of manhood all men will strive to reach. When women collectively respond to good men who are superior in their demonstrations of honesty, integrity, respect, compassion, generosity, courage and hard work, women will influence other men to strive to reflect those same values.

Whose genetic line will control the future? This is an ongoing battle among men, a battle that will ultimately be decided by women. The dominant male is the male who attracts the females. If women want a fair and just society that is compassionate toward the poor, protects children and makes knowledge and opportunities available to all, then women must select men who reflect those values. Otherwise they will find themselves at the mercy of cruel men, who have seized power by brutalizing others.

Men who are confident, self-assured, and secure in their own capabilities don't need discriminatory laws and customs to give them a false sense of superiority. They don't fear competition from other men, because they are confident in their own abilities to excel. Only the weak and inferior strive to maintain a social and economic system that gives them an unfair advantage and allows them to exploit other people.

Systematic racial injustice is imposed by desperate men, who fear the strength, intelligence and skills of other men and therefore strive to prevent them from developing them. Their imposition of unjust laws and practices is a confirmation of their own feelings of inferiority. It exposes their unwillingness to compete on an equal basis with other men, whom they fear will supersede them, and perhaps attract their women.

Men of good character will speak out against injustice toward men, women and children. They will support laws and practices that protect the rights of others. They will not seek to take unfair advantage of those who are less educated or less wealthy.

They will teach their sons respect for women and will not participate in any activities designed to embarrass, humiliate, or physically injure any woman.

When determining which men are desirable as husbands, fathers, and leaders in society, women must judge the character of a man. The best men are those that honor the sanctity of marriage and preserve the dignity of womanhood.

When a man has learned to see himself as without value, he will not value his offspring enough to strive to provide for them. Women must select men who value themselves and their children.

By nature, it is the female's role to select the male that has demonstrated his worthiness to reproduce. When a woman has learned to see herself as without value, she will not value her offspring enough to make sure she selects the best father for them. She will not set high standards for a man to reach in order to be worthy of her.

Women can change the course of an entire country by the men they select to father their children. Those who capture the hearts of the women, by treating them with the honor and respect they deserve, will create a better future for mankind than those who abuse other women or strive to dominate other men through oppression and violence.

Women are the majority population in most parts of the world. In many democratic societies, they have the majority vote and can choose heads of governments. But above that, women choose husbands and fathers. Women choose heads of households. Women determine which men are powerful.

Women are the prize in the ongoing contest between men. It is only through a woman that a man may reproduce himself and continue his existence through his children. What makes a man worthy to be a husband, father, and head of household is not a matter of race or color, but of character. In this contest of intelligence, strength, skill, and endurance, the best men are those who are best in their treatment of their fellow human beings.

It's the women's choice. So, may the best men win.

What Traits Do You Inspire in Men?

Men's actions are often motivated by their desire to attract women. This means that men's behavior tends to reflect women's values as well as their own. What values do you encourage in the men in your life? Answer the following questions truthfully.

1) You enter a small crowd of young women and notice that a handsome young man is making jokes. You realize that the butt of his jokes is a heavyset young man with glasses, who is sitting silently, not responding. With every joke, the crowd laughs. You:

   a) Laugh also. The jokes are funny.

   b) Turn away and pretend not to hear

   c) Give a cold, angry stare at the handsome young man and pointedly walk away.

2) You meet an attractive man at a party given by a friend. He drives a very expensive car, dresses extremely well, and is wearing an expensive watch. He says he would like to get to know you better. When you inquire about him, your friend informs you that he makes his money in ways that are illegal. You:

   a) Go out with him anyway – he has money!

   b) Talk to him on the phone. Who knows? He may be nice.

   c) Tell him thanks, but you're not interested.

3) A man you have been seeing for several months informs you that a woman from a previous relationship has contacted him, claiming that she is pregnant and he is the father of her child. He says that she is just somebody he was with one night at a wild party, and he plans to just ignore her calls. You:

   a) Agree with him – he shouldn't even respond to her, she's probably lying anyway, and doesn't know who the father is.

   b) Tell him to urge her to get an abortion.

   c) Tell him to take a blood test, and if it shows that he's the father, he should take care of his financial responsibilities.

4) The very attractive husband of a friend of yours calls you up one day and informs you that he and his wife have been having problems in their marriage and will probably get a divorce. He says he has always been interested in you, and would like to invite you to have lunch with him. You:

    a) Accept the invitation. After all, he did say he was getting a divorce, and he's very good looking.

    b) Tell him you'll think about it and call him back later.

    c) Tell him "No." He's married.

Analysis:

*If you answered **a**:*   A man's ethics aren't as important to you as his looks, his money, and what he can do for you. You don't care that he mistreats others, so don't be surprised when he mistreats you as well.

*If you answered **b**:* Although you know that a man is doing wrong, you hesitate to take a firm stand because you don't want to lose him. Ask yourself: is he really worth holding on to?

*If you answered **c**:* You have principles that you live by, and the men in your life either live up to those principles, or they leave. If they leave, you haven't lost anything of value.

    Men reflect the values of the women in their lives. Mothers and wives play a key role in reinforcing values such as honesty, integrity and respect. If women are cruel, greedy, selfish or dishonest, they encourage these traits in the husbands they marry and in the sons they raise. A culture reflects the values of the women.

    Think about the man in your life. What positive qualities does he have that you could recognize and praise? What positive things is he doing that you could encourage and support?

Chapter 5
The Protective Stallion
Guard Your Daughters Until They Find Suitable Mates

It is early Spring. The zebra stallion stands atop a hill and surveys his family grazing on the slope below. He is the proud father of many strong young colts. Other young stallions graze further away on another hill, keeping a respectful distance from his mares. The young stallions tussle and wrestle each other, slamming against each other's necks in displays of strength, specifically designed to capture the interest of the young females of the herd.

The elder stallion suddenly lifts his head and sniffs the air. His nose captures a familiar scent and he turns his head. It's his oldest daughter, standing downwind so that all the stallions might get a whiff of her and dare to come a little closer. She stands with her legs slightly apart and lifts her tail, turning her back to the stallions every so often so that they might get a clear view of her condition. She is fertile.

Her father watches warily as one stallion trots closer. She lifts her tail invitingly. He trots closer. His legs pick up speed and he is galloping toward her with full force. It is a clear invitation for her to run away with him. But before he can reach her, her father charges at him, teeth bared. He snaps at his daughter's would-be suitor and rears up on hind legs, raising two deadly hooves to show he means business. The young stallion swerves to avoid a painful blow and gallops off, with the young mare's angry father in full pursuit. He chases the young stallion clear across the plains, forcing him to run a safe distance away from the mares.

Before the father of the fertile young mare can trot triumphantly back to his hilltop, another excited stallion is in hot pursuit of her. Again, the father must chase away a daring young male, lured across the pastures by the seductive motions of his eager young daughter. Just as he manages to chase away the second admirer, a third one decides to make his move.

The father ferociously fends off this bold young stallion, even as his daughter's alluring posture invites another's pursuit. The determined father chases off another, then another, while his equally determined daughter boldly advertises her desire to mate.

At the end of the day, an exhausted father surveys his herd in weary triumph. His daughter is too young, and not yet ready to leave her family. But, more importantly, the young stallions who desire to take her away from his herd are too slow, too weak, and not worthy of her. She will remain under the protection of her father until the day comes when a strong young stallion is fearless enough to face him, strong enough to stand up to him, and fast enough to outrun him in order to take away his daughter.

Puberty is the Springtime of youth. The body experiences a new awakening. It is a time to plant seeds and create new life. It's an exciting time for children emerging into adolescence. But it can be a frightening time for parents who wonder how to control this new person that suddenly looks, thinks and acts differently.

At the onset of puberty, certain traits develop that are universally attractive to the opposite sex. Signs that indicate emerging fertility in women – the enlargement of breasts, the widening of hips and curvature of the buttocks – attract human males. Similarly, signs that indicate emerging virility in men – the broadening of shoulders, the enlargement of muscles, the deepening of the voice – attract human females. When boys experience the physical changes that signal the coming of manhood, their natural instinct is to seek the attention of women and to challenge the authority of other men.

Physically, girls' bodies begin to mature about two years before boys'. The hormonal changes that occur in a girl's body activate all the sexual urges that culminate in the instinct to procreate. Her mind is stimulated by the presence of males in a way that did not exist before. Many girls become, to use a common phrase, "boy crazy."

This is natural. In fact, it's necessary for the chemical

mechanism within the female to trigger a strong sex drive during this critical stage of development. A small baby grabs at things to touch and feel, in order to exercise finger muscles and to develop hand/eye coordination. An older child runs and plays to develop motor skills and muscular control. Similarly, as a child passes into the next phase of life before adulthood, new senses are developing that need exercise. The ability to emotionally bond with the opposite sex is created by a biological change that triggers a strong attraction and motivates adolescent girls to practice being seductive.

At puberty, a girl's body produces hormones that cause her to emit a new scent that actually attracts males. It is imperceptible on a conscious level to human males, but among animals, when a female is approaching fertility, males are first attracted to her scent. Human males are more conscious of the visual signs of a female's fertility, such as the enlargement of a girl's breasts and buttocks.

So, in the process of developing a look and smell that attracts the opposite sex, girls are also developing the emotional capacity to form romantic relationships. The natural magnetic attraction between males and females makes a harmonious union possible. By the time their menstrual cycle starts at the ages of 11, 12 and 13 years old, girls are practicing beautifying themselves. They are already exercising their ability to be sexually alluring, even though they are not emotionally mature enough for sexual intimacy. It is a natural female instinct. Females seduce males. They attract males with their scent, their voices and their body movements. Although these behaviors are instinctive, they are also influenced by observation of other females in ones culture. Young girls learn most by imitating their mothers, aunts, older sisters, older cousins, and older friends.

This is a critical period for parents. Sex too soon will arrest a girl's emotional development even as it quickens her physical development into womanhood. At this stage, the body is still in the process of perfecting the regularity of menstrual cycles. Sex at the onset of puberty is not physically healthy, and a baby conceived during this time stands a greater risk of being born premature. Emotionally, a girl is not prepared to be a responsible parent. Maternal skills are learned, they don't just appear because a girl gets pregnant. Even though the sex drive is present, a girl of 11, 12 and 13 years old is still undergoing childhood phases of emotional and financial dependence upon her parents.

In many parts of the world today, popular culture promotes sex in every form of media – movies, television, radio stations, newspapers, books, magazines, and billboards. Young girls are encouraged well before puberty to think in terms of being "sexy." Popular designers that influence the clothing industry create revealing garments that accentuate a girl's blossoming breasts and buttocks, encouraging her to be sexually attractive.

Parents have almost given up the battle to prevent teenage sexual experimentation, and are permitting schools to provide, along with sex education, access to birth control. Girls receive a bundle of mixed messages. Parents may tell their 11, 12 and 13 year old daughters that they are "too young" for sex, yet they continue to buy them revealing, sexually alluring clothing. They expose them to sexually stimulating TV shows, movies and songs. Then they allow their sexually aroused daughters to engage in unsupervised social activities with sexually aroused boys. Why are they surprised then, when their young daughters start having sex?

In the animal kingdom, fathers that act as heads of families know they have to guard their young daughters against the advances of anxious male suitors. In a herd of zebras, the stallion watches over all the females and their colts. When young female mares are approaching fertility, the stallion is very protective, making sure they are not easily approached by other males. Perhaps human fathers can learn something from the zebra stallion.

Fathers Give Daughters Healthy Self Esteem

The relationship between a father and a daughter is critical to the formation of a girl's self-confidence, self-esteem and sense of self worth. It is also critical to the development of a man's ability to express love and affection in a way that is non-sexual. Fathering daughters helps men mature emotionally in ways that no other experience can.

In his book *Dads and Daughters,* author Joe Kelly observes that having daughters helps men develop their ability to express deeper emotions:

> *Fathering is emotional territory.   There's no getting around it...Having daughters can help us learn about and identify our emotions.   Communicating this to other fathers can deepen, cement and affirm the process.   We may get more emotional than we want to be, and start to choke up in front of our friends and then be embarrassed about what they'll think of us.*
>
> *If our friends are honest men concerned about being good fathers, they'll probably think we are brave to bare our softer sides...*
>
> *Having daughters provides countless opportunities to widen our notion of what it means to be a successful man.   Our daughters bring out what many dads call their "feminine side." That's the side where life with a daughter stirs up a father's intense and unaccustomed feelings of longing, love, fear, incompetence, affection, and other emotions usually considered "unmanly."   Often, we get disturbed and confused by all this turmoil. We feel weak or stupid or like failures.   After all, children furnish daily reminders of our fallibility.*
>
> <u>*Dads and Daughters*</u>, *Pages 228 and 229*

Father's have a natural instinct to protect their daughters. For most little girls, Daddy is the big strong hero that keeps her safe. A girl's relationship with her father lays the foundation for her later relationships with men once she reaches adulthood. When fathers are present in the home and are supportive and encouraging, daughters grow into confident, self-assured women who tend to make good choices in their personal and professional lives. Fathers who provide a model of descent male behavior enable their daughters to recognize it when they see it.

Many women complain that there are no decent men. The

fact is, there are many decent men, but women have to be able to recognize a good man when they see one. You can't find something if you don't know what it looks like.

In the classic Dr. Seuss tale, *A Cat in a Hat*, a cheerful cat comes into the home of two children on a rainy afternoon and asks them to help him find his "moss covered, three-handled family gradunza." They agree to search for it, but the problem is, they have no idea what it looks like.

Many women make mistakes in their relationships because they don't know what a decent man looks like. They didn't see one in their own homes.

The cat in *A Cat in a Hat* suggests to the children that since they don't know what a moss covered three-handled family gradunza looks like, and therefore don't know where it is, they can begin by crossing off all the places where it *isn't*. This is good advice for women who can't recognize a good man when they see one. At least they should know where one isn't – namely at sleazy singles bars and night clubs where men go in the hopes of picking up a "one night stand."

Children learn how husbands should behave toward their wives by watching their fathers and mothers interact. A man who is violent and abusive is teaching his sons to abuse women and is teaching his daughters to accept abusive men. When fathers are physically or emotionally absent and uninvolved in their lives, girls become accustomed to being neglected by men. They grow into women who tolerate men that won't make a commitment to them.

According to recent statistics, 82% of teenage girls who get pregnant come from fatherless homes. This makes a statement. A father in the home protects a teenage daughter from irresponsible boys and men who take advantage of her blossoming sexuality. A father in the home is a signal to young men that they must approach a daughter with respect.

Girls need love. They need love like they need air, water and food. There is a special kind of love that only a father can give to a daughter. It helps her learn how to bond with the opposite sex.

A father's love gives a daughter that unique reassurance

that she is a valuable human being worthy of good treatment. Women tend to be attracted to men that remind them of their fathers. When fathers are absent or emotionally distant and non-affectionate, daughters often spend their entire adult lives searching for the love of a man to fill the void left by their fathers.

Teen poet Ebony Williams of Chicago powerfully expresses this feeling in a poem:

Without A Father

'Cause you don't have a father
You look for a father image
'Cause you look for this love
You look in the wrong places.
'Cause you meet someone
You fall in love
'Cause you're now in love
The relationship gets deeper
'Cause you think you're ready
You begin to have feelings
'Cause you have feelings
You want to have sex
'Cause you have sex
You end up pregnant
'Cause you get pregnant
The boy runs away.
And now since the boy is gone
Your baby is looking for a father figure.

By Ebony Williams
Residents Journal, November/December 2004 edition, page 17
(Reprinted by permission)

Girls are becoming sexually active at younger ages. This is a reflection of a society that does not protect its young women, but instead, exploits them. Lonely, insecure girls seeking love are in desperate need of guidance from older, wiser women.

Popular music videos promote a common image of nearly naked young women gyrating suggestively to the beat, creating a cultural environment where respect for womanhood is rapidly disappearing. Many critics of popular culture say that young women have become far too accepting of being called vulgar names.

Monique Caradine Kitchens, Chicago talk show host and community activist, suggested that more women need to act as mentors to young women to prevent them from being led astray:

"Conscious women have to counteract this negative image. Every opportunity we get, we need to take a little sister under our wing. We can take her to dinner and talk to her. A lot of these girls are from homes where mothers stay out all night. Some have mothers that are in jail. We need to spend time with them, take them places, mentor them. If we just did that much, that would make such a difference. We have to start by helping them understand they are unique human beings. We can introduce them to historic women, let them know, so many women paid a price for them to be here.

"We have to tell them their bodies are sacred temples. They have to consider themselves the perfect gift to a man. They have to think, 'I am the most precious gift.' When you think that, you start to question who you give that gift to. This body is the essence of your being, the core of who you are. Think, 'Does this person deserve the essence of who I am? Is he worthy of allowing his spirit to come inside of me?' You have to see it as that. You are deciding to blend your spirit with his spirit."

Monique recalled how her father had a strong influence on the shaping of her values as she was growing up. A political activist in college, she later became known as a conscious-raising radio commentator and television talk show host.

"My dad is the person who influenced me most. He would always say, 'I can tell who you are by the company you keep.' That made me always think about what I was doing.

"My husband had a strong impact on me. He's very detailed and driven. He's made me more driven and assertive about what I want. That's what a husband should do, make you a better person.

"I hope our son grows up to have his father's drive. He's eighteen months old now. When he's older, we're going to talk about the act that men and women engage in when they love each other, that it's a very sacred act. When my son grows up, he'll seek out a woman who is nurturing, patient and compassionate. He's going to sit down and talk to the girl's parents, meet the father. He's going to know how to treat a lady."

When fathers demonstrate high moral values, their daughters become dignified, self-respecting women. Women who respect themselves earn the respect of their children. They provide a positive role model for their daughters to emulate and a model of the kind of woman their sons should marry.

Daughters With Good Fathers Choose Good Spouses

Women who have positive relationships with their fathers are more likely to choose spouses that are emotionally well adjusted and are able to form good relationships with children.

Cheryl Charles, Sports Copy Editor for a major daily newspaper, remembered her father as a man of honesty and integrity, who worked hard to provide for his family:

"Those are the values that I got from my father, honesty, hard work, integrity. I remember that he was always supportive of me. I was on the drill team, the "Titanettes" when I was at Fenger High School in Chicago. We performed at half time at the football games. He came to every single one of my performances.

"People have to know what to look for when they want to get married. If you have low expectations, that's what you're going to get. I know I wanted somebody who was intelligent, who made me feel good about my self, who wanted a family.

"I look at my daughter and my husband now. They have their own little love affair. She loves her father. They do little silly things together, like skipping down the street, things he would never have done before. She brings out different qualities in him."

Just as marriage civilizes men, fathering children, particularly daughters, sensitizes men, and makes them more careful about saying and doing inappropriate things in public. In the past, men were conscious about not using profanity or telling crude jokes in the presence of women and children. Today, however, it is often the women and children who are publicly using profanity and telling the crude jokes.

Cheryl noted that over the years, attitudes about respect for women have drastically changed. Working in a field dominated primarily by men, she observed that men's behavior is often influenced by the way women carry themselves.

"I've been here for over 15 years. I'm used to working around men. I'm pretty strong. I listen to a lot of rude comments, but I don't stoop to that level.

"When women are crude and rude, that raises the level of immaturity in the men. One woman used to act so crude, it was like she was trying to out-crude the men. Whenever she was around, their comments would get worse. When she was absent, they weren't so bad. Some women feel they have to act that way to get attention. It's a sign of insecurity.

"It's just like wearing inappropriate clothing. Women are taught to value themselves based on how they look. Even if they're intelligent and talented, they feel like they need that kind of attention. It's like a child who acts out and misbehaves. Women wear inappropriate clothing to get attention, then get offended if somebody makes a crude comment.

"People don't even know what polite conversation is anymore. The expression 'that sucks' has a sexual connotation. It's nasty. Just like the expression, 'pissed off.' It's a vulgarity.

"I noticed one time when I went down to work in another

department, the men were a little older. I was in my 30s and they were all over 50, part of that "Old School" era where men tipped their hat to you and didn't say crude things in front of women. Things have changed. I think men's attitudes toward respect of women is very much a matter of age."

Men call women vulgar names, in public, on television, and in movies. Words that used to be considered profanity are now a part of regular speech. Men curse around women because women curse even more.

A young woman who wears clothing that exposes her body to the public to generate sexual excitement, uses foul and vulgar language and engages in lewd behavior in order to get attention is making an announcement:

"I HAVE NO FATHER IN MY HOME WHOM I RESPECT AND WHO HAS TAUGHT ME TO RESPECT MYSELF."

When women project such signs of vulnerability, they are ripe for exploitation by unscrupulous men (and women), who introduce them to sex, drugs and various forms of prostitution, often disguised as "modeling" or "entertainment." No matter what it's called, the outcome is the same: an attractive girl with low self esteem ends up selling her body to attract men in the hopes of finding love. She often goes from one disastrous relationship to the next, unable to acquire the one thing she is so desperately seeking: a sense of self worth.

Author Joe Kelly asserts that fathers who have a wholesome attitude toward female sexuality are better able to cope with their daughter's emerging maturity in a way that is helpful and reassuring.

When we take a positive approach to our daughters' emerging sexuality, we take a huge step in raising healthy, happy bold and savvy girls. But we also take a huge step toward keeping our relationships with our daughters relevant to them and us both. Although it may seem hard to imagine, that unconditional love we feel from our young daughters can survive adolescence and flour-ish in adulthood. We make that happen by remaining true to them, even as they develop into sexual beings...

As boys and young men, we had more permission to ex-press and act on sexual desires. In my high school, a guy with a reputation for sleeping around was a stud. A girl with a reputation for sleeping around was a slut. That double standard continues today, and girls know it. Meanwhile, the media sells sex as the way to rebel and be cool, while cultural mores and many parents continue to treat girls' sexuality and sexual desire as bad. This creates a confusing, contradictory environment where it's easy for girls to feel confusion, anger, self-doubt, and like their getting un-fair treatment.

One way girls may try to escape from that frustration is with alcohol or drugs... Girls may use alcohol as a tool (albeit an unhealthy one) to explore their sexuality—and to ignore the double standard that restricts their desires and denies their legitimate adolescent yearnings. They may also use drugs and alcohol to drown out guilt about their sexual desires and sexual behaviors...

It's a fair bet that you want your daughter to be valued for reasons other than her sexuality, especially by the boys and men with whom she has significant relationships. But she learns how to properly value her sexuality when you also want your daughter to be valued for reasons in addition to her sexuality. In other words, value her without denying her sexuality. She is likely to feel more in control of her sexuality, less vulnerable to abuse and more able to fulfill her desires in healthy ways...

Sexual desires are not the only yearnings our daughters have. Girls yearn to be themselves, seek justice, be creative, make the world better, and have a host of other longings.
<u>*Dads and Daughters*</u>*, pages 133, 168 and 169*

Girls have a need to feel beautiful and loveable. A father that shows his daughter affection and tells her she is beautiful helps her to develop healthy self-esteem and still maintain her modesty. If she does not hear compliments from her father, she is more likely to expose her body in order to get the male attention she needs to confirm her to herself that she is attractive.

Cultural Traditions of Repressing Womanhood

Men often do not know how to address the blossoming womanhood of their daughters. In some cultures in the past, men were so afraid of the powerful affect of women's sexuality that they tried to suppress it in unnatural ways.

During the Middle Ages in Europe, the philosophy of the Roman Catholic Church heavily influenced European culture and attitudes toward sex. According to Church doctrine, lifelong chastity, or abstinence from sex, was a sign of purity and holiness. The single, celibate life was preferable, but marriage was permitted for those who did not possess the spiritual discipline to remain single. This philosophy was largely based on the writings of the Apostle Paul, who himself never married:

"Now, concerning the things whereof ye wrote me: It is good for a man not to touch a woman. Nevertheless, to avoid fornication, let every man have his own wife, and let every woman have her own husband...

"I say therefore to the unmarried and the widows, It is good for them if they abide even as I. But if they cannot contain, let them marry: for it is better to marry than to burn."
The Bible, 1 Corinthians 7: Verses 1, 2, 8 & 9.

Religious orders were created for men and women who chose to live a celibate life and devote their lives exclusively to the study of religion. Monasteries were institutions for men, and Convents were institutions for women. Each man and woman took a vow of lifelong chastity, poverty and obedience in order to serve the Church in a secluded community of religious devotees. Men were trained to become monks or priests and women were trained to become nuns.

Over a period of time, Convents, or nunneries as they were

called, became places for parents to send their wayward girls to protect the family from public shame, should the girl show signs of promiscuity. Virginity was an absolute requirement for any young woman hoping to get married. Of course, the contradiction was that men were expected to have some sexual experiences before marriage. They sought to practice on somebody, if not a prostitute in a brothel, then someone's daughter.

For girls whose families sent them away out of fear of an out of wedlock pregnancy, placement in a nunnery was like a life sentence in the penitentiary. As the power of the Roman Catholic Church spread throughout England and Ireland, so did the number of monasteries and nunneries housing supposedly celibate men and women living to serve "the Church."

Repressing female sexuality became an obsession for Church leaders. Church teachings expounded endlessly on doctrines that emphasized the "sin" of "fornication" and the "evils" of "adultery." The "original sin" of Adam and Eve was interpreted to mean that Eve, the deceptive, seductive woman, led Adam astray with her feminine charms. Female sexuality was evil and sinful, according to church leaders. The female Jezebel in the Bible was the subject of many preachers' scornful sermons admonishing women to be chaste.

Families that had daughters that developed into physically attractive young women often banished their daughters to the nunnery. It was akin to prison. The girl's hair was cut off, and she was forced to wear drab, old clothing. Celibacy was her vow and she was bound to serve the Church for the rest of her life.

Despite religious teachings and social pressures, women still developed normal desires for physical intimacy. Men whose work required them to travel far from home feared the infidelity of their wives. In England during the Middle Ages, a restrictive fettered girdle was developed for women, known as the "chastity belt." It actually locked around a woman's genitals, preventing anyone from touching her private parts. Usually only the woman's husband held the key. Of course, such a contraption also prevented the women from practicing proper hygiene.

Just as a repressive European culture twisted the teachings of the prophets in the Holy Bible to justify traditions of mistreatment of women, so did a repressive Arab culture twist the teachings of the Prophet Muhammad and the revelations contained in the Islamic scripture, the Holy Quran.

In early Arabia, the birth of sons was considered a blessing, but the birth of daughters was considered a source of shame. For centuries it was a practice among Arab men to bury their infant female daughters alive. Arab men did not allow female children to be educated. They gave their daughters in marriage almost like they were selling property. Violent, ill-tempered men beat their wives, forcing them to cower into submission.

The coming of Islam in the 7th century brought a religious scripture that declared equality of men and women in the sight of God. It condemned the barbaric practice of female infanticide. Verses in the Quran also address domestic violence, but these verses have often been misused to condone the violence against women that was always part of Arab culture.

Men are guardians over women because Allah has made some of them excel others, and because men spend on them of their wealth. So virtuous women are obedient and guard the secrets of their husbands with Allah's protection. And as for those on whose part you fear disobedience, admonish them and keep away from them in their beds and chastise them. Then if they obey you, seek not a way against them. Surely Allah is High and Great.

Holy Quran, Chapter 4, Al Nisa, Verse 35

The words "Men are guardians over women" clarify men's roles as providers, responsible for the financial maintenance of the family. Men are commanded to take care of women. Women are commanded not to squander the wealth their husbands provide, nor publicly humiliate their husbands by exposing the intimate things that only a wife would be privy to.

The words "And as for those on whose part you fear disobedience" are addressing *domestic conflicts when the wife is the ag-*

gressor. According to the *Holy Quran English Translation and Commentary* by Malik Guhlam Farid (published in 1981) the word "disobedience" is translated from the original Arabic words, *Nashazat al-Mar'atu 'ala Zauji-ha* meaning, "the woman rose against her husband." This implies a woman's actual physical attack on her husband, not merely a verbal disagreement.

The idea of Almighty God advising men to beat their wives for "disobedience" is repugnant to women, especially in light of frequent cases of domestic violence that end in tragic murders. But this verse, rather than condoning violence against women, is actually advising men to exercise restraint when responding to violent tempered females, and to take steps that would restore peace.

Emotions between husbands and wives can be volatile and if unchecked can escalate into fights that end in homicide. In most cases women are the victims. In his review of Linda G. Mills' book on domestic abuse, reporter John DiConsiglio examines the violence behind the current wife-killing epidemic. He states in his article published in the August 2003 issue of *Glamour Magazine*:

Linda G. Mills has an unsettling proposal to combat wife killing. "Acknowledge that domestic abuse is not one-sided. Women have to admit that they are bringing some violence to the table."

A professor of social work at New York University and the author of the book Insult to Injury: Rethinking Our Responses to Domestic Abuse…Mills speculates that intimate murder continues because examining it more seriously would mean recognizing that "There's a tremendous amount of aggression coming from both sides in the intimate sphere." Women's aggression may take a different form than men's – manifesting itself as a slap or constant belittling – but it's still harmful. "That slap across the face she gives him is meaningful and humiliating, " Mills says. "But we don't recognize it as abuse. In some cases, her actions are a powerful trigger. If we can stop the slap, maybe we can prevent the violence from escalating."

Glamour Magazine, August 2003, page 221.

Women that constantly belittle the men in their lives are often expressing unresolved anger and hostility at their own fathers, who may have hurt and disappointed them. Constant verbal abuse whittles away a man's self esteem, and kindles suppressed rage in a man that is easily triggered by a small act of violence, such as a slap or hit.

Some women become extremely violent with their husbands, slapping, kicking, scratching, even biting in uncontrolled anger. When that happens, men are often too ashamed to talk about it. Instead they may retaliate with even worse violence, despite the fact that they are physically stronger than the women and capable of doing worse damage.

But, according to the verse in the Quran, what is a husband advised to do if his wife physically attacks him? Keeping in mind that the husband is supposed to be the guardian, the protector, and the provider, he is *not* to retaliate with violence. First *admonish them* (tell her to stop it); next, *keep away from them in their beds* (withdraw affection, and she'll miss you enough to control her mouth and her temper); and if that fails, *chastise them* (physically stop her from hitting you.) Every human being has the right to stop physical assault against themselves.

However, the English translation "disobedience," in this verse leaves so much room for a man's subjective judgment. If his wife expresses a difference of opinion, is she being "disobedient?" Men whose intention is to physically abuse women twist the meaning of this verse to use it as an excuse to beat their wives at whim.

Verbal or physical abuse on the part of either a husband or a wife is wrong, in that it kills the love between them. Marriage is meant to be a peaceful, harmonious union. Families are urged to help couples solve disputes in a respectful manner:

And if you fear a breach between them, then appoint an arbiter from his folk and an arbiter from her folk. If they (the arbiters) desire reconciliation, Allah will affect it between them. Surely, Allah is All-Knowing, All-Aware.

<u>Holy Quran</u>, *Chapter 4, Al Nisa, Verse 36*

Despite Quranic injunctions to read and seek knowledge and understanding, in many Muslim countries women are kept illiterate and uneducated so that they cannot read their own scriptures and cannot even protest their own mistreatment.

Abused Girls Become Abused Women

When fathers mistreat daughters, they set in motion patterns of behavior that may continue for generations. Girls learn from their fathers that they have no value as females, so they grow up and select men that treat them as if they have no value. When enough girls are raised with this kind of low self-esteem, mistreatment of women becomes an accepted part of the culture. When women have been conditioned from childhood to accept abuse, they eventually become the ones to perpetuate it.

Other cultures also developed abusive practices toward women to keep them under control. In China, the ancient practice of "foot binding" continued into the twentieth century. The feet of female infants were tightly bound with cloth to prevent them from growing naturally. This process was not only painful; it distorted the bones and hindered girls from walking for the rest of their lives. Foot binding was done at first to prevent women from wandering and being unfaithful to their husbands. Over a period of time, these abnormally small feet came to be considered a mark of daintiness and beauty. Nearly two thirds of the females in China were subjected to this practice until it was prohibited at the beginning of the twentieth century.

In many East African cultures, female circumcision was practiced as a means of controlling the female sex drive. Female circumcision is an operation that removes the clitoris, the most sensitive part of a female's genitals. Men believed that women who enjoyed sex would be more likely to commit adultery. Once her circumcision healed, sexual intercourse was an unpleasant experience for a woman.

This operation sometimes led to infections that caused complications during childbirth. In some societies, female circumcision is still a common practice. Surprisingly, it is the women who insist upon it, as a means of protecting their daughters' morals.

Most cultures with a long history of abuse of females will continue to abuse them until the women themselves become enlightened. Women set the standard for what is culturally acceptable male behavior by what they allow to occur in their own homes. Therefore, women have a moral responsibility to select good husbands who will treat them and their children with love and respect and thereby set a good example of proper conduct.

One cannot stand up for justice for others if one is also being oppressed. If a woman is being beaten by her husband, she cannot protect her children from assault, which is her responsibility as a mother. Many boys who were beaten by cruel fathers grow up to be cruel men. They abuse women, partially out of the contempt they feel for their mothers who were too frightened to protect them from a violent father.

In nations throughout the world, women find themselves the victims of oppression and brutality at the hands of cruel, insensitive men. How is this possible? Worldwide, women outnumber men. Men by nature will strive to please women, in order to win the love of women. So why are women oppressed?

Oppression is a consequence of disunity. An organized minority can oppress a divided majority, when the oppressed people are fighting among themselves to gain higher status or recognition. They will allow others from their group to be mistreated, believing that this somehow elevates their own position. It doesn't.

When a group of people is suffering oppression, that group must come together to collectively resist their mistreatment. The greater the oppression, the greater their unity must be in order to end the oppression.

When some women allow other women to be mistreated for the sake of distinguishing themselves as belonging to a higher social class, they are in fact creating a culture of disrespect for women. Women who encourage men to rob, steal and make slaves of other men and women in order that they may lead a life of extravagance; women who permit the mistreatment of servant girls in their homes; women who allow poor widows and young orphan girls to be neglected and exploited; women who let other women suffer so that they may feel superior to them; these women are in fact conditioning men to abuse women. Eventually, the abuse spreads from just the poor women and engulfs all women. Oppression of women becomes an accepted part of the culture.

Women raise boys to manhood. They are responsible for making sure that the natural aggression of their sons is not perverted into cruelty and oppression of women. They must not designate other women as "low class" or "bad girls" or any other description that would make rape or any other violence toward them seem permissible. An abusive man is a reflection of a mother who either over-indulged him and made him arrogant, abused him, or allowed him to be abused by others. Mothers must make sure their sons treat their own wives with kindness, fairness and respect.

Women's Rights vs. Right to Life

For centuries, European male intellectuals had argued that the nature of women made them inferior to men. In the eighteenth century, European female intellectuals began to question these traditions. English writer Mary Wollstonecraft, author of *Vindication of the Rights of Women*, argued that those who claimed the rule of Monarchs over the people was wrong must also recognize that the rule of men over women was equally wrong. She declared that women should have the same rights to education, economic and political power as men. She is widely considered the founder of modern European feminism.

The feminist movement grew and expanded to address centuries of mistreatment of women. Modern day feminists sought to address the right of women to control their own bodies and the power to choose whether or not they would reproduce.

In response to centuries of sexual repression, women today insist on enjoying intimate relationships with men outside of marriage. Some women have decided to remain single and sexually active, rejecting society's pressures for marriage and children.

They intend to experience sexual pleasure without fear of conception. If conception does accidentally occur, today's pro-abortion activists have demanded, "the right to choose" whether they will allow the baby to live.

Various religious and political groups find themselves on opposite sides of the fence regarding the very controversial issue of abortion. Cruel practices, such as the killing of female infants in Arabia, are horrible reminders of what can happen when human life is not properly valued.

Animals are driven to fight to stay alive, to procreate, and to protect their offspring so that their species may survive. Unless their natural instincts have been altered by extreme illness, starvation, or domestication by humans, female animals are the most ferocious when it comes to protecting their young. Females will often fight animals many times their size to protect their babies. All animals understand that their basic function is to continue to exist.

Something has gone dreadfully wrong when women demand the right to kill their children.

"Say, 'Come I will recite to you what your Lord has forbidden, that you associate not anything as partner with Him; and that you do good to parents, and that you slay not your children for fear of poverty—it is We who provide for you and for them—and that you approach not foul deeds, whether open or secret; and that you slay not the soul the slaying of which Allah has forbidden, save in accordance with the demands of justice.' That is what He has enjoined upon you, that you may understand."
                    Holy Quran, Chapter 6, Al An Am, Verse 152.

No matter what the laws regarding abortion state, the decision to give birth rests with a woman. The life she carries has been entrusted to her, and either she is willing to fulfill that trust, or she is not. When something valuable is entrusted to you, you have the power to protect it, or the power to destroy it.

Consider this:

You graduate from high school at age 18 and take $500 to open a savings account at a savings and loan that promises to pay 10% interest. This money represents your entire life savings. You plan to eventually buy a house. You let it remain safely in your savings and loan account for the next 10 years, calculating that the money is earning $50 per month. Over the years, you have gotten married and started a family. At age 28, you figure that after 120 months, you should have $6,000 in your savings account. This would be your down payment for a new home.

You haven't received a statement on your account for a while, and you begin to hear rumors that the company is having problems. You rush to the savings and loan to withdraw your money in anticipation of putting a down payment on the beautiful home you and your spouse have found. But the teller looks up your account and says, "I'm sorry, your account has been closed." Puzzled, you are sure there has been some mistake and ask to talk to the manager. The manager comes and confirms the same thing. Finally, you demand to talk to the owner.

The owner sits down with you and calmly explains, "Your money is gone. There was an investment we decided to make, and we took your money to do it. Things didn't work out, though, and all your money was lost. Sorry." He dismisses you with a polite nod and you sit devastated as he gets up to leave.

"But, that was my money!" you protest.

"But it was in my savings and loan company," he replies.

You trusted the savings and loan company with $500, which represented your future. When the owner lost your money, whatever good you intended to do with that $500 was prevented from happening.

Nothing can stop a woman from destroying the life in her womb, not a law, not social pressure, nothing. The only thing that stops her is the understanding that the life she carries does not belong to her, but to the Creator. She has been entrusted with that life and all its potential for growth.

When a woman chooses to end the life of an unborn child,

whatever good that person would have done on earth is prevented from happening.

There are times when a pregnancy could actually endanger the mother's life. Or the child was conceived through an act of incest or forced sexual intercourse. In such circumstances, a woman must be the one to choose whether to risk her life to give birth. However, most abortions that occur are not because the mother's life was at risk or because the pregnancy was the result of rape. Most abortions are performed to remove accidental pregnancies. Women engaged in sexual intimacy without the intention of producing life. Women do this because they really don't understand the value of their bodies and the power they have to change the world by the creation of a life. This understanding is something that must be imparted to them by their parents.

Teach A Daughter The Value of Her Body

Girls become sexually active too soon often because no one takes the time to explain to them why they shouldn't. In an article entitled *Where Do Kids Learn About Sex* published September 29, 2002 by Web MD with AOL Health, author Salynn Boyles states:

You may think they're tuning you out when the talk turns to birds and bees, but they're not, according to two studies released in April by the National Campaign to Prevent Teen Pregnancy (NCPTP) that reinforce the role of parental advice and role-modeling in determining the sexual behavior of teens. In those studies, more teens, 38%, pointed to their parents as the biggest influence on their sexual behavior – more than friends, the media, educators, siblings, or religious organizations.

In recognition of this, the organization urges parents to engage their children "early in discussions of sex, love, relationships, and values."...

Although teen pregnancy and birth rates in the U.S. declined significantly during the 1990s, approximately 1 million American teenage girls still get pregnant each year. This is by far

the highest rate of teen pregnancies of any industrialized nation –
and 8 out of the 10 are unplanned, according to NCPTP figures.
                    <u>*Where Do Kids Learn About Sex*</u>*, by Salynn Boyles*
                              Copyright 1996-2002 WebMD

How does a girl learn the value of her body? In a society where older women are making so many bad choices themselves, it is difficult for girls to get a clear message. Sometimes mothers, in their anxiousness to preach to their daughters, are unable to establish the kind of trust that allows open, honest communication. Daughters need to confide in their mothers, but may be reluctant to face possible criticism.

As they approach womanhood, girls must know how to avoid abusive relationships. This is difficult for daughters whose own fathers were emotionally defective (due to drug or alcohol addiction), physically abusive, or simply absent.

In her book *The Power of Beauty*, author Nancy Friday observes how men use crude remarks to make women feel insecure:

When the boy eventually learns women's absolute control over whether or not there will be sex, his crude and embarrassing remarks to girls increase; what he would prefer, most of the time, is simply to adore the woman's body. When he is abruptly put in his place and made to feel like an animal, well, he responds like one: Two men stand talking to each other on a street, all the while their eyes drawn to a woman walking by, all splendor. Feeling their gaze, she glares at them. Awe turns to anger. "Hey Harry," one guy says to the other, "look at those jugs!" "Crude brutes!" the woman says, consoling herself, hunching her shoulders forward.

What kind of war is this? When did it begin and why? Men should not yell crude remarks at women, but they are playing on a sensitivity that has always been there, at best, a fear of inadequacy that women learn from other women.
                    <u>*The Power of Beauty*</u>*, Pages 111-113*

When women learn to value themselves based only on what they look like, they are ripe for this kind of psychological warfare. Men use insults to tear down a woman's self esteem, particularly a woman that has made them feel inferior because of her superior skills or intelligence. When women have relationships with men that are less educated or earn less money, men may become jealous and resentful. Men who feel inferior to women express their hostility through insults, usually targeting a woman's looks.

Fathers can fortify their daughters against this kind of attack, by giving their daughters a healthy sense of self worth. Fathers need to tell their daughters that they are beautiful, intelligent, talented and loveable.

When fathers are absent, daughters interpret the absence as a personal rejection. A girl whose father is uninvolved in her life comes to feel, "If I'm really beautiful, intelligent, talented and loveable, why doesn't my father want me?"

Daughters whose fathers make them feel special are less likely to engage in teen-age sex out of an unfulfilled need for male affection. They are also less likely to end up in relationships with men that insult and abuse them.

Date Rape, Sexual Assault and Pornography

Fathers that are extremely protective of their daughters send a signal to young men: *My daughter is very precious to me. I will not allow you to mistreat her.*

While some teenage girls may find the strict rules laid down by their fathers extremely annoying, they are in fact a girl's best protection against physical harm.

When fathers allow their daughters to roam the streets freely with no restrictions, no curfews and no supervision, they send another signal to young men: *My daughter is not that important to me. I don't care what you do to her.*

Too many fathers have sent this signal to young men. Date rape has become a common phenomenon. Men with hostility toward women commit sexual assault because they believe they can get away with it. Current statistics state that one out of every three women under thirty has been sexually assaulted! What kind of effect is this having on male/female relationships?

Rape crisis counselor Sedia Mathis is often called after a victim has contacted a Rape Crisis Center. She sometimes escorts the victim to the police station or to the hospital. She explained the emotional devastation for women who are victims of rape:

"Rape is used to control and humiliate you. That's why it's done. It's about power. Often, it may be someone you know, it might be a family member, or a friend of a friend.

"Sometimes police make it worse by they way they treat you. Your body becomes a crime scene. You want to wash the stench off your body, but you can't. If you're not severely injured, police act like you're not telling the truth about being raped. Some cops are nasty just because they can be. The last thing you need to be told is that you're not believed.

"No one has the right to harm you. When I offer counseling, the first thing I tell them is 'It's not your fault.' It's hard to talk about, but it's even harder not to talk about. I tell them 'You have a right to be angry.' I tell family members, 'She's going to need you.' If the woman is a virgin I reassure them that they have not lost their virginity. No one can take that from you, that is something you choose to give.

"In a rape, you don't just have primary victims, you have multiple victims – family members, friends. Sometimes family members are more traumatized than the victim. They say, 'I can't believe someone did that to my loved one!'"

Victims often suffer from "Rape Trauma Syndrome" in which something triggers a memory of the rape experience. Something as small as a smell that was in the air, or a sound, or even a place near where the assault occurred can trigger a traumatic memory. Sometimes women are unable to experience normal sexual relations because the sex act itself triggers an unbearable memory of the rape.

Another aspect of Rape Trauma Syndrome is a victim's attempt to control what happened to her by continuously reenacting the sex experience. This takes the form of extreme promiscuity, as the victim carelessly engages in sex as if her body has no value. Many so-called "bad girls" with "reputations" are in fact sexual assault victims acting out because they are suffering from Rape Trauma Syndrome. Some victims turn to alcohol or drugs to numb the emotional pain of the assault.   Some, feeling that their bodies have no worth anyway, turn to prostitution. Sedia observes:

"Your body is the only thing on this earth that is yours. This is your vessel for life. When they violate that, they take everything from you.

"Healing is possible. Of course, nothing happens over night. It's like healing from a knife wound. If the knife is still stuck in your arm, you can't heal. You have to get rid of the source of pain.

"In some families, the same person keeps assaulting people for generations. You should confront the attacker, even if they don't acknowledge what they've done. Families should ostracize the attacker and embrace the victim.

"You have to heal at your own pace. You have to choose to get help. People must go through a spiritual transformation to heal."

Rape is not a normal male instinct. Something happens in the mind of a man that triggers violent aggression that is acted out through forced sexual contact. Rapists often go unpunished when men and women buy into the notion that the victim somehow caused the rape. Women don't cause rape; society conditions men to rape. One of the things that condition men to rape is society's confusion about what it is. Rape is not "accidental sex" occurring as a "consequence" of a woman's flirtation or teasing. Rape is a hate crime. Men who harbor contempt for women commit rape.

In court, lawyers argue over whether or not the act was "consensual sex." Rape and sexual intimacy are not the same thing.

Rape is a prelude to murder. Rape and murder often go hand in hand, just like robbery and murder. A robber demands money. The implication is, "Give me your money, or I'll kill you." Often the victim, after handing over the money, is killed anyway.

In cases of rape, the implication again is, "Allow me to use your body for my sexual pleasure, or I'll kill you." Often, the rapist, after sexually assaulting his victim, kills her anyway.

Eighty percent of rapists motivated by displaced anger come from fatherless homes. For boys who are angry and resentful at mothers and other women who dominate their lives, sex becomes a weapon to use to demonstrate power over a woman.

The epidemic of fatherlessness makes the traditional "father-son" talk about marriage and sex almost non-existent today. Now, many boys are introduced to sex through pornography. Sexually arousing music videos, songs, movies and magazines in which women are referred to in insulting terms create unrealistic fantasies in the minds of boys. Pubescent boys are initiated into manhood with constant sexual stimulation and degrading impressions of women.

Boys who have been improperly introduced to sex grow up to be men who are unfit to be husbands and fathers. Women sometimes make the mistake of bringing such men into their homes. These men, rather than feeling paternal instincts to protect the women's daughters, see them as easy sexual conquests. Girls are often victimized by their mother's live-in boyfriends. Some women, desperate for an intimate relationship and financial support, choose to look the other way. Some even blame their daughters for initiating the sexual advances.

In a society saturated with pornographic images, too many men have learned to disrespect the sex act altogether. They have been conditioned to see all women as potential sexual conquests.

Articles published in the July 22, 2003 edition of *Awake!* Magazine explore the harm pornography causes to society. One article, entitled <u>Pornography: Opposing Viewpoints</u>, points out that those who insist pornography is the hallmark of an open, mature society create confusion about its destructive effects:

Antipornography activists point to...the degrading effects of pornography. It destroys relationships, they claim, demeans women, abuses children and engenders a perverted and harmful view of sex. On the other hand, supporters defend pornography as free expression and view the detractors as prudish...

Many are ambivalent toward pornography because it has now entered the mainstream.

"It is already a vastly bigger cultural presence than all our opera, ballet, theater, music and fine art put together," says writer Germaine Greer. Modern attitudes toward pornography may be reflected by the 'prostitute-chic' fashions many celebrities sport, the music videos that increasingly flaunt sexual imagery, and the advertising media's adoption of a "porno aesthetic."...

The fact is that like all successful advertising, pornography's main purpose is to create appetites where none existed before.

"Pornography is about profits, pure and simple," write researchers Steven Hill and Nina Silver. "And in this marketplace gone amok, anything is considered an exploitable and expendable resource, particularly women's bodies and human sexual relations."...

Some doctors claim that pornography can spark an addiction that is far more difficult to overcome than drug addiction...

Researchers at the National Foundation for Family Research and Education concluded that "exposure to pornography puts viewers at increased risk for developing sexually deviant tendencies." According to the report, "the rape myth (belief that women cause and enjoy rape, and that rapists are normal) is very widespread in habitual male users of pornography."

Awake! July 22, 2003, pages 3, 4, and 5
Published by Watchtower Bible and Tract Society of New York

Pornography creates a danger for women in society. In her book, *Against Pornography: The Evidence of Harm*, Dr. Diana Russell studies the effects of pornography in causing men to rape. She examined the responses of men who admitted to having fantasies about raping women after having read articles that described the rape of a woman or having viewed films in which women were raped. Some men expressed the desire for a feeling of power over women, but said they hesitated to actually rape someone because they feared getting caught and punished.

In excerpts from two chapters of her book entitled, *The Role of Pornography in Predisposing Some Males to Want to Rape* and *The Role of Pornography in Undermining Some Males Social Inhibitions Against Acting Out Their Desire to Rape*, she states:

> *I define pornography as material that combines sex and/or the exposure of genitals with abuse or degradation in a manner that appears to endorse, condone, or encourage such behavior...*
>
> *Sexual objectification is another common characteristic of pornography. It refers to the portrayal of human beings –usually women – as depersonalized sexual things ...*
>
> *However the sexual objectification of females is not confined to pornography. It is also a staple of mainstream movies, ads, record covers, songs, magazines, television, art, cartoons, literature, pin-ups, and so on, and influences the way that many males learn to see women and even children...*
>
> *A man may want to rape a woman and his internal inhibitions against rape may be undermined by his hostility to women or by his belief in the myths that women really enjoy being raped and/or that they deserve it, but he may still not act out his desire to rape because of his social inhibitions. Fear of being caught and convicted for the crime is the most obvious example of a social inhibition...*
>
> *The common portrayal in pornography of rape as easy to get away with probably contributes to the undermining of some males' social inhibitions against the acting out of their rape desires. If there were more effective social sanctions against pornography, this would almost certainly increase the reluctance of some people to participate in the pornography industry.*
>
> *Excerpt from <u>Against Pornography: The Evidence of Harm</u>*
> *www.csus.edu/indiv/m/merlonos/dianarussell.html*

Introducing boys to sex through pornography under the guise of "entertainment" degrades women and conditions men to rape. If women want to end sexual assault, they must work to remove the things in society that condition men to rape.

Pornography deteriorates intimate relationships between men and women by introducing artificial images of female sexuality, conditioning men to respond to often unrealistic standards of beauty. They gradually lose the capacity to respond to the natural beauty of the women they love, and become addicted to the artificial images they see on the television or computer screen or printed in a magazine. The more their addiction to pornography increases, the more men become emotionally detached from their spouses.

In the book *Pornography: Private Right or Public Menace?* edited by Robert M. Baird and Stuart E. Rosenbaum, author Harry Brod contributed a chapter entitled "Pornography and the Alienation of Male Sexuality." He asserts:

In terms of discourse of what it understands to be "free" sex, pornographic sex comes "free" of the demands of emotional intimacy or commitment...

This puts a strain on male sexuality. Looking to sex to fulfill what are really nonsexual needs, men end up disappointed and frustrated. Sometimes they feel an unfilled void, and blame it on their or their partner's inadequate sexual performance...

To the pornographic mind, then, women become trophies awarded to the victor. For women to serve this purpose of achieving male social validation, a woman "conquered" by one must be a woman deemed desirable by others. Hence, pornography both produces and reproduces uniform standards of female beauty. Male desires and tastes must be channeled into a single mode, with allowance for minor variations which obscure the fundamentally monolithic nature of the mold. Men's own subjectivity becomes masked to them, as historically and culturally specific and varying standards of beauty are made to appear natural and given...men are dominated by desires not authentically their own.

<u>*Pornography: Private Right or Public Menace?*</u> *pages 118, 119*

Women play an active role in perpetuating their sexual objectification. The advertising industry offers great financial incentives for women who will slip on revealing clothing and pose seductively before a camera in order to help sell a product. The entertainment industry promises fame and fortune - something many love-starved girls yearn for - to those who will partially or completely disrobe and titillate viewers with glimpses of their bodies.

Women who need attention, affirmation of self worth, love from a man, admiration from other women, or the sense of power that the feeling of being beautiful and desirable gives them, become willing tools in an industry that exploits women for profit.

"However we may detest admitting it, the fact remains that there would be no exploitation if people refused to obey the exploiter. But self comes in and we hug the chains that bind us. This must cease."

Mohandas Gandhi

Women define a society's culture. Women must redefine their sexuality as something to be honored in the sanctity of marriage and not merely used to sell products.

Fathers who love their daughters must protect them from the young men that are being programmed by a profit-driven mass media to treat women as worthless sex objects. Fathers must be actively involved in their daughter's personal lives, making sure that young men who express interest in their daughters have honorable intentions. They must be as diligent as the zebra stallion in watching, protecting and supervising their daughters to ensure that young men treat their daughters with the utmost respect. They must guard their daughters from premature sexual involvement, and thereby enable their daughters to find suitable mates - emotionally mature men who are able and willing to make a commitment of marriage.

When a father shows love, compassion, sensitivity, affection and understanding toward his daughter, she will know to look for a spouse who possesses those same manly qualities.

Looking For A Father Figure

Women make choices in their personal lives based on the influence of their fathers. A healthy relationship with ones father increases the likelihood of a choice of a good, compatible mate. Women - consider your father's influence in shaping your image of a husband/wife relationship. If you cannot answer yes to at least eight of the following 15 questions, you may have difficulty making good choices when it comes to relationships with men. Seek the company of a happily married couple that you can observe as an example of what to look for in a healthy male-female relationship.

1.   My father was present in my home.
2.   I had a good relationship with my father.
3.   My father spoke to my mother respectfully.
4.   My father never hit my mother.
5.   I never saw my father intoxicated, high, or otherwise not in his right mind.
6.   My father provided regular financial support for our family.
7.   My father was encouraging and supportive of me and my activities.
8.   My father never cursed, made vulgar remarks or used profanity in my presence.
9.   My father and mother showed love and affection towards each other.
10. My father made me feel cute and loveable.
11. My father helped my mother around the house.
12. My father never hit me.
13. My father never did anything lewd, crude, or inappropriate to me or any of my siblings.
14. I am comfortable having private conversations with my father about matters that are important to me.
15. I want to marry a man that has the positive qualities that my father has.

Chapter 6
What The Lioness Knows
Raise Your Sons To Head Families of Their Own

It is a bright sunny afternoon on the East African plains. A mother lioness leads her three cubs through the tall, dry grass where a small gathering of antelope graze peacefully in the distance. Members of the herd are not expecting an attack in this midday sun, when most predators are somewhere stretched out under the shade of a tall tree.

But this is training day. The lioness is careful to remain upwind where the antelope cannot detect her scent. She walks softly through the grass and motions her cubs to keep their tails down low. Her eyes search the landscape, seeking just the right opportunity.

She spots it. It is a fawn, not more than a few days old, walking on spindly legs behind its mother. The mother's back is turned and the brown and white spotted fawn is wandering dangerously far away from the herd. The lioness signals her cubs to stand still and quietly observe.

She crouches low. Each deliberate step brings her inches closer to her unsuspecting target. The fawn, oblivious that its mother has moved a step farther away, is momentarily distracted by a butterfly. Now is the time to strike.

The mother lioness suddenly leaps out of the tall grass. The herd scatters. She charges toward the fawn, who, for an instant, is frozen in fear. Suddenly, panic brings speed to its little legs. It desperately darts away, twisting and dodging to allude capture. But the skilled lioness swipes at its legs, sending the fawn tumbling into the grass. Quickly, the lioness clutches the fawn by the throat. She raises the fawn's dangling body out of the grass for her cubs to see. The cubs watch intently.

If she holds her grip for a few more moments the struggling fawn will cease to move. But instead, the mother lioness

*loosens her jaws. The dazed fawn, hardly believing its good for-
tune, staggers a moment and stumbles away on trembling legs.
The lioness signals her cubs. It's their turn now.*

*One lion cub clumsily pounces at the fawn, but the fawn is
able to dodge out of reach of his sharp teeth. Another cub charges
at the fawn, but she cannot outrun the skinny little legs. The third
cub manages to leap upon the fawn's back and grasp it by the
neck. But it is not the suffocating death grip his mother demonstrated, and the fawn wrenches away.*

*With a burst of speed, the fawn dashes across the plains
toward the safety of the herd, to the relief of its mother who is observing the scene from a safe distance. The cubs regretfully watch
the fleeing fawn with panting tongues and empty stomachs. The
lioness also watches, but does not follow. She could have caught
the fawn and made a quick meal of it. But her cubs must learn: if
you miss a kill, you go hungry.*

*There will be other chances to practice. The cubs must
watch and try and try again until they master the techniques that
will enable them to survive.*

The Lion. Often called the King of Beasts, most likely because of
his proud posture, his majestic main, his rousing roar and his fearless fighting when facing an enemy. People often use the lion as a
symbol of strength and courage.

Every mighty lion was once a helpless cub, protected by its
mother. The lioness knows that she must raise him to one day be a
powerful predator.

Lions primarily live in family groups called "Prides." Females that are connected by blood ties, (mothers, daughters, sisters,
aunts, nieces), make up the pride. A male lion, or sometimes a pair
of male lions (blood brothers) head the pride. As with all animal
families, the most important function is the protection of the children. Lions must protect their cubs from hyenas and other natural
predators until the cubs reach adulthood. The lion pride makes a
fascinating study, and demonstrates a few principles regarding the
training of children that some human families can learn from.

Distinct Roles and Responsibilities of Males and Females

The males and females have distinct roles in the pride. The females do all of the hunting. Males know how to hunt, but their primary job is to protect the pride's territory from other predators. That means they must be ready and willing to fight off hyenas, wolves, jackals and others whose hunting might diminish the family's food supply. Also, a male lion's mane makes it more difficult for him to camouflage himself in tall grass while stalking prey.

A solitary male lion has less chance of a long, healthy life than one who lives in a pride. There are always greater advantages to having a family than being single. A single male must hunt for himself, limiting the kind of prey he can capture. A pack of three or four lions can bring down a large buffalo or zebra, whereas a single lion stands a greater chance of being kicked or gored to death in the struggle.

The only way a lion can take over a pride is that he must fight and defeat the head of an existing pride, unless he finds a pride in which there is no male head. Often, when a male or a pair of males becomes old and weak, a younger, stronger pair of males will attack them and kill them. They also kill all young male offspring. Otherwise, these males may grow up to overpower them. It's one of nature's harsh examples of survival of the fittest. This insures that the lionesses are under the protection of the strongest males, and that all male children in the pride are the sons of the current male heads of the pride.

The lioness understands that she must train her sons well so that they can survive on their own. Female cubs will grow up and remain with the pride. But by the age of three years old, males have reached adulthood, and must leave the pride. If they don't leave voluntarily, the other lionesses will drive them out. Even the lioness realizes that grown males cannot stay at home and challenge the authority of their fathers.

The extended family structure of the lion pride enables a pregnant lioness to stay in a den with her cubs after giving birth, while the other lionesses hunt and bring back some of the meat to her. Soon, when she is able to hunt with the pride again, she instructs her cubs to remain safely hidden while she leaves to hunt for food. She nurses her cubs until they begin to grow teeth. Then, she brings back small pieces of meat for them to chew, getting them accustomed to the smell and taste of fresh meat.

When they are old enough to keep up, the cubs are allowed to follow along with the pride when they go on a hunt. The cubs remain safely in the tall grass or hidden in a tree while the family hunts. Lionesses are quite organized hunters. Like a championship football team, they give signals and execute specific plays designed to successfully tackle their target. The cubs watch while their elders silently stalk unsuspecting prey and swiftly execute the kill. Survival for the lion pride is a matter of teamwork.

The lion takes his share first, and the lionesses wait until he is finished. The logic in this, of course, is that if the one who protects the territory is well fed, he will remain strong enough to continue to protect the territory. His job is to fight off other predators so that there is enough prey for his family to eat.

The lionesses eat next, and then the cubs eat whatever is left. During meals, members of the pride must fight for their share. Survival means aggression, so cubs learn early that to be timid is to starve. Lions become quite ferocious at mealtimes. Yet with all of their growling, snarling and biting during meals, lions are very affectionate toward family members. They groom each other, take long naps together, and are fiercely protective of the cubs. When two adult males are head of the pride, they will both mate with all the females and will protect all of the females' children, regardless of which male is the father.

Training Children By Demonstration and Practice

Training children is a matter of demonstration. Children are born imitators. They watch their parents and mimic everything they see. Human parents often make the mistake of telling their children what to do without actually showing them. The children don't learn and the frustrated parents wonder why their children aren't following instructions.

The lioness knows that teaching children is a combination of her demonstration and their practice. When they are old enough, she takes them to the fields and shows them how to stalk and kill. First she lets them practice on smaller animals, giving her children many opportunities to perfect their hunting skills. Even though a male lion may one day have females to hunt for him, he must still know how to kill his own prey. Shortly after the males reach puberty, they must leave the pride and make it on their own. If their mother taught them well, they will survive until they are big and strong enough to take over another pride. If they failed to acquire the necessary hunting skills, they will be unable to catch enough prey and will slowly starve to death.

A pride may be large, consisting of ten or twelve females and two or three adult males, or it may be small, consisting of just two or three females and one male. Young male lions understand the adult male's role as the protector of the territory from observing their fathers. They know that their father's roar and his scent markings serve to warn predators to stay off of the family's property. They know that their father fiercely attacks any predator that dares to challenge his authority. Young cubs play fight as part of their preparation for adulthood. They are honing fighting skills they will need not only to survive but to conquer other rival males.

Human females often make the big mistake of trying to stifle the instinctive male aggression in their sons. They fail to realize that such aggression is necessary for a male to fulfill his later role as protector and provider of the family. Successful men must aggressively pursue knowledge, aggressively acquire skills, and aggressively perform the work that will enable them to get paid, so that they can feed, house, and clothe their wives and children. In order to channel that aggression in a constructive direction, the son has to see a model of the appropriate adult male behavior. The father must teach him by demonstration.

The lioness knows that any male who earns the right to lead the pride must demonstrate strength, courage, and skill. Children learn their roles by what they see the parents do, not by what parents say. If a woman has a son by a man who is absent from the home, the son cannot know how to perform the role of husband and father. If the son grows up in a home where the mother is the only one who works and brings home money, the son only knows that women work and bring home money. Very often, the grown man who seeks to live off of women was once a young boy whose father was either physically absent or chronically unemployed.

Just as the proper training of her cubs is the lioness' role, the proper rearing of children is the human mother's role. Teaching children is a job that requires time, effort, patience and skill. Just as the lion must do his job of keeping the territory safe from intruders so that the lioness can do her job, the man must do his job of providing a living so that the woman can do her job. This is not sexist thinking. An infant requires specific care from the mother.

For human beings, the training of children is an extensive process. After children are weaned, not only must they be taught survival skills, they need morals and ethics to enable them to make the right decisions, so as not to bring harm to others.

Single mothers face the challenge of being expected to do both their jobs and the jobs of the fathers. If a woman is under constant stress because she is forced to be both mother and father to her children, or if she is being abused and neglected, she cannot do her job properly. Husbands must give love to their wives, so that wives can give love to the children and enable them to grow into kind and loving human beings.

Hussaifa Kikelomo Olajumoke Sunmonu, Retired Director of Pharmaceutical Services for the Lagos State Ministry of Health in Nigeria, observed that women have placed so much emphasis on equality with men in the workplace that they have neglected the critical job of raising children at home:

"God Almighty has given a division of labor and he has given what is expected of men as husbands as sons, and he also told us in the scriptures what is expected of us as wives, as mothers and as daughters.

"But, unfortunately, what we have in the world today,

we've turned the whole thing upside down. So, the values are lost. Women are seeking liberation, women's liberation. But Almighty God has liberated us a long, long time ago, because every man in whatever position, in notable positions all over the world, passed through the laps of women. And these men in authority all over the world, they go back home to consult with either their mothers or their wives. Those mothers and wives are women.

"The problem with the world is with us women. We have left our jobs undone. We are so busy trying to rub shoulders with the men that we have gone overboard.

"It is the duty of the woman to bring up the children at home, so whatever it is we have to do, we must remember that that is our primary objective in life, because that is what Almighty God has mapped out for us, to be able to bring up the children properly. So that when they go out in the society, they behave like human beings, they don't behave like animals, and they behave with so much love. If you give the children love, then they will be able to give it to the world.

"If you want something from me, it must be something that I have. If I don't have it, I cannot give it to you. If I don't have enough love in me, I cannot give you love.

"So, the women, us women, mothers, must go back to their primary assignment and that is the building of the home, the rearing of the children properly. It's only when they rear the children properly that they can build a good society."

Women have spent so many years fighting against mistreatment of wives and mothers that they have mistaken the role of wife and mother as a weak position. But, it is actually the wife and mother who has the power to shape the world by what she teaches in the home. However, she cannot use this power for the good of humanity unless she has wisdom and insight. Mrs. Sunmonu points out that a woman must have moral and ethical training herself in order to impart it to her sons and daughters.

"First of all, it is very important that the women should go

back and say, "Why am I a woman? What are my duties, my God-given duties that are expected of me? The various religions of the world, the Christians go to Church...the Muslims go to the Mosque...the Jews go to the Synagogue...all the various religions of the world, they're teaching something. If only we can listen, the world will be a better place.

"I am a Muslim woman and I know that it is my sacred duty to bring my children up properly. And when you bring up children properly, and they see the happiness you radiate in the home, they also want to have their own home. Charity begins at home. Whatever it is, it is for us women who want to be good wives and good mothers to live by example."

With five grown children and four grand children, Mrs. Sunmonu pointed out that older, more experienced women must share their knowledge with younger women who may not know how to properly raise their children. Older, wiser women must be able to lovingly give advice and guidance to those who need help and support.

Female-headed households create confusion for sons trying to understand their future roles as husbands. Boys, seeing their mothers perform the housework, may perceive it as unmanly, especially if they never see any men around helping to do it. Sons need to know how to work outside of the home, but they also need to know how to perform inside the home as well.

Boys must be trained to be good husbands, just as daughters must be trained to be good wives, Mrs. Sunmonu noted. She encouraged her sons to practice cooking and cleaning, reinforcing the idea that they would one day grow up and get married:

"I would come home from work and I would say to my son, 'I want you to prepare my dinner.' He would say, 'Oh, Mom, why don't you tell my sister to do it?' And I would say, 'No, I want you to do it.' He would prepare the food, and I would say, 'Oh, your wife is going to be so pleased with you!'"

The lioness teaches her sons to hunt so that they have the skills to survive while they are living on their own. A good human mother will teach her sons how to survive on their own as well. Sons must know how to clean a home, shop for food, wash and iron clothing and pay the bills while they are bachelors. They'll need to use these skills when their wives are weakened after childbirth and need help around the house. Some of the biggest conflicts between men and women erupt because men have not been taught homemaking skills.

In a society that often requires women to work outside of the home, men must know how to share household responsibilities. Too often, however, men's own mothers do not teach them. Mothers may teach the daughters, but they carelessly neglect to impart these very critical skills to their sons. The frequent result is that women find themselves working outside the home as providers and working inside the home as homemakers, while the men only work their eight-hour jobs outside of the home.

Marriages often end in divorce soon after a man loses a job. Conflicts are exacerbated by the fact that the man, although he is at home, performs few of the housekeeping activities necessary to manage the home. Wives leave home in the mornings to go to work and come back in the evenings to find beds unmade, floors unswept, dishes unwashed and food uncooked. They are furious. Working wives expect their husbands to know how to do chores, and are frustrated when the men don't do them.

Husbands, never having been properly taught these skills, are frustrated that their wives are so critical. Men interpret their wives' criticism as an attack on their manhood. Women interpret the neglect of household chores as laziness and inconsiderateness. Both men and women are angry at what they perceive as unfair treatment.

Fussing at children for not making their beds, cleaning their rooms and washing their clothes is not the same as teaching them how to do it. A mother must learn what the lioness knows: Teaching your children requires taking the time to demonstrate how to do a job, letting the children do it, letting them learn from their mistakes while they do it, and letting them practice it until they get it right. Household management is not "women's work." It is "adult's work." Both men and women have to be taught how to do it and how to do it well.

Preparing Boys For Independent Manhood

When an adult male lion leaves the pride, he must seek out and claim his own territory. He announces his presence with a roar and marks a space of land with his scent, urinating around the boundaries of his property. If any other male in the vicinity challenges his claim, they must do battle. The strongest predator wins the right to claim the territory as his hunting ground.

Once he secures his territory, the lion must then capture his food, using the skills he learned from his mother. If he misses a kill, he goes hungry. If too many days pass with no food, he will be too weak to hunt and could die of starvation. There is no lion pride to kill for him. Fighting off rivals and hunting for food are skills a young lion must have when he leaves his family to live on his own.

Just as in the case of the adult male lion, human males need to leave home after they reach the age of maturity. They need to prepare to head their own families. Some people make the mistake of kicking their sons out of the house at the age of eighteen, with the idea, "he's a boy, he can make it." Parents ignore the fact that they have taught the youth no survival skills whatsoever.

Even if a high school graduate found a job that paid a living wage, few parents have taught their teenage child how to remain a reliable, hard working employee, locate a reasonably priced apartment, furnish a home comfortably on a limited budget, buy and maintain clothing, manage and save money, pay bills on time, and establish good credit in order to purchase a home in the future. Earning a living and maintaining a dwelling are the skills a young man must have when he leaves his family to live on his own.

A young man is ready to take on the responsibility of starting his own family when he is willing to use his earnings to make sure a wife and children are fed, properly clothed, and living in a secure, comfortable space. He must also be able to assist in the maintenance of the home and the rearing of children. When he can do this, he is demonstrating the proper role of a male head of household.

"A woman who does not raise her sons properly is abusing other women."

Hazrat Mirza Tahir Ahmad, Khalifatul Massih IV

Too many mothers lament the fact that the fathers of their children are little more than children themselves. They are lazy and irresponsible, the women complain. They won't get a job. They won't help around the house. They hang out with their friends rather than take care of the children. The question is, who raised these boys to manhood? Why were they not taught how to be hardworking heads of households? Where were their fathers, who were supposed to model the correct behavior for them? Why didn't their mothers prepare them with the proper skills to take care of a family?

Women who do not raise their sons properly are, in fact, abusing other women. They are forcing the women who marry their sons to have to work harder in order to compensate for their son's defective behavior.

So, why are women allowing immature, ill-prepared men to father their children? Again, it comes back to choices. Women have a responsibility to choose mature men who can demonstrate the appropriate behavior for a male head of household. If a woman does not, she will be forced to try to become both "father and mother" to her children. No matter how hard she works, how much money she earns, or how many expensive clothes and toys she buys for her children, she cannot do it.

Some women insist they can do it all – career, housework and childrearing – without a man. This is a fallacy. The best of day care centers and private baby-sitting services cannot replace two parents in a home. As part of their upbringing, boys must learn their defined roles of husband and father – and if they don't, once they reach adulthood, they'll create great torment for the women who live with them.

Mothers and Fathers Provide Emotional Balance

Boys may learn certain aspects of manhood, such as courage, leadership, teamwork, and professional skills, from other men. Uncles, teachers, coaches and scout leaders might serve as good role models. But boys can only learn how to be husbands and fathers from watching their own fathers in the home. Inside the home is where children are trained in family roles and responsibilities. An absent father can only demonstrate how to be an absent father.

Some single mothers, trying to compensate for the absence of a father in their son's lives, will try to imitate what they believe is "manly" behavior. They will be cold, unaffectionate and harsh to their sons, believing that this is how a father would act. They think that being harsh will make their sons tough and strong. It doesn't. It actually weakens, even cripples boys emotionally, making them insecure and lacking in a sense of self worth. People who don't feel worthy of love often don't know how to love others.

In his stage play entitled *I Didn't Think*, Chicago Hip Hop artist, playwright and actor Hashim Hakim expresses the frustration of a young man whose non-affectionate mother rejected him for an abusive boyfriend:

"I wrote this play because I knew what I was going through in my life was common. There's a large percentage of households with no father.

"When I was growing up, it became normal for us how we were raised without a father. Whenever men came around, it became abnormal. We made it very difficult for my mother to have a relationship. She tried to discipline us, she used extension cords, switches, everything. Nothing worked. There really should have been a father there.

"I was raised in the church, but it was the same thing – no

fathers, no male figures.

"*My mother tried to compensate for her lack of a man. She acted real hard and mean. People in the neighborhood would make jokes, they'd say, 'Your mama's a man.' I don't remember her ever showing me any affection. I was so starved for affection, when I brushed my hair, I would pretend it was a woman's hand, stroking my head.*

"*I knew a hug was a symbol of love. So, when my cousin gave me a hug, I associated it with love. That's how I got introduced to sex – trying to get affection. I was five years old. We started playing 'house.' That went on for years. I don't remember ever getting that kind of love from my mother.*

"*I witnessed my stepfather physically abusing my mother. I tried to stop him, but my mother didn't appreciate my defense of her. She sided with him. I became a vicious child. I did things to get any kind of attention. Once you kill the kindness in a child, you leave the bad. When you don't acknowledge the good a child is trying to show the parent, the evil becomes the dominant force. I didn't get acknowledged for trying to defend her.*"

Hakim entered his teen years as an angry, rebellious young man. He was violent and cruel to his sisters. Prematurely introduced to sex by his cousin at age five, he sought to keep repeating the experience with other girls. He was considered the "black sheep" of the family, the one that would never amount to anything. He saw himself headed down a path of self destruction. He said when he joined the Nation of Islam, his perspective changed.

"*I would have no knowledge of how to maintain a family if it were not for the Honorable Elijah Muhammad and the Nation of Islam. In the Nation of Islam, there are detailed solutions for every situation. I studied the life of Malcolm X. Malcolm reminded me of myself, living the street life, then coming into the knowledge. The Nation gave me the discipline I lacked. I still struggle with the sex thing, though, but I'm not at the point where I can't say 'no.'*

"The two children I have now, I acknowledge everything they do, whether it's 'Dad, I picked you some dandelions' or 'See, Dad, I washed the dishes.' I make a big deal over it. You have to set the right foundation from childhood.

"I had to find someone to study, to learn from. I clung to Malcolm. I related to what he went through."

When fathers are in the home, they provide a balance, allowing mothers to be warm and affectionate without fear of making their sons too "soft." Boys need female affection and nurturing in order to learn how to express affection, not just sexual desire, toward their wives. Many sexually promiscuous men were once love-starved little boys who didn't receive enough affection from their mothers. Often improperly introduced to sex at a young age, they learn to equate sex with love, and end up using sex as a means to fulfill a need for physical affection.

Boys learn how to treat women from watching how their fathers treat their mothers. When sons watch their fathers or other men being violent, verbally abusive, or neglectful towards their mothers, they learn that women are not worthy of respect. When a young man spews out foul language, wears his pants hanging off his rear end, and calls women vulgar names, he is making an announcement:

"I HAVE NO MOTHER IN MY HOME WHOM I RESPECT AND WHO HAS TAUGHT ME TO RESPECT MYSELF."

If mothers don't raise boys to respect women, there will be no descent men to become husbands and fathers in the future.

Many single mothers repeatedly remind their sons not to imitate their father's inappropriate behavior. While their intentions may be to encourage better behavior in their sons, this denigration of fathers has an emotionally crippling effect. One cannot teach a negative: "Don't be like your father." So, what positive image does this give a son? None. Sons need to see a positive father image in order to imitate one. A mother cannot be a father; a mother can only be a mother.

Good parenting is important. But what many single parents are not recognizing is that mothering and fathering are two different jobs. There is a point in a son's physical and emotional development where he needs to talk to his father, a man he has bonded with, a man he trusts, who has gone through the same awkwardness of puberty and can comprehend what he is experiencing. A woman, no matter how sensitive she may be to her son's feelings, cannot tell him how it feels to be a man.

Just like a single father's pubescent daughter may feel uncomfortable in discussing the onset of her menstrual cycle, a single mother's pubescent son may not feel comfortable discussing his wet dreams, spontaneous erections and other bodily functions signaling the coming of manhood. The frustration of not having a father present is what prompts many adolescent boys to exhibit anger and resentment toward mothers.

Society has been most unfair to single parents, expecting two distinct jobs to be done by one person. Is your doctor and your dentist the same person? No. Is your carpenter and your auto mechanic the same person? No. So, why do we expect a mother and a father to be the same person? Even when single parents do an outstanding job, the fact remains that the children in the home do not learn how to function as a spouse in a marriage. This is perhaps one reason why many children raised in single parent homes never marry.

Mothers Must Engage In Appropriate Behavior

Sons need to see their mothers as examples of decency and goodness, models of what they should look for in future wives. Mothers have to be conscious that when their sons are approaching puberty they are very easily aroused by the sight of a female body. It is embarrassing and humiliating for a pubescent boy to discover that he is becoming sexually aroused by the sight of his seductively dressed mother. Mothers need to make sure that they remain properly covered in the presence of their sons (no see-though negligees), and that all visiting female friends are also properly covered.

This encourages boys to maintain respect for women.

In her book *Between Mothers and Sons, The Making of Vital and Loving Men*, author Evelyn S. Bassoff, Ph.D., points out that single mothers who are openly sexually active create great distress in their sons:

> *In the previous chapter, I included a lengthy quote from Allen, a fifty-one-year-old man, who, drawing from his own boyhood experience as the son of a single parent, was able to describe the rage he had felt toward his mother's many lovers and his sense of personal powerlessness from being unable to protect her against their advances. Allen also told me how painful it was for him to live in a home that seemed to be always sexually charged. With his bedroom separated from his mother's by paper-thin walls, he was exposed to the sounds of his mother's sex acts night after night; and even when his mother was not engaged in sexual activity his mind would spin out of control with sexual images of her. Continually stimulated sexually, he would brace himself against the forbidden sensations of arousal.*
>
> *The consensus among child psychologists and family therapists is that children are distressed when their parents flit from partner to partner and are indiscreet about their sexual activities; open talks about love and sex are not enough to soothe this distress; good communication is not the salve that quells all emotional pain... Every culture sets limits around sexual expression in order to assure the well being of children and of the community as a whole.*
>
> <u>Between Mothers and Sons</u>, *Page 144*

Married parents express affection towards each other, but are usually conscious about keeping their sexual intimacy private. Single parents, on the other hand, tend to be more openly passionate when they are dating, forcing children to recognize their parents' sexuality in a way that makes them extremely uncomfortable.

Women must select men who model the appropriate behavior for a husband and father. Women with live-in boyfriends teach their sons that it's okay to be uncommitted and irresponsible. They are teaching their sons that having sex, not taking care of children, is the main objective in a relationship. Many men do not marry because they have not been raised to be husbands. They have been raised to be grown men with girlfriends with whom they engage in social activities and with whom they enjoy sexual intimacy.

In a society where more marriages fail than succeed, many men are fearful of the pain of divorce. They may have witnessed their own father's emotional and financial devastation after a divorce; they may have some vivid childhood memories of bitter arguments between their parents. Whatever the case, many men cannot visualize themselves as husbands, and will remain bachelors throughout their 30s, 40s, and 50s. By the time they realize the benefits of a permanent relationship, many men have lived well past their prime and are not likely to ever marry and have children.

When a single mother chooses to have an intimate relationship with a man who resents her children, the results can be disastrous. Such a man will not likely forge a paternal bond with the children. Just as a lion when taking over a pride kills the male cubs fathered by another lion, men who resent the sons of other men will destroy them, if not physically, emotionally. The child is a constant reminder of another man, and a possible rival. An older son will challenge the man's authority in the home. A woman finds herself having to choose between her mate and her son. If she chooses her son, she loses her mate. If she chooses her mate, she loses the respect of her son. Her son's hurt and anger will affect his relationships with other women, perhaps causing him to be physically or emotionally abusive.

Too many women have made the mistake of having their boyfriends baby-sit their children. It is unlikely that one who is emotionally unprepared for marriage will be emotionally prepared to act as a parent. A man who is lacking in maturity and patience will become angry and frustrated when children cry. He may beat the children, sometimes injuring them, even killing them. There is an even greater risk that a man will injure a child that is not his own, due to underlying hostility towards the child's father.

Boys with absent or uninvolved fathers may desire to be good parents, but because of the lack of a role model, they simply don't have a clue as to what fathering is. In her book *Where's Daddy? How Divorced, Single, and Widowed Mothers Can Provide What's Missing When Dad's Missing*, Claudette Wassil states:

> *During her interviews with families, Arlie Hochschild, author of* The Second Shift, *asked fathers what they felt their role was with their children. The least involved fathers (and most of the fathers she interviewed had little involvement with their children) said they felt fathers should discipline and teach about sports, current events, or cars, or described "good fathers" as men who were "around." Despite their vague descriptions of fathering, these same men had no difficulty describing the role of the mother in great detail. According to these men "good mothers" were patient, warm, caring, physically attentive, intellectually stimulating and emotionally supportive. As we can see, it is not that men don't know what children need or what "parents" should do, they just could not relate these traits to their own roles or responsibilities. They often drew on the images of their own absent fathers in their search. For many men parenting now, fathers were the parent who left in the morning, came home for dinner, and then sat and watched TV. That's not much to go on.*
>
> <u>*Where's Daddy?*</u> *Page 10*

When a boy has no memory of a father who was actively involved in helping him with homework, teaching him how to play games, showing him how to repair things around the house, or just having a lighthearted conversation, the boy often grows up to be a man who does not know how to interact with his own children.

Women, particularly if they are single parents, often don't know how to instill qualities of manhood in their sons. Following is a list of Dos and Don'ts to help women avoid mistakes and to recognize and correct mistakes they may have made.

Guidelines For Raising Sons To Manhood
DO:

1. Encourage your son's aggressive behavior. He is instinctively striving to exercise his muscles to develop body strength and coordination. Find space for him to run and play. Channel his energy toward positive competitive activities, like sports or martial arts.

2. Teach your son how to cook, clean, and care for younger siblings. Just as little girls visualize themselves as wives and mothers, boys must envision their future roles as husbands and fathers. Praise your son for mastering homemaking skills. Tell him he is becoming a strong man who can take care of his family.

3. Give your son wholesome expectations of sex within marriage. Schools will give him clinical information. Television, movies, and women on the street will give him sexually stimulating images. His body will urge him to satisfy natural desires. You must teach him that manhood means marriage before sex.

4. Show your son plenty of affection. Even though boys may go through a phase where they withdraw from a lot of hugs and kisses, they still need physical affection from their mothers. They need to learn how to be affectionate, not just sexually aggressive, toward their wives. If they never receive affection, they will not know how to give it to their wives or their own children.

5. Get to know your son by taking time to listen. Parenting isn't just lecturing all the time. You can learn a lot by listening. Have lighthearted conversations; let your son tell you about his friends, his activities and his opinions. Listen to him without being critical and judgmental. Let him know his thoughts are important.

6. Give him opportunities to earn his own money. Allowance should be earned, not just given freely. Even if it's just a few dollars for mowing the lawn or washing the windows, children need to learn the value of money. When they reach their teen years, they should be allowed to get a safe part-time job. Boys have a natural instinct to be self-sufficient. Parents need to encourage it by giving them the independence to earn money honestly. Parents must teach sons how to save and how to budget their expenses.

DON'T:

1. Criticize your son's father in your son's presence. Whatever his father is, you made the selection, so take responsibility for your choice. Point out positive things about your son's father, to raise his self esteem. He needs to feel that he comes from a person who has good qualities.

2. Allow your son to tease, bully or hit girls. Boys need to learn that there is a distinct difference in the way they should treat the opposite sex. Even though little girls may sometimes be just as rough and aggressive as little boys, a male child must be taught never to hit a female. Men must develop an early aversion to violence toward women, so that they will never abuse their wives.

3. Bring men into your home to spend the night. If a son perceives that his mother is having sex outside of marriage, he will conclude that marriage is not necessary in order for him to fulfill his own sexual desires. He will not respect other women. He will also perceive that men do not respect his mother, and this will cause anger and hurt.

4. Marry a man who cannot bond with your son. If you have other children together, such a man will not be able to hide his preference for his own offspring over your child from a previous relationship. He may mistreat your son. Underlying resentment will fester and explode, eventually destroying family relationships.

5. Let your son visit girls when their parents are not home. It is your responsibility to know where your child is at all times. Don't let your son run wild, and then blame the girl for getting pregnant. Most teenage sexual activity occurs in the home when parents are absent. You should know the parents in every home he visits.

6. Ignore your son's emerging manhood. When your son reaches puberty, you must recognize that your relationship will change. You cannot keep him a little boy by babying him or intimidating him. Let him know that you recognize he is becoming a man. Respect his privacy. Give him more responsibility. Recognize that he is aware of your femininity. Always dress appropriately in his presence and demand the same of your female friends.

Chapter 7
Harmony in the Buffalo Herd
Form Extended Families to Protect the Children

The intoxicating smell of fresh grass, damp with the morning dew, lured the young calf a few steps away from its mother. He lowered a long thin neck and, standing shakily on spindly legs, tasted a delicious mouthful. He was not yet weaned, but in between feedings of his mother's warm milk, he enjoyed the succulent taste of the long green blades that spread across the field as far as the eyes could see. In a moment he had stepped an unsafe distance from the protective flank of his mother and the rest of the buffalo herd as they silently grazed under the bright orange haze of dawn.

Suddenly he stopped, his ears pricking up in alarm. It wasn't a smell or even a sound, it was more of a feeling. He was being watched. Suddenly he froze. There, in the clump of bushes ahead, a pair of dark eyes met his own, the spotted fur almost invisible in the tall patch of grass. It was a leopard.

In an instant the calf sprang away, and in fractions of a second all of the moves his mother taught him back came to him— run left, turn right, fake left, run right, turn left, fake right, run left, sprint...sprint...sprint...

The young calf forced his little legs as fast as they could go, struggling to reach the safety of the herd. He had strayed too far, making himself an easy target. The leopard leaped toward him, with powerful front legs reaching out to trip him. The calf stumbled, trying desperately to regain his footing. The black bodies scattering in the distance were so far away. He couldn't make it...he couldn't make it...

Suddenly a big black figure came charging out of the crowd. The male head of the herd lowered his horns at the snarling leopard. Suddenly, the angry snarl turned into a yelp of pain, and the leopard stumbled away, wounded. In a rush, the calf saw a mass of bodies surround him. His mother and the other cows en-

*circled him protectively, their horns facing outward, as the leopard
scrambled to his feet. The leopard searched for an opening in the
wall of cow horns shielding the calf. But the cows stood firm.*

*Again the bull charged at the leopard and the leopard
whirled around, sinking sharp fangs into the bull's shoulder. But
this bull meant business. He lowered his powerful head and
jabbed full force at the leopard.*

*With a yowl of pain, the leopard slinked stealthily into the
bushes. This hunt was over. One young, inexperienced leopard was
no match for a huge buffalo bull, and eleven determined buffalo
cows, not when it came to protecting a young calf.*

*Slowly the cows moved away and resumed their peaceful
grazing. The young buffalo calf, legs still shaking nervously, stood
close to his mother and began to nurse, calming his racing heart.
He was safe in the care of his family.*

*The calf turned his head to search for his father, the strong
and fearless bull. There he stood across the plains, head erect, the
tip of his horn stained with the blood of the leopard, his muscular
chest heaving as his flaring nostrils breathed out hot breaths. The
bull's eyes searched the plains for any more signs of danger, but
there were none. The leopard had slipped away into the tall grass
to nurse its wounds. The bull stood protectively beside the cows
and their calves, his head held high. Blood dripped from the
small gash on his shoulder, but there he stood in proud triumph.*

Among herd animals -- buffalo, wildebeests, zebras, elephants
and others -- females instinctively group together for the collective
safety and upbringing of their children. It is one of the most basic
female survival instincts.

This same instinct exists among human females as well. It
is no accident that mothers are most often the active members of
block clubs, Local School Councils and Parent Teacher Associa-
tions. Women work together for the sake of their children. They
organize programs and look out for each other's children. They
have the social skills to cooperate and compromise, skills that are
necessary in order to get a job done.

Males and females are created differently by nature, in order that they may complement each other, rather than clash with each other. When it comes to raising children, males and females have to work together in complementary ways in order for the family to remain in harmony.

Animals form family groups based on the ratio of males to females. If the numbers are pretty evenly matched, such as in the case of most flocks of birds, there is usually a male for every female. But in the case of most migrating herd animals, there are usually more females than males. Animals that provide food for many other animals must produce enough offspring to maintain the population. This keeps a balance in the earth's ecosystem. This means that all females must have an opportunity to mate and give birth. So, among most herd animals, females form family groups and seek out the strongest males to father their children, to give their children the best possible chances of surviving to adulthood.

A strong male head of household is important to human families as well. Children are instinctively drawn to strong males, as a natural survival instinct. They admire men who are fearless. A father's presence in the home means that the house is secure.

Both sons and daughters are negatively affected when fathers are absent. In her book *Where's Daddy? How Divorced, Single, and Widowed Mothers Can Provide What's Missing When Dad's Missing*, author Claudette Wassil notes that the reason for a father's absence has just as much of an emotional impact on the child as the absence itself:

A child whose father is living nearby but who never chooses to visit him will have a greater sense of personal rejection than a child whose father has died. A child whose father lives at home but is always away on business or spends his evenings down at the office may feel more abandoned than a child whose father lives three states away, due to divorce, but sends for the child twice a year and enthusiastically spends every minute of the day with the child for two weeks.

<u>*Where's Daddy*</u>, *by Claudette Wassil, page 5*

Whatever the cause for the absence, there are some common signs of distress in children without fathers, she observes. Boys often have difficulty making friends with other boys and are reluctant to engage in rough play. They also tend to be anti-social and exhibit poor self-control.

Girls without fathers tend to be either extremely shy around men, or extremely flirtatious. Both boys and girls tend to experience poor academic performances in school.

A father's presence has a great effect on the development of a boy's self esteem, direction and purpose. In his book, *A Season of Afflictions*, Dr. Kenneth Nave reflects on the profound effect of a father's absence:

A boy's world loses so much of it's meaning, so much of its truth, when a father dies or is absent. The absence of a father sends a resounding echo though the soul of a young man and separates him from his history, his past, and his roots. Single mothers often perform outstanding jobs raising fine young men in the absence of the children's fathers. Their efforts assure that a male child survives, lives, learns and possibly even loves. But there is something spiritual and divine about the relationship between a father and a son. Nothing can replace it: not an uncle, not a stepfather, and not the greatest efforts of a mother. This is a relationship ordained by God. The loss and damage caused by the severing of this tie can only be overcome with the aid of the God that <u>allowed</u> it.

A father bestows manhood and masculinity. Every stop on a boy's journey into manhood is to be heralded by his father's many gestures of approval and his gentle (or sometimes harsh) coaxing along the way. When there is no father, there is no clear journey.

A Season of Afflictions, pages 22 and 23

Many boys fail to live up to their potential, socially and academically, because of the low self-esteem they experience as a result of the absence of a father's encouragement and reassurance.

Sons Rebel Against Single Mothers

When children do not have a father in their homes, they feel vulnerable. They will often rebel against a single mother who, by herself, appears weak. This rebellious attitude translates into rebellion against all female authority figures. Female schoolteachers find their authority being challenged by the boys in the classroom. As boys raised by single mothers grow into manhood, the only way they know how to assert their masculinity is by trying to dominate women, as opposed to being dominated by women, as they had been throughout childhood. Such rebellion is a young man's way of expressing independence.

Street gangs flourish in neighborhoods where men are not in the home. Absent fathers cannot help their sons make the important transition to manhood. Boys seeking strong men to emulate often find role models in those who can show them how to survive.

In her book *The Other America: Gangs*, author Gail Stewart interviews a number of youth who provide a glimpse of life inside the street gangs. Tajan, son of a single mother, reveals how his estrangement from his father, mother, stepfather and younger step siblings made gang life attractive. Regarding his relationship with his father, Tajan responds:

"My dad? You mean my real dad? I don't know much about him. He left when I was, like, two or three and went back to where he was from. Someplace in Ohio, I think. He came back when I was about thirteen, trying to be all in my life and whatever, but I had no time for him. I was busy. I got to take care of my own business."

This final statement is spoken solemnly, and he pauses a moment, thinking.

"I really don't know what the deal is with my mom now. I got a stepdad, her little husband or whatever," he drawls, rolling his eyes. "I don't know what their deal is, though, if they're like, separated or divorced. He stops through and stuff, because these little kids here, they're his and everything. I don't pay much atten-

*tion.   I'm just looking out for my own, for myself, you know?
That's what I'm doing these days."*
The Other America, Gangs, by Gail Stewart, page 14

When fathers are absent and stepfathers or boyfriends do
not effectively bond with them, boys seek out other men to serve
as role models. Despite the violence and drug trafficking associated with street gangs, many fatherless youth find in such organizations the kind of support they missed at home. Tajan and his
friend A-Loc explain to Ms. Stewart the advantages of being
members of the Gangster Disciples:

*"It's not all that stuff you read about in the newspapers. It
really isn't," he (Tajan) maintains.   "It's not all about gang-
banging and stuff like that. To me, GD could stand for Growth
and Development. It's more like an organization. See, the GD's
was started by a Black Panther in Chicago named Larry Hoover.
That's what the stuff was that I read, like five or six pages' worth,
explaining it all. It started out as the BOSs, the Brothers of the
Struggle. I mean, from that, you can kind of tell what his beliefs
are. It's like, we're here to help out the neighborhood. We're
more into protecting than anything. It's a pride thing, a pride and
loyalty to the neighborhood where you live...A-Loc tell her how
this brotherhood works."*

*A –Loc smiles. "Yeah, it's like everything you learn—the
handshakes, the signs, everything. I learned it from this older
dude, someone who'd been in the gang a long time before me. And
he taught me how to survive, how to make money. Then I teach it
to somebody else, some younger guy later. It's a circle, a rotation.
That's the beauty of it."*

"Exactly," murmurs Tajan, nodding his head.
The Other America, Gangs, pages 20, 28

A father shows his son how to succeed as a man. If there is
no father in the home, a young man will instinctively look for a
male substitute. Girls who are raised in fatherless homes also tend

to seek a male substitute and often are attracted to drug-dealing, womanizing, gang-banger types. Having no positive strong male image, fatherless girls sometimes mistake rebellion for strength.

The Feminization of Fatherless Boys

Children prepare for their adult roles by imitating the mannerisms and behavior of the same sex parent. But what if the same sex parent is absent?

Many boys who are raised by single mothers begin to develop feminine mannerisms. They are not homosexual. They simply have no one to regularly reinforce male behavior. Subtle things, such as the way a boy sits or stands, a wave of the hand, even a voice inflection can reflect a decidedly feminine influence.

Chicago playwright, actor and hip-hop artist Hashim Hakim recalled how his manager on a job first made him aware of the noticeable feminine influence in his personality. He began to realize the difference between the behavior of men who have been raised with fathers in the home and men who have not:

"What made me realize there's a big difference is when I had an argument with my manager. We were going back and forth, then he stopped me and said, 'You've been raised by a woman, haven't you?' I said, 'Yes, how did you know?' He said, 'You keep trying to have the last word. A man's way of handling things is different. It's his reasoning, his rationale. Women are more emotional, more argumentative.'"

Among African American youth, hairstyles and jewelry that were at one time exclusively feminine styles are now being worn by muscular men with facial hair. Men wear fancy braided hairstyles with beads, dyed hair, straightened hair with curls, earrings, necklaces and polished nails, reflecting a strong female influence, quite possibly the dominant influence of a single mother.

In the book *Souls of My Brothers*, by Dawn Marie Daniels and Candace Sandy, former police officer and consultant Robert

Roots writes a chapter entitled "Can A Woman Raise A Man?" He points out that there must be a difference between the roles of men and women, and addresses the question of whether single mothers can successfully guide their sons into manhood.

> *Black males are beginning to look and act more like their mothers. They have gone from no earring to two earrings. And more women are saying they don't need a man to raise a child, that they can do it alone. The ones who are suffering are the children. And when the children suffer from this kind of dysfunctional thinking, society as a whole feels the consequences...What we are developing are strong women and weak men...*
>
> *Can a woman raise a man?...No, a woman cannot raise a man. As much as she tries, a woman is still a woman. It is up to the father to assume his role and raise his son to be a man. And when the father is not around or is failing to show leadership, then other men in the family need to be men and act as role models.*
>
> <u>*Souls of My Brothers*</u>, *"Can A Woman Raise A Man?"*
> *Pages 158, 159*

Boys whose parents separate because their fathers are violent, alcoholics, drug addicts, convicted criminals, or possess any number of other negative traits, are left to deal with the emotions of their single mothers. Too often, a mother's anger and frustration is directed at her son, who must listen to constant criticism of his father, the only man who represents his own male identity. This is quite destructive to a boy's self-esteem.

Actor/Screenwriter Kevin Green contributed a chapter to the book *Souls of My Brothers* entitled "A Culture's Cancer," in which he recalls being raised by a single mother following the break up of his parents when he was five years old. After years of hearing his mother's friends vent their anger at all the "no-good" men in their lives, he entered his teen years with nothing but negative images of manhood. He became a drug dealer and a robber and eventually got arrested.

After avoiding conviction and jail, he developed a new hustle: women. He learned how to manipulate rich, beautiful women, spending their money and living a lavish lifestyle among the celebrities. His philosophy on women was, "If they couldn't be used, they were useless."

And then, he met the daughter of a TV station executive, and discovered a whole new world that completely changed his life. He developed a relationship with her and eventually they got engaged to be married. She got pregnant by someone else and he recalls that he was emotionally devastated when they broke up, but not because he was so much in love with the woman:

My intention of course was to squeeze her like all the others, but when I met her father it was love at first sight. I was starstruck in his presence. He embodied all the qualities of my mother's description of a perfect man. Suddenly that ache to fill my father's shoes returned...

The world I'm talking about had nothing to do with money. It was the world of an African American family that included a father—trust me there is a difference. My joy was so overwhelming that I confused it with love and treated her with nothing but respect. I was loyal, kind, considerate and didn't want a dime...

So what was it that hurt me so much, you ask? Her father—I loved him as my own and didn't want to lose him.

Time spent with him was short, but the revelation that came with it could touch the sky...he talked to me about everything from his militant role in the civil rights movement to his fear of God to his respect for women. I was a sponge and soaked up more than just his words. I studied his gestures, his posture, his confidence. I watched how he handled the waiter, his family, his friend and confrontation. Unknowingly he exposed me to the fact that I was ill-equipped in almost every area of my being. The revelation that slapped me cold in the face was that I was not a man. That reality was the source of pain that no one knew of...

Had I been raised by a loving, positive father whom I idolized and confided in, I would've been a different person coming up regardless of my environment. My self-worth would've been above dealing drugs. My respect for women would not have allowed me to use them...Yes, losing my ex's father was tough, but the lesson learned was an indisputable fact: No boy should ever be raised without his father!

<u>*Souls of My Brothers*</u>*, "A Culture's Cancer," Pages 5 and 6*

Eighty-five percent of all youths sitting in prisons grew up in fatherless homes. Seventy five percent of all adolescent patients in chemical abuse centers come from fatherless homes. Eighty five percent of all children that exhibit behavioral disorders come from fatherless homes.

Where are the men to help raise these children? According to a May 15, 2001 report issued by the U. S. Census Bureau, within the decade between 1990 and 2000, families maintained by women with no husband present increased three times as fast as married couples with families, 21% verses 7%. Married couple families dropped from 55 percent to 52 percent of all households.

Today's families are in a state of crisis. Current statistics show that 53% of the nation's children are being raised in single parent homes. The vast majority of these single parents are mothers, trying to juggle financial responsibilities, household management and childrearing. They are condemned by an unforgiving society every time one of their children suffers physical harm as a result of being improperly supervised. Rarely does the public exclaim when a child falls out of a window, "Where was the father?" But the mother is almost always the parent who receives the blame when things go wrong.

It's not enough to keep lamenting the fact that the men are not in the home. A series of social and economic conditions have contributed to this crisis. Deaths from war, homicide and poor health care contribute to the numerical imbalance between men and women. In many communities chronic unemployment among young men further decreases the prospects for stable marriages.

Despite these conditions, we must move toward a viable solution, a solution that brings responsible men into the homes and into the lives of children.

Extended Family Offers Balance and Support

Women have the power to end this crisis and get all that they desire…a loving husband, a comfortable home, and an extended family in which to raise their children. By observing the harmony in a buffalo herd, women can learn a lot about how females strengthen the family by cooperating with other females. Women can work together to insure that all children are raised in a household that includes a mother and a responsible father.

Buffalo family groups are basically matriarchal. If a calf is orphaned, often the other females in the herd will adopt it and raise it. This is the advantage of being a part of an extended family. One has many mothers to turn to for help and support.

Buffalo calves are born in the spring of the year, when grass and water are plentiful. Calves stay with their mothers until they are weaned, sticking close to them for protection as the herds migrate across the plains. When young males reach puberty, they join the group of older males, forming a protective shield around the cows and calves as they move across the open fields.

Young buffalo males learn their role in the buffalo community by watching older males. They learn that they must graze constantly to build up muscle mass, and must sharpen their horns and prepare themselves for the rutting season, in which only the strongest males will be allowed to sire offspring. The next generation of calves must be strong enough to make the long trek across the prairie and robust enough to survive the winter cold. Females teach their calves survival skills from the moment of their birth. Migrating herds are targets for all kinds of predators, and a calf must know how to stay close to the herd, how to sense danger, and how to run for its life.

Besides the day-to-day drama of staying alive and avoiding becoming someone's dinner, life in the buffalo herd is peaceful. Hundreds, thousands, even hundreds of thousands of buffalo once moved swiftly across the North American countryside in unison, never trampling a single calf. For the buffalo herd, each child is precious and worth fighting for.

There is harmony in the buffalo herd because there is harmony among the females. They walk side by side, always keeping a watchful eye out for danger. The females don't fight each other over who should have the right to have a mate. Those who are fertile share the best males among themselves and form family groups in order to collectively raise the children.

Human children also need to be raised in families – extended families, where there are fathers, mothers, uncles, aunts, grandparents and cousins. A family should not be just one parent struggling alone, trying to be both mother and father. No matter how valiantly a single parent may strive, one parent cannot provide the same support for a child as that of an extended family.

Children need to see, in their own families, how husbands and wives interact with each other in order to understand their future roles as husbands and wives. The epidemic of single mothers can only be corrected by bringing responsible men into the home, to be husbands and fathers.

There are many human societies in which women outnumber men, yet all women have husbands and are part of a family. This system, known as polygyny, allows men to have more than one wife. The purpose of this system is to insure that all children are raised within the protection of a family that includes a mother and a father.

Multiple Wives, Not Multiple Husbands

Polygyny specifically means the marriage of one male with more than one female.

Poly: many, several
Gyne: (Greek) woman, wife

This is not to be confused with the word Polygamy, which means having more than one spouse, either husband or wife, at a time. Whenever the subject is brought up of men having more than one wife, some women demand, "Well, why can't women have more than one husband? If men can have a bunch of wives, this gives men more power over women!"

This basic misunderstanding of marriage is one of the main reasons why our marriages are not working. Marriage is not a power struggle between a husband and wife. It is a bond between a man and a woman that provides for the mutual fulfillment of needs. It is the core of the family structure.

When a man marries a woman, he is establishing a friendship, a partnership, a spiritual union, a physical relationship and a legal entity recognized by the government.

In a polygynous system, if a man marries another woman, he is establishing all of the same things he had with the first wife. The purpose of marriage is the same for each marriage between a man and woman. The children are recognized as brothers and sisters of the same family, regardless of which mother they have.

If a woman was to have different husbands and she became pregnant, the question of paternity would arise. Which man is the father? Which man is financially responsible? Men, unlike lion brothers in a lion pride, do not have a social structure in which they comfortably share wives and share responsibilities for each other's children.

There are biological reasons why it is unhealthy for a woman to engage in sex with different men simultaneously. Unlike the combination of sperm and ovum, the sperm of two men are not a compatible biological mixture. When a woman is receiving sperm from two or more men simultaneously, it may trigger her body to develop diseases, some of which can be sexually transmitted to other men and women.

And the divorced women shall wait concerning themselves for three courses; and it is not lawful for them that they conceal what Allah has created in their wombs, if they believe in Allah and the Last Day; and their husbands have the greater right to take them back during that period, provided they desire reconciliation. And they (the women) have rights similar to those (of men) over them in equity. But men have a degree of advantage above them. And Allah is Mighty and Wise.

Holy Quran, Chapter 2, Al Baqarah, Verse 229

When women are divorced, it is advised in this verse that they wait three menstrual cycles, or courses, before establishing another relationship. This is to give a woman's body a chance to cleanse itself, and to give her the opportunity to make sure she is not pregnant with her ex-husband's child. If she marries someone else while pregnant, how will it be determined whether the child belongs to the new husband or the ex-husband?

If a pregnancy does exist, reconciliation is advised if possible and if desired by both the husband and wife. The "degree of advantage" spoken of in the Quran refers to the fact that the husband is financially responsible for the maintenance of his wife and children. He therefore has a greater right to keep his family intact than his wife has to take his children away, provided his wife is not divorcing him because of abuse or mistreatment.

Men should recognize that there is in fact an advantage to being financially responsible for the maintenance of their families. They earn respect from society and they earn the love, respect and admiration of their wives and children. They feel better about themselves as men.

In today's society, when women lose respect for their husbands, many use divorce as punishment. Rather than seek counseling in hopes of reconciliation, they break up the family because they are angry with their husbands for some fault, mistake or bad decision. Divorce becomes an act of vengeance, with little regard for the long-range consequences for the children. In such situations, men often find themselves powerless as women refuse to allow them to see their children, yet demand money from them for childcare. Both men and women tend to dismiss the critical importance of a father in the home.

In his book *Fathers' Rights*, author Jeffery M. Leving observes that even after the courts provide visitation rights to fathers, mothers sometimes purposely interfere with the fathers' visitation, effectively removing fathers from their children's lives. He states:

No other country in the world has a higher divorce rate than the United States. Over the past decade, an average of one million divorces have occurred each year, involving 1.2 million children annually.

According to the Census Bureau, 18 million U.S. children now live in single parent homes. Only 3.5 percent of these kids live with their dads. Unless my calculator is broken, that means we have 17.4 million children growing up fatherless...

Because 20 percent of custodial mothers see no value in maintaining the father-child relationship, visitation interference is common...Only one in six divorced fathers sees his children once a week or more. Almost 40 percent of children who live with their mothers haven't seen their fathers in at least a year. The bottom line is, fathers are vanishing from the social landscape, and, as the following facts compiled by the National Fatherhood Initiative demonstrate, father absence has dramatic and extremely serious effects on us all:

- *Seventy two percent of all teenaged murderers grew up without fathers...*
- *Fatherless children are twice as likely to drop out of school as their classmates who live with two parents...*
- *Three of four teen suicides occur in single-parent families...*
- *Eighty percent of the adolescents in psychiatric hospitals come from fatherless homes...*
- *A growing body of evidence establishes a high correlation between fatherlessness and violence among young men (especially violence against women.)*

Knowledgeable social scientists have linked fatherlessness to a wide range of social nightmares and developmental deficiencies. Among these problems, judging by the results of numerous studies, are substantial increases in juvenile crime, drug and alcohol abuse, teenage pregnancy, promiscuity, truancy and vandalism.

Fathers' Rights, pages 45, 46, and 47.

Court battles make a bigger mess of marital break ups by creating emotional distress for children. In her book, *Where's*

Daddy? How Divorced, Single, and Widowed Mothers Can Provide What's Missing When Dad's Missing, Claudette Wassil notes how lawyers often encourage parents to use the children in a power struggle for higher alimony payments or better visitation rights:

> *Lawyers are programmed to be even less helpful in "keeping the peace" between the divorcing parents. They are trained in adversarial approaches – in which one party is assumed to be the bad guy – and are predisposed to winning for their clients at any cost. Stories are common of lawyers advising men to ask for custody, whether or not they want it, because they can often get the ex-wife to settle for less money. Meanwhile, opposing counsel advises women to postpone the divorce or ask for more money than they actually want in a kind of open-market "bargaining" stance. Divorcing spouses who might want to negotiate are advised not to speak to each other about the matter because it will weaken their positions. Lawyers, paid by the hour, get richer as the conflict draws on, and less money is available to children when the court battle finally ends.*
>
> <u>*Where's Daddy?*</u> *Page 34*

The legal system has reduced fatherhood to little more than a child support check. Many men have learned to avoid responsible fatherhood altogether. They want intimate relationships with women, but they don't want to be the father of any woman's child. Some women get pregnant after relationships with a series of men.

Women who think that any kind of order can come from having several men at the same time need only to look at some of today's bizarre daytime talk shows, where the nation's worst sex scandals are aired. A popular theme is the DNA test, where a woman has accused several men of fathering her child. Men nervously await the results of a DNA test that will determine the paternity of the child. By the end of the show one of the men, quite often to his regret, is proven to be the child's father.

In healthy communities, fatherhood is respected because men marry women before producing children. Marriage is an act of respect for the woman and her family, insuring that her children will be recognized as the man's legitimate heirs. Marriage connects children to a greater extended family, and provides them with protection, security and a sense of identity.

Polygyny: What it is, What it isn't, Why it's needed

When women vastly outnumber men, such as often happens after a war, society must make a way for women to still get married and have families that include both a mother and a father in the home. Some religious teachings provide specific guidelines for the practice of polygyny.

> *O ye people! Fear your Lord Who created you from a single soul and of its kind created its mate and from them twain spread many men and women; and fear Allah, in Whose name you appeal to one another, and fear Him particularly respecting ties of kinship. Verily, Allah watches over you.*
>
> *And give to the orphans their property and exchange not the bad for the good, and devour not their property by mixing it with your own. Surely, it is a great sin.*
>
> *And if you fear that you will not be just in dealing with the orphans, then marry of other women as may be agreeable to you, two, or three, or four, and if you fear you will not be able to do justice, then marry only one or marry what your right hands possess. Thus it is more likely that you will not do injustice.*
>
> Holy Quran, Chapter 4, Al Nisa, Verses 2, 3, and 4

These verses, revealed after a major war left behind many widows and orphans, emphasize the importance of fair treatment of women and children. The verses address the critical need for children to be raised under the protection of a family. At that time, many war orphans were heirs to wealth and property, and in addition to warning their guardians against taking unfair advantage of them, the verses advise men to marry women who can help raise the children. Men are urged to marry female servants and prisoners of war (as designated by the term "what your right hands possess") rather than exploit them as concubines. However, men are warned not to marry more than one woman if they cannot be fair and just to all the women.

Today, with so many men in prison, on drugs, or just too dysfunctional to be responsible husbands and fathers, single mothers are like widows struggling alone to raise children; the fathers of their children are mentally, if not physically dead. The children are like orphans, deprived of strong fathers that can protect them and guide them into adulthood. Children need good men to marry their mothers, to love their mothers and to love them, and to be living examples of what it means to be a husband and a father.

Polygyny, if instituted correctly, can solve the crises created by the growing shortage of men who are able and willing to get married and take care of children. However, in order to really understand what polygyny is, we first have to be clear about what it *isn't*.

1) **It isn't adultery.** This is not an opportunity for a husband to run off and have an affair with another woman, then tell his wife later that he has taken on a second "wife." Polygyny is a system that requires first a discussion between the husband and wife even before a courtship with another woman takes place, inasmuch as another woman is being considered to be brought into the family. Just as in the first marriage, any second or third marriage must meet the family's approval. Particularly in this age of AIDS, and other deadly sexually transmitted diseases, men and women who engage in secret extramarital relationships are jeopardizing each other's lives.

2) **It isn't an orgy.** Many men may get all excited when they think of the prospect of having two or more women. Their minds conjure up all kinds of fantasies. But polygyny is not "ménage le trois," a sexy threesome with a man and two women. In a polygynous family, every wife has her own private quarters, her own home in which she has her own scheduled time to be with her husband. The husband

has to provide equal private time and an equally comfortable dwelling for each wife.

3) **It isn't pimping.** Some men, chronically unemployed or underemployed, may visualize themselves latching on to several professional women and living in a luxurious home at their expense. This is not an opportunity for a man to sweet-talk some women out of their paychecks. Just as in a monogamous marriage, the man must provide finances for the family's maintenance. Even if a wife works or earns more than her husband, marriage is a partnership and the husband must strive to bring his share of resources to the table. He must share his income with every single wife.

4) **It isn't multiple sex partners.** Men who have fathered children out of wedlock with several women may see this as an opportunity to legitimize their irresponsibility. It isn't. If you didn't marry your baby's mother before she got pregnant, and you get another woman pregnant, you are in fact destroying two families. Being a "baby's daddy" is not the same as being a husband. Being a husband means getting married, establishing an exclusive relationship and providing a home for your wife and children. It doesn't mean just coming by a woman's house for sex and dropping off some money and a few presents for the children. It doesn't mean going out and finding another sex partner in between arguments with the mother of your children. Marriage is a declaration of responsibility, a vow before the Creator to be faithful. In a polygynous family, each marriage is an exclusive commitment, with full knowledge and approval of each spouse before pursuing another relationship. There is still to be no sex outside of marriage.

5) **It isn't a harem.** Old movie images of scantily clad women running round at the beck and call of an Arabian prince flash into some men's minds and they think, "Yes, I could do that. I have money, I could afford it." Forget the fantasy. This isn't about who has a lot of money and can "buy" women, even though financial stability is necessary

for marriage stability. Polygyny is a system that is instituted to benefit women, to make sure that every women that wants a husband is able to have one, even if there is a shortage of good single men.

The last three generations have witnessed major wars that depleted the male population in many nations. Those countries that failed to address this condition experienced a great moral decline. Women who desired permanent relationships with good men found themselves in competition with each other for what became a precious commodity.

Who could be the most beautiful, the most alluring and the most seductive? The cosmetic industry, the clothing industry and every other industry needed only to advertise that their product would guarantee the capture of a man. Women rushed to the shopping malls, spending whatever it took to beautify their hair, nails, faces and bodies in order to be one of the few to win that prized possession – a good man.

The desire for the love of a man often drives women to go straight to the path of least resistance: Sex. So, women offer sex. Men accept sex. Men leave them after sex. Women are angry. They want love, they hope for commitment, they get neither. This crisis causes some women to act out of desperation. They make bad choices because they believe they have no other options. Some conclude that the best way to avoid heartbreak is to avoid too much emotional attachment. They decide to keep relationships casual and non-committal. That way they are not too disappointed when, even though they desire love, all they can get is a temporary sex partner.

Women need love. They need love like they need air, water, and food. They are being deprived of legal spouses for themselves and legitimate fathers for their children, because the current marriage laws in many U.S. states will not permit legal polygyny.

When you don't provide an honest way for people to get what they need, you create a climate for theft.

Consider this:

A friend owns a cabin near a ski resort and invites you and another friend to join her for a weekend skiing trip. The day you arrive, a terrible snowstorm hits the area, knocking out all power lines. You are totally isolated and completely snowed in. There is no electricity, telephone lines are down, your cell phones won't work, and according to your only means of communication, a little battery operated radio, all roads will be closed for at least a week until snow plows can get through. All you have is running water.

Your friend says, "That's okay, we have plenty of water. Plus, there's a loaf of bread in the cupboard. We should be able to last for the next seven days."

That evening, your friend passes out cups of water to you and your other companion. She pours herself a cup of water and pulls out a slice of bread. You and the other friend ask for your slices of bread, but she says sternly, "This is my bread. It has to last me for seven days. You two can drink water, that'll keep you alive for a week."

She chomps happily on her slice of bread while you and the other friend resentfully drink your water.

The next morning, the two of you wake up hungry, while your friend is happily munching on her bread. She pours both of you a cup of water, and sips her water while eating her bread, ignoring your hungry stares.

"I figured it out," she says cheerfully. "I can eat three slices a day for the next six days until the snow plows get through, so I should be fine."

"But what about us?" you ask in alarm. "We're hungry!"

"You have your water. You can drink plenty of water. That should fill you up. But this is my bread," she says decisively.

At noon, you and your other friend fill your empty stomachs with water while your friend chews and swallows her slice of bread. Again, in the evening, two of you drink your cups of water, while your friend has another slice of bread with her water.

On the third day, you are starving and angry. But your friend stands firm.

"This is my bread. I'm not sharing my bread with any-

body. Drink your water!" she snaps. You and your other friend watch with simmering rage and growling stomachs while she noisily enjoys each bite of bread, one slice in the morning, one slice at noon and one slice at night.

By the fourth day, what do you think will happen between you, your companion, and the friend who refuses to share her bread?

Your relationships with family members and female friends, like water, may sustain you. But a relationship with a man, like bread, is what you hunger for when you don't have it.

Desiring a mate is not a sign of weakness. It is a natural part of life that should be fulfilled for ones physical and emotional well being. Stable marriages lead to stable communities.

Adultery is widespread among women. Adultery is basically theft of someone's spouse. In their desperation, women have become predatory in the pursuit of men. They are actively stealing other women's husbands because they want good men, the kind of mature, stable men that marry women and take care of children.

"The good ones are all married," many women say. And so they go after the married ones, sometimes unknowingly, but often knowingly. This has such a corrupting effect on men, that a vast number of married men don't really expect their own marriages to be monogamous relationships. Other women, hungry for love and willing to settle for a little attention part of the time, provide so many opportunities for extra-marital affairs.

Think about it: Do you know a woman that has had a relationship with a married man? Have you ever tried to attract a married man? Has another woman ever tried to attract your husband?

If you are a married woman who has experienced the betrayal of adultery, you are probably angry with both your husband and the other woman. If you are the "other woman" you probably believe that the wife, (or perhaps now the ex-wife) didn't deserve the man as much as you did. Regardless of who's to blame in these situations, our society has failed to address the reality that the numbers of men who are seeking marriage have drastically decreased over the decades.

This is because so many women are providing sex outside of marriage. Much of today's social behavior is influenced by the intense competition between women over the dwindling numbers of eligible men. Women are often afraid that if they refuse to become sexually intimate, they will lose a man to another woman.

Major Wars Deplete Male Population

Current attitudes regarding marriage and family seems to have begun with the generation known as "the baby boomers," those born after World War II, from 1946 to 1964.

According to a March 13, 1996 Census Bureau report, entitled *Marital Status and Living Arrangements*, between 1970 and 1994, the years when baby boomers reached adulthood, the number of never married persons doubled from 21.4 million to 44.2 million and the numbers of those currently divorced quadrupled from 4.3 million to 17.4 million. Unmarried persons 18 and over rose from 28% to 39%. The percentage of currently married adults declined 72% to 61%.

"The delay in first marriages and the rise in divorce among adults are two of the major factors contributing to the growing proposition of children in one-parent living situations," said Arlene Saluter, the report's author.

World War II ended in 1947. In the two decades following, America was again embroiled in wars overseas. The Korean War in the 1950s and the Vietnam War in the 1960s snatched away two generations of young men, leaving single young women struggling to find suitable men to marry. For widows with children, there was a major shortage of available men who were willing to take on a ready-made family.

During the last several decades, the depletion of large numbers of young men from the population created this common scenario: A single woman on the job, seeking a relationship with a desirable man, is attracted to a married co-worker. The married man has an intimate relationship with the single woman. The wife discovers her husband's unfaithfulness. The husband and wife divorce. The family is broken apart.

Who's at fault here? Some will say it's the men's fault - they need to have better morals and learn how to be faithful to their wives. Some will say it's other women's fault – they need to respect the wives and leave married men alone. But the fact is, wars kill large numbers of young men, creating an extreme imbalance in the population which, if not addressed properly, will always lead to this kind of social disorder.

In many parts of the country, women over forty already outnumber men their age by more than three to one. To make matters worse, these current wars are drastically depleting the numbers of young men, creating many widows and orphans and condemning countless numbers of young women to either remaining single for the rest of their lives or committing adultery.

This is cruel. We must enact a more humane marriage law to enable every woman who desires a husband to get married. Statistics show that eighty-five percent of all youths sitting in prisons grew up in fatherless homes. Women must cooperate with each other, so that all children are raised in the safety and security of a household that includes a mother and a father.

This is the female solution to single parenthood. Strong, decent, responsible, God-fearing men must prepare themselves to marry more than one wife.

Just as women have the capacity to have several children and love them all, men have the capacity to have several wives and love them all. Nature has made it so, in the event that women outnumber men, as is often the case after major wars deplete the male population. The government must support laws that encourage family stability.

Many women react with alarm at the thought of men, particularly their own husbands, having the legal right to marry more than one wife.

"This is my husband. I'm not sharing my husband with anybody!"

This common reaction comes from an inability to distinguish the difference between polygyny and adultery. Women respond with anger because they envision having to tolerate their husbands having extra-marital affairs. Unfortunately, many women have learned to view each other as competitors and men as trophies that verify their worth as females.

For some women, their self-esteem is based upon whether or not they have a relationship with a man. Some women have such low self esteem that they cannot develop sincere friendships with other women, all of whom they view as competition for male attention. The cattiness, the gossip and the two-faced backbiting among women are all symptoms of low self-esteem.

Secure Women Can Share Without Jealousy

In communities where polygyny is practiced correctly, women are secure and content in their marriages. They also have better relationships with each other. When there is respect and trust, women can develop a true sisterhood. In communities where women can cooperate, responsible fathers are in the home.

Gheliyah Eshet Haraymiel, a long time member of the Original Hebrew Israelites of Jerusalem, discussed her experiences as the second wife of three wives in a religious community where polygyny is widely practiced.

"The name Gheliyah means 'My joy is in the Lord.' 'Eshet' means 'Wife of'. I'm the second wife of Dr. Haraymiel Ben Shaleahk. Haraymiel means 'The elevated of Yah.' Yah is Hebrew for God. Haraymiel's first wife is named Nasiyah, meaning 'The miracle of Yah.' His third wife is named Yahlee, meaning 'God is my God.'

"I was born and raised in America. Prior to my involvement in this community, I had no relationships with women. There was always a lot of jealousy and infighting. For the past ten years since I've been here, I've experienced friendships, loyalty and trust – all of these things developed in my life.

"There's a difference between being a second wife and be-

ing 'the other woman.' I know. For five years I was in a relation-
ship where I was the other woman. The wife didn't know about
me. The man was Egyptian. We traveled together. There were
material benefits in the relationship, but it was very lonely. There
were no fringe benefits, like being able to meet his family. It was
also very selfish, it wasn't sisterly at all. When the wife found out
about me, it was very stressful."

When her relationship ended abruptly in 1985, Gheliyah
began to question her values and her lifestyle. She realized that
something was missing in her life. She joined the Original Hebrew
Israelite Community in 1988 after attending a few of the Sunday
afternoon services in Chicago. Admitting that she first thought the
Old Testament Hebrew religion-based group was a cult, Gheliyah
said that after listening to the teachings she realized that there had
been a spiritual void in her life. She met Haraymiel during one of
the meetings and became interested in him. An international busi-
nessman, he informed her that he had a wife in Israel and before
they could discuss marriage, he would need to go and tell her in
person that he was considering another wife. He traveled to Israel
and discussed the matter with his wife Nasiyah, then made arrangements for Gheliyah to go and meet her.

"They had been married for 25 years. When I got there, I
was very happy to meet her. He had told me a lot of good things
about her, so I had a very high regard for her. I really admired
her, she had stuck with him through a lot. I took gifts and things to
her. I really tried to endear her.
"In our community, we have three phases of the marriage
process: First there is Divine Pursuit, which is the equivalent to
the courtship. Next is Divine Mechodeshet, the engagement pe-
riod. This is when the couple is planning to get married. It's a
period when very in-depth discussions and observations are made.
You have to have ten sittings with a priest and other wives. If the
woman observes problems with the man, they need to discuss it,
bring it out into the open. If the other wives see problems with the

sister, they need to iron them out. Next is Divine Marriage. Sometimes the previous wives participate in the ceremony.

"In marriage, there have to be guidelines, structure, accountability. We already know, before marriage, what the guidelines are. Before marriage, we go through a 12 week absorption period, with classes and counseling, to thoroughly understand the mechanisms of marriage and to be ready to take on the responsibilities."

Gheliyah had been married for eight years when her husband Haraymiel told her he was considering a third wife. She met Yahlee and was able to welcome Yahlee into the family.

"Why should I be jealous? I already have him. When you're secure, you don't feel threatened because someone else is coming in. When you come into an extended family, everybody brings what they have. A woman has to be secure in herself. You have to know who you are, what you're bringing to the table. Whatever another woman has doesn't diminish what you have. Whatever you bring to the table strengthens the family economically. Nasiyah is an accountant. I have my own business, a greeting card company. Yahlee is in education.

"There are a lot of advantages in this system. The first one is marriage. You come under the protection, the love, the security of a man in your life. The woman who is already in the man's life doesn't have to lose him. A man doesn't have to forsake his children for another wife.

"The women recognize all the children as their children, because they're the husband's children. We breastfeed all the children. Of course you have a special bond with your own biological children, but you're a mother to all the children.

"We have shared responsibilities. We rotate in terms of who prepares meals. You don't have to worry about if your husband is taken care of; sometimes the other woman is handling it. You have more time for yourself. You can pursue your own personal interests, you're not just tied to the house and the chores.

"This is another advantage over monogamy – you have people to help you. With monogamy, you don't get any help unless you can afford to hire somebody. A lot of things get left undone.

"As we come to grips with the reality of the need, as we count heads, we realize it is numerically impossible for every woman to have her own man by herself. How many choices do we have? How many men are in prison? On drugs? Homosexual? On the 'down low'? When a woman does finally find a real man, out of the few real men that are left, the scriptures say 'Seven women will take hold of one man.'.

"We teach sisterhood. Treat others the way you want to be treated. We all want love, friendship, companionship, someone to be there for us. We should want for our sister what we want for ourselves."

In some southwestern U.S. states, such as New Mexico and Arizona, people are already practicing what they call "plural marriages." This is basically polygyny, the marriage of one man to more than one wife. These states also have large Native American populations. Native American cultures stressed the importance of marriage and family for young men and women. In some Native American communities, if women greatly outnumbered men, the men would marry more than one wife. Today, although some State governments might not officially recognize a man's second marriage, the people still fulfill the need to provide husbands for the surplus of women.

Marriage defines ones legal rights to joint ownership of property, inheritance of wealth and possessions, child custody, and the authority to make life and death decisions regarding a spouse's health care. Without a legal marriage recognized by the State, one has problems securing these rights.

Current marriage laws require both the husband and wife to sign the marriage license. One minor adjustment could be added to authorize a man's marriage to additional wives: The husband and all wives must sign each marriage license. This means that if a man takes a second wife, the first wife must also sign the marriage license. If he takes a third wife, the first and second wives must sign the license. If he takes a fourth wife, the first, second and third wives must sign the license. All wives would have the same legal status of a lawfully wedded spouse as the first wife.

Legalizing polygyny would not threaten the stability of existing marriages. There is no compulsion to marry anyone. Not every man is interested in having more than one wife. Not every man is emotionally or financially capable of having more than one wife. Some men are not emotionally or financially capable of having even one wife. Not every married woman is emotionally capable of permitting another woman to have an intimate relationship with her husband. Those who do not desire to practice polygyny should not. Such an arrangement must be mutually acceptable by both the husband and the wife.

This is a point that must be taken seriously by men. Polygyny is not an opportunity for men to play two women against each other in the hopes of manipulating them both. Jealousy between women is nothing to play with. It can be deadly. Just look at the situation between Abraham, Sarah and Hagar of the Bible.

God promised Abraham that his descendants would inherit the land of Canaan. His wife Sarah didn't see how this was possible – he had no descendants because she had been unable to conceive a child. Still, wanting her husband to see the fulfillment of God's promise, she allowed Abraham to produce a child with an Egyptian woman, Hagar.

And Sarai Abram's wife took Hagar her maid the Egyptian, after Abram had dwelt ten years in the land of Canaan, and gave her to her husband Abram to be his wife.

The Holy Bible, Genesis 16:3

Hagar gave birth to a son, Ishmael. After becoming Abraham's wife and having his baby, Hagar's attitude toward Sarah changed – she wasn't acting like just the maid anymore. Sarah got jealous and ordered Abraham to kick Hagar and her baby out of the house. Abraham took Hagar to the desert and left her there with

Ishmael. (To this day, Muslims who make the Hajj to Mecca have as part of the ceremony a re-enactment of Hagar running back and forth across the desert in a desperate search for water.)

Abraham was an elderly man and Sarah was an elderly woman when God promised Abraham that his wife Sarah would also conceive a son. God caused Sarah to become pregnant. She gave birth to a son, Isaac.

Neither shall thy name any more be called Abram, but thy name shall be Abraham; for a father of many nations have I made thee. And I will make thee exceeding fruitful, and I will make nations of thee, and kings shall come out of thee.
The Holy Bible, Genesis 17: 5 and 6.

Ishmael and Isaac were brothers. The question was, which one was the son promised by God to be the father of a great nation? The answer depends on whose side of the family you talk to.

Ishmael is considered an ancestor of the Arab people, the founders of Islam. Isaac is considered an ancestor of the Jewish people, the founders of Judaism.

Those who claim to be Arabs today say that the land of Canaan, in what is now known as Palestine, belongs to them. They say that it was promised to Ishmael, who is the first-born son of Abraham.

Those who claim to be Jews today say that Palestine belongs to them. They say it was promised to Isaac, who they say is the legitimate first-born son of Abraham. Jews claim that Hagar was only Sarah's maid. Muslims claim that Hagar was Abraham's second wife.

God fulfilled his promise to Abraham through both sons. Both were the progenitors of great nations. Both the Jewish nation and the Islamic nation were founded upon spiritual laws that commanded obedience to God. The followers of those great religions could have peacefully co-existed. But, instead, the Jews and Arabs are at war over a piece of land that both claim was promised to them through their ancestor, Abraham.

This family feud has been going on for centuries. Now, nations around the world, including the USA, have been dragged into it, and are still taking sides in the battle, engaging in bloody conflicts and suffering heavy casualties. Will there ever be peace in the Middle East? How many thousands, hundreds of thousands, even millions of lives have been lost over the centuries, and continue to be lost today, as a result of a conflict that was basically caused by the unresolved jealousy between two women?

When a man chooses to marry a second wife, the family will prosper only if the women are in agreement. Polygyny must be practiced correctly, with the consent of each wife, in order to benefit the family. If a man takes a second wife without his first wife's consent, rather than enjoy peace and harmony, he will endure hell in his home, a hell that may plague his family for generations to come. This is the husband's punishment for disregarding his wife's feelings. Jealousy and resentment between women will create feuds between the children. There will be fights over money and property, and the children will grow up to be enemies of one another. There will be so much infighting that eventually the family will lose all its wealth in legal battles against each other. The feuding family members might even go to war. It's that serious.

Give Financial Incentives to Men Who Marry More Wives

When men and women make decisions based on mutual consent, the family receives great benefits. Just as corporate mergers lead to increased wealth for the company's owners, when men and women combine their resources, they increase their financial stability. Divorce, on the other hand, often leads to poverty for women and children, and is sometimes the cause for economic hardship for men. Many men, without the stabilizing influence of a wife and family, tend to be less organized, less disciplined, and less responsible. But when men are in the home with their families, less money is spent on outside childcare, restaurant meals, and home maintenance. Couples who live together tend to do things for each other, rather than having to hire outside support.

Unlike the welfare system that gives financial incentives to women who don't have husbands, encouraging women to remain single and have more babies, a pro-family system would give financial incentives to men who married additional wives, particularly if they married women with minor aged children.

This system, if instituted properly, will have a positive effect on men. When manhood is clearly defined as responsibility for the care and maintenance of a wife and children, men will become more mature in their approach to relationships. Rather than seeking women only for companionship and sex, men will prepare themselves for marriage and fatherhood. They will strive harder to be financially and emotionally stable upon reaching adulthood.

People really do have the ability share that which they value. When natural disasters, such as floods, fires, earthquakes, tornadoes and a devastating tsunami cause overwhelming damage to life and property, people are moved to give unselfishly to help the victims. They may not have much themselves, but they give generously to those who are in desperate need. They do this out of love for humanity, realizing that although they may have little, they can afford to share with those who have absolutely nothing.

It is with this spirit of love and compassion that women must approach each other and openly discuss their needs and the needs of their children. We must be honest with each other in order to create honest, respectful men.

Men who demonstrate exceptional emotional maturity, intelligence, patience, honesty, and integrity should be allowed to spread their positive influence to more than one family. They can be good spouses to other women, as well as good fathers and role models for other women's children.

Many social problems could be solved if women would simply learn to work collectively in the care and upbringing of children. Many conflicts between women would disappear if they stopped seeing each other as rivals for the attention of men. Decent women deserve decent men. If women cooperate with each other rather than compete with each other, all women can enjoy a happy marriage with a good man.

An Honest Dialogue About Polygyny

Raising children is a family affair. Husbands and wives need to work together harmoniously. We must engage in an open dialogue to seriously examine how to build good relationships and create lasting marriages, despite the numerical disparities between men and women. When men and women are mature enough to discuss the issues intelligently, lawmakers will be able to consider changing the laws. Is polygyny a workable solution for you? Following are a few questions to honestly discuss:

1. **Single women** – Think of a man that you really wished you could marry, but he is already married. If the man was willing to marry you, and his wife consented, would you consider it?

2. **Single men** – If no woman would permit any physical intimacy between the two of you unless you married her first, is there any woman you would seriously consider marrying? How long would it take you to decide?

3. **Married women** – Think of a woman that you respect, that also is compatible with your husband. If she was interested in marrying him, and he was willing to marry her, would you consider it?

4. **Married men** – If the government paid you a cash bonus as a financial incentive to marry another woman, particularly a single mother, would you consider taking an additional wife?

5. **Married women** – How do you feel about your husband marrying a younger woman? How do you feel about your husband marrying an older woman?

6. **Married men** – Let's say you are considering marrying a woman who already has children from a previous relationship. How do you feel about raising another man's children?

Chapter 8
The Elephant Matriarch Never Forgets
Learn from the past to build a better future

The bright noon sun beat down mercilessly on the dry, dusty plains, producing a glittery haze in the air that flickered off the smooth landscape, creating the illusion of puddles of water on the ground. But it was only an illusion.

The heavy, padded feet of the old elephant matriarch plodded on, kicking up dust with each slow, methodical step. She raised her trunk, searching the air for signs of water while flapping her ears back and forth to generate a breeze around her head. A desperate band of tired, thirsty elephants plodded doggedly behind her, the smallest children stumbling along in weak exhaustion.

It was the dry season, one of the most severe dry seasons in many years. The herd had already lost one, a newborn calf, who collapsed during the long trek across the dry, dusty earth. The herd had tried to lift up the weakened baby daughter, but she lay still, her body unable to draw another breath. It was a hard loss.

But faithfully they marched on behind old grandma. She remembered, long, long ago, when the dry season was so harsh that there was no water for many miles. But somewhere under the ground there was a spring of fresh water. She searched her memory for the signs she knew marked the spot. Her family, younger sisters, brothers, sons, daughters, nieces, nephews, grandchildren, and great grand children, along with distant cousins and longtime friends made up a herd of sixty eight elephants, all trudging resolutely behind her.

Suddenly, she stopped. The small clump of bushes in the wilderness was a welcomed sight. Slowly the old matriarch reached into the earth with her trunk and scooped up the dirt. She tossed it aside and scooped up more, the tip of her trunk cupped like a hand as she dug in and tossed. The others followed suit, digging deep into the dry, loosened earth and tossing aside dirt. Slowly, the hole in the ground got deeper and deeper.

Soon the ground underneath began to get moist. Dry dirt was turning into mud. The elephants worked diligently, loosing up the hardened earth below with their tusks and pulling up scoops of mud with their trunks. Finally water seeped into the hole, forming a small pool. Sure enough, there was a spring of water running deep under the soil, and the elephants continued to dig, widening the hole that slowly filled with water.

The old matriarch and her family waded into the muddy water hole, splashing their dry skin with relief. This little pool of water meant survival during the most severe drought that some of them had ever known. Old Grandma's memory of this precious underwater spring had saved their lives.

There's an old saying: "An elephant never forgets." It has been observed that elephants remember every dangerous incident, every confrontation, and every enemy they encounter in their lives. From then on, they will avoid whoever or whatever it was that threatened their safety. They pass this experience down to their children, who will also avoid the danger. Elephants demonstrate how to learn from your past mistakes.

Elephants have been known to live as long as 60 years or more. In terms of family structure, the oldest, wisest female elephant is the matriarch that leads the herd. Most of the members of the herd are connected to her by blood, either as younger siblings, children or grandchildren. Brothers and sons, once they get older separate from the herd and form independent bachelor groups, only joining the greater herd for mating. But during severe weather conditions, everybody looks toward the old grandmother of the herd, the one whose wisdom comes from the collective knowledge of the ancestors.

Human societies all over the world are in trouble today. Where are the wise elders to help us find the way out of this mess we're in?

Just like in elephant herds, among humans, females tend to outlive males. In most families, the oldest living relative is the grandmother, who may be a great grandmother or even a great, great grandmother, the matriarch of three generations of children.

Grandmothers play a critical role in the family. They are the voice of experience for daughters who are trying to learn the art of childrearing. They are the voice of reason for sons who are trying to learn how to take care of family responsibilities. They are a source of love and comfort to children, who need a seasoned grandma to buffer the impatience of youthful parents.

Many notable individuals credit the grandmothers who raised them for their success in life. Grandma combined love and discipline to instill character.

The grandmother influences the direction of a child's development from the very beginning. A woman understands her role as a mother from watching her own mother. Wise grandmothers show love and affection as they teach simple lessons in life, demonstrating that a mother's first job is to guide the spirit of the child to the Creator.

In his book *The Soul of an Indian*, Charles Alexander Eastman (Ohiyesa), describes how Native American mothers imparted the principle of respect for life to their children. Simple walks in the woods, observing nature, gave mothers an opportunity to teach their children reverence for the Creator.

The Indian mother has not only the experience of her mother and grandmother, but the accepted rules of her people for a guide, but she humbly seeks to learn a lesson from ants, bees, spiders, beavers, and badgers. She studies the family life of the birds, so exquisite in its emotional intensity and its patient devotion, until she seems to feel the universal mother-heart beating in her own breast.

She continues her spiritual teaching, at first silently – a mere pointing of the index finger to nature – then in whispered songs, bird-like, at morning and evening. To her and to the child the birds are real people, who live very close to the Great Mystery. The murmuring trees breathe its presence; the falling waters chant its praise.

If the child should chance to be fretful, the mother raises her hand. "Hush! Hush!" she cautions tenderly, "The spirits may be disturbed!" She bids it be still and listen – listen to the silver voice of the aspen, or the clashing cymbals of the birch; and at night she points to the heavenly blazed trail through nature's galaxy of splendor to nature's God. Silence, love, reverence – this is the trinity of first lessons, and to these she later adds generosity, courage, and chastity.

In due time children take of their own accord the attitude of prayer, and speak reverently of the Powers. They feel that all living creatures are blood brothers and sisters; the storm wind is to them a messenger of the Great Mystery...

At the age of about eight years, if her child is a boy, the mother turns him over to the father for more disciplined training. If the child is a girl, she is from this time much under the guardianship of her grandmother, who is considered the most dignified protector for the maiden.

                                     The Soul of An Indian, pages 23 and 24.

Grandmothers generally have more time and are unstressed by the day-to-day requirements to get out and earn a living. They are the best baby sitters and caregivers, because they have a vested interest in the proper development of their grandchildren.

They can pass down valuable family traditions. They tell the stories that acquaint children with their family's history. They give children a sense of being connected to a history and a people. Children tend to lose a great deal of their culture and heritage when grandparents are missing from their lives.

Youth Oriented Culture Ignores Wisdom of Elderly

The elderly are highly respected in most cultures around the world, but in today's western culture it is youth, not age, that is admired. Gray hairs, rather than being a sign of emerging wisdom, become a source of panic for men and women who fear their youth is slipping away. Hair dyes and wigs help to preserve the illusion of youth for aging women and men.

The "baby boomers" are becoming senior citizens, but many are not prepared to age gracefully. Some men and women, although well into middle age, are desperately clinging to adolescence. They are going out to parties at the clubs, looking for an exciting interlude of sex, oblivious to the children they have left at home. Some are parents of young children. Some are parents of older children. Some are grand parents. Men and women in their 40s, 50s, and 60s are seeking to relive their long lost teen years, staying out all night, coming home drunk, and waking up with a hangover the next morning.

In families where children respect the elders, it is because the elders demonstrate wisdom and maturity. In families where children don't respect their elders, it is because the elders are acting irresponsible and immature. How can "grandma" advise her grandsons and granddaughters on proper conduct when she is staggering in drunk from a tavern? How can she advise them on relationships when she is having violent fights with her boyfriend?

The grandma of yesterday who baked cookies in the kitchen and told the children bedtime stories is seldom seen today. The baby-boom generation of grandparents are often divorced men and women seeking personal relationships. They are too busy with their own personal and professional lives to help raise grandchildren. Some grandparents are frequenting the same nightclubs as their sons and daughters, who are out partying while a hired baby-sitter watches the children.

Some teen mothers later become young grandmothers when their own daughters follow their example and become pregnant, unwed teens. Women in their thirties find themselves becoming grandmothers, but are hardly emotionally ready to fulfill the role.

So to whom does a child turn for wisdom and advice? Where is the wise grandparent to listen patiently to a child's dilemma and gently help the child figure out a solution?

Families are so fragmented that grown children don't want to live with their parents and don't want their parents to come live with them. Grandchildren are disconnected from the past. They don't experience history through the stories of family members who lived it. They don't learn to appreciate what the family has achieved over the years and how the family has sacrificed for their benefit. For some children, Grandparents are merely distant voices on the telephone. If grandparents are youthful, they are likely to be living their own lives, and don't want to be bothered. If grandparents are elderly, when they become incapacitated they are placed in a nursing home.

Dysfunctional Parents Abandon Children to Grandparents

A June 2005 ABC-TV special report entitled *"Family Lost, Family Found"* examined the growing phenomenon of grandparents who are forced to raise grandchildren that have been abandoned by parents. In some cases, the mothers were drug addicted and living in the streets and the fathers were in jail, on drugs or simply missing. The children, traumatized by the abandonment, coped the best way they could. Some acted out in school, becoming chronically disobedient to express the anger they felt. Others withdrew inside a shell, becoming very quiet, or even silent, to express their emotional pain. Grandmothers, as dedicated as they were to raising the abandoned children, were physically, emotionally and financially overwhelmed.

Some grandparents in the ABC-TV report lamented that perhaps there was something they did wrong in the rearing of their own children, the reason why their children had become dysfunctional and unable to act as parents themselves. This is something the current generation of older adults, the "baby boomers" have to seriously examine. While society has always had its problems, this latest breakdown of the family and the disappearance of wholesome values seem to have occurred within this generation.

Certainly, the drug culture played an important part. In his book *A Season of Afflictions*, Dr. Kenneth Nave reflects:

America was changing in every venue and on every level. Nowhere was this more evident than in our inner cities...the re-

laxed social morals of the '70s planted the first seeds of a scourge that would flourish and overtake our nation – a plague our country has yet to address or recover from. Was it all an amazing coincidence, or a part of a dark conspiracy?

The rationale that marijuana smoking, alcohol imbibing and hallucinogen taking were socially acceptable behaviors began our nation's drug problem. Before anyone knew it, before it could be seen and recognized, our country was in the grip of an intoxicant use craze. It seemed as if everyone was getting high on something...

As the process of enslavement to free-base cocaine continued, formal casual drug users, accustomed to smoking a "joint" and "cooling out" with a glass of their favorite alcoholic drink, became obsessed with the procurement and use of this drug. Evenings once spent just "chilling" with friends became weekends or weeks locked in dark apartments with the shades drawn and dank basements filled with drugged out acquaintances, all caught in the trap of this new kind of drug addiction. Fifty-dollar Fridays spent free-basing cocaine became entire-paycheck weekends, money gone in a cloud of cocaine vapors. There would be nothing left to show for one's labors except empty pockets, hungry children, and despondent spouses wondering "What happened to the person I married, the person I fell in love with?"

<u>*A Season of Affliction*</u>*, pages 192 and 193*

A large percentage of marital breakups are triggered by alcohol or drug use. Many adults are suffering from the pain of unresolved childhood traumas. They use drugs or alcohol to numb the pain of hurtful memories and experiences. They try to compensate for low self-esteem and insecurity by using mood-altering drugs. Not only does the pain of the past remain, greater problems are created in the present, insuring the eventual destruction of families and friendships.

Alcohol has always been a destructive element for those who consume it. However, new and more potent drugs have made the devastation of ones life more immediate and more complete.

Cocaine addiction is on the rise, and with the availability of it's cheaper form known as "crack," many adults are becoming hopelessly addicted, leaving behind small children to fend for themselves. The escalation in the numbers of incarcerated females reflects the increased numbers of women addicted to crack. Many of these women are mothers with young children.

What has happened to cause such a rapid increase in the number of female drug addicts? Growing up without a father increases the likelihood that a woman will develop addictive behavior, observed author Jonetta Rose Barras. In her book *Whatever Happened to Daddy's Little Girl?* she reflects on the food addiction she and her friend Sandra suffered. She noted that they were addicted to food for the same reasons other women became addicted to drugs - trying to compensate for the emptiness of growing up without their fathers.

It took Sandra and me years to learn that it didn't matter how much food we loaded onto our plates or how many gold brick candies we ate in one day; our father hunger could never be satisfied by eating.

Conversely, if we starved ourselves – to death even – we would never instigate the attention we wanted from our fathers, nor could we control the pain we felt...

Where food fails, some women hope drugs – marijuana, heroin, cocaine, or a host of prescription drugs and other chemicals among the plethora now available in the United States – will succeed; these women turn to these substances to kill the pain. When a tooth hurts you use Orajel or some other medication; you may shun the dentist until your pain gets so unbearable that the over-the-counter drug is of no consequence. Similarly, the fatherless woman uses that double shot of Chivas Regal or a thin line of the white powder for medicinal purposes. Not unlike the Orajel user, or Sandra and me, the fatherless woman continues to use these substances, believing she is adequately coping with her emptiness and suffering.

<u>*Whatever Happened to Daddy's Little Girl?*</u> *pages 131 & 125.*

When drug addicted mothers abuse, neglect or abandon their children, state agencies sometimes get involved and remove the children from the home. Or, other family members step in. Grandparents are often the ones who must pick up the pieces of a child's broken family. Too often, by that time, the emotional damage has been done, and the love-deprived child is already on his or her way to becoming an alcoholic or drug addict also.

Surviving The New Plague

In addition to drugs and alcohol, sex becomes another opiate to ease the pain of depression and despair. This is why unwed pregnancy is so widespread among the poor. Young women are seeking comfort in the way that is easily available to them. Poverty makes marriage difficult, but sex becomes an easy escape from hopelessness into the fantasy of what many young women convince themselves is love.

Today, many are dying of a plague that is sweeping the continents of the world because they engage in behavior that often has fatal consequences. This plague is wiping out a large portion of the human population. It is spread a number of ways, including blood transfusions and unsterilized hypodermic needles. But mostly it is spread through sexual contact. This plague is AIDS – Acquired Immune Deficiency Syndrome.

In America, the fastest growing population of new AIDS cases is young African American women between the ages of 14 and 24. Part of the reason is the large number of young African American men who are incarcerated in America's prisons, where homosexual rape is rampant. The AIDS virus is transferred between infected men having sex with other men. These men, infected with AIDS, come home to unsuspecting wives and girl friends, and spread the virus to women. Another reason for the spread of the disease among the youth is the increased peer pressure to engage in sex. Young women feel that if they remain celibate, they will not find a male companion. Young men feel that if they remain celibate, they will be taunted as "gay." AIDS is sweeping college campuses, where widespread sexual activity has become a cultural norm.

People disagree about strategies to stop the spread of AIDS. A common debate centers on whether to teach abstention from sex outside of marriage or to promote "safe sex" with regular condom use. Condom manufacturers profit from the AIDS epidemic by convincing people that greater condom use will make the problem go away. The fact is, the fibers in a condom (no matter what brand you use) are not closely knit together enough to completely prevent the passage of body fluids from one individual to another. Many who thought they had engaged in "safe sex" will find themselves carrying the AIDS virus

Regardless of one's belief about the issue, nature's law does not change. "Survival of the fittest" is nature's law, and the "fittest" are those who use their intelligence to learn from past mistakes. People who fail to learn will die. They are dying now. They will continue to die, painful, sad, heartbreaking deaths that could have been prevented had they made correct choices. What's even more tragic, they will spread this deadly virus to innocent people, including unsuspecting spouses and innocent children born to AIDS infected mothers.

Children orphaned by the deaths of AIDS infected parents are left alone to fend for themselves in many countries across the world. Particularly tragic is the sweep of AIDS in countries across the continent of Africa, where colonial exploitation, prostitution, and poverty create a climate for promiscuity to escalate.

The only people who are safe from this plague are the people, men and women, who practice abstention from sex until marriage. Their challenge is to find compatible mates, either within their own faith-based community or somewhere that people share their values and principles. This is particularly challenging in that, while more girls are urged to abstain from sex, so few parents are raising their sons to do likewise. This further decreases the availability of eligible men for the upcoming generation of women. Why would a woman want to keep herself chaste until marriage, only to be infected with the deadly virus by her previously sexually active husband? With so many sexually active youth and adults now carrying the virus (which can lay dormant for up to seven years) sex has become like Russian roulette: one risky sexual encounter just might be the fatal one.

Young people must somehow sift through all of the contradictory messages and determine what is true wisdom from the elders. Not all adults are wise. In the animal kingdom, survival depends on ones skill in avoiding danger. The world of tomorrow will be populated with those who make the right choices today in order to survive this new plague.

Maintaining Family Relationships

Wisdom is passed down from generation to generation. When children are fortunate enough to have wise grandparents who take the time to teach them life's lessons, they start out with a strong foundation that enables them to survive difficulties.

Paternal grandparents (the father's parents) need to be involved in their grandchildren's lives, just as much as the maternal parents (the mother's parents). When a marriage breaks apart, children can overcome the devastation of divorce much easier if relationships with both grandparents are not severed.

Unfortunately, when couples divorce, or when children are born to couples in which marriage never took place, there is sometimes extreme bitterness between the man and woman. Too often, in their anger over the break up, women refuse to allow fathers or even family members of the father, to have contact with the children at all. Grandparents, cut out of the lives of their own grandchildren, are unable to bond with them and give them a sense of belonging to their father's side of the family as well.

Some fathers, angry that they are being denied access to their children, refuse to pay child support. As a result, they become more and more estranged from their children. This becomes a vicious cycle, in which the children suffer greatly in the long run, as author Jeffery Levin points out in his book *Father's Rights*:

Many estranged fathers believe that withholding of child support is the only weapon they have to counteract the banishment, visitation obstruction, harassment, and alienation suffered at the hands of former spouses. Unable to obtain relief for legitimate grievances from biased or uncaring family courts, these fathers, essentially, are trying to use support funds to buy parenting time. It's a desperate measure by desperate men.

Other non-custodial fathers, frustrated and defeated by vindictive ex-wives and a useless judicial system, simply drift away from their children, overwhelmed by intolerable feelings of anger, failure, hatred and loss. They stop paying child support because their children, their children's mothers, and the courts have stripped them of fatherhood...

Our legal system's definition of "support" it seems to me, must be expanded – to include the love, nurturance, discipline, guidance, and companionship a child needs from both parents. Financial support is only one contribution parents can make to a child's well being, and it turns out, the money is not nearly as important as we've been led to believe. In academics and in tests of social competence, children from low-income two-parent families consistently out-perform kids from wealthy single-parent homes.

<u>*Father's Rights*</u>, *page 49*

In healthy families, parents try to help their grown children work out marital differences rather than seek divorce. Divorce sets in motion a pattern of family break ups for the next several generations. Daughters are not learning to resolve problems in a marriage; they observe their mothers and learn to get a divorce and then get vengeance on their ex-husbands by suing for child support. They learn that by denying visitation rights to the fathers of their children, they can force the fathers to pay more money.

Sons, even after experiencing the pain of abandonment, after a divorce they often end up doing the same thing to their children that their fathers did to them: they walk away from their families and refuse to pay child support. Angry mothers and fathers both contribute to the emotional devastation of the children.

Some adults are too bitter to care how much their feud has hurt the children over the years. Divorced couples sometimes spend the rest of their lives attacking each other, and actually punishing the children, by not letting children see their other parent or relatives. The fragmentation of our families makes it difficult to raise children with expectations of lasting marriages when they reach adulthood.

Today's grandparents, even if they are single parents themselves, must change the pattern that has been set for the next generation: We must encourage our children to get married before they have children, and help them work out difficulties so that they can stay married. If we have grown children who are already single parents, we must encourage them to allow the other set of grandparents to be involved in the child's life as well.

Good Parents Teach Respect For Life

The values a child learns at home are what the child gives to the world. A child who is taught that things are more valuable than people is a child who will not value other human life. A child who is taught that people who have more things are better than people who have less things will grow up to be a greedy, selfish, arrogant adult. When people teach their children that other people are unworthy of respect, this is where the problem starts.

In a world overflowing with abundance, why is there still no peace? How are leaders of nations able to so casually destroy human life, exploding bombs on people they don't even know? How can leaders of nations permit the jailing, torturing and killing of other human beings? War is the consequence of a sick society, where human life no longer has value. The only winners in war are the leaders who orchestrate it. Everyone else on both sides are the losers.

The elders who lived through World War II, the Korean War and the Vietnam War know first hand how the devastation of war destroys families for generations. Men are dead, women are widowed, children are orphaned, schools are dysfunctional, businesses are failing, religious institutions are ineffective, and communities are destroyed.

Elders in our midst remind us of the mistakes of the past, so that we may learn from them and not repeat them over and over again. But in a society that teaches its children to value things, money, wealth and status over wisdom, we select people as leaders because they are wealthy and attractive rather than wise and experienced.

Too often, men and women are elected to public office based on their professional or business connections, and the money they are able to generate in order to create a persuasive advertising campaign. This is why the government seems to have so many greedy, self-serving business people who cannot agree on sensible public policies. If ones real intention is to hoard all the wealth for ones own family and friends in order to feel superior to other people, one can never agree to divide up the nation's resources in such a way that is fair, equitable, and eliminates suffering. When those elected to public office purposely deny people access to basic necessities for the sake of personal profits, they reflect a poor upbringing, where correct values were not taught in the home.

Good government leaders who were raised properly are compassionate enough to want to end suffering and intelligent enough to know that a nation cannot be at peace when too many people are deprived.

In many simple rural communities where leadership is selected from among the elders who have demonstrated patience, compassion, intelligence, and concern for the welfare of others, decisions are made that benefit the whole community. In these societies, people live close to the earth and strive to maintain the basic necessities of life (food, clothing, and shelter). Anthropologists may call them "primitive," yet they live in more peace and harmony than people in so-called "developed" areas where the only objective seems to be to acquire more "things" than ones neighbor.

Like the elephant matriarch who saved her community from the drought, a good leader draws on years of experience and lessons learned from the past. In order for a society to progress, age and wisdom must be respected. However, the respect and deference generally afforded to the elderly in other cultures is, in American society, reserved for the wealthy and famous.

This is one of the major problems in modern western culture. Ones age does not automatically trigger respect from youth. Instead, young people are indoctrinated with the idea that aging, and even the appearance of aging is something to avoid. Old people are often the targets of purse-snatchers, who know that an elderly person is not likely to sprint down the street after them.

In other cultures, particularly in African and Asian cultures, respect for elders is an intricate part of daily life. Such respect is even reflected in the language. Linguist Obadele Kwame Kambon explains:

"In many African languages, such as the Akan language, Yoruba, and Wolof, the elders are addressed with the plural form of "you" as a sign of respect. It means that the elder represents the collective wisdom of the people. They represent themselves and all the ancestors. Whenever there is a ceremony or gathering, one must ask permission of an elder before beginning the program. This is out of respect, for ones elders and for the ancestors."

Respect for elders is conveyed in other languages as well. In Spanish, when addressing an individual using the word "You," the formal term "Usted" is used when speaking to an adult and the more informal word "Tu" is used when speaking to children. Likewise, in the Pakistani language of Urdu, when addressing someone as "You," the word "Tum" is used for children, the more formal word "Ahp" for adults. In Urdu, Japanese, Yoruba and several other languages, when requesting someone to do something, different forms of the verb indicate whether one is speaking to a child or to an adult. In Yoruba, as in many African languages, the respectful title of "Mama" or "Baba" is used when addressing an elder. Likewise, in Japanese, the term "San" meaning "honorable" is added to an adult's name or title to denote respect.

But in the contemporary English language, there is no such

distinction between youth and elderly. In fact, in some areas, people don't even teach their children to address adults using the titles "Mister" or "Miss", considering such titles as too formal. Instead, children are allowed to address adults by their first names, just as if they are talking to one of their peers.

In a society that disdains the physical signs of aging (gray hair, wrinkles), how can the young learn to respect the elderly? How can elders, shut out of the lives of their grandchildren when relationships break up, perform their roles of guiding the next generation? Where are the wise elders that can lead us out of this drought of ignorance into the refreshing waters of understanding?

Until we raise children with a better set of values, we will continue to ride non-stop on the road to self-destruction.

Discerning Correct From Incorrect

Every experience in life serves as a lesson to help one develop good judgment. Some people make bad decisions because they simply cannot discern what is correct from what is incorrect. They not only fail to learn from other's mistakes, they fail to even learn from their own. Given the health consequences of activities such as drug and alcohol use, or even cigarette smoking, one would think that these self-destructive acts would be abandoned. But so many people insist that they have a right to do wrong. They not only endanger their own health, but also endanger others.

Some young people have decided to follow a way of life different than their parents. They have recognized the mistakes their parents made and they are making better decisions, regarding health, relationships, and values. Their greatest challenge is to avoid the consequences of other people's bad decisions.

How many people die from automobile accidents caused by other drunk drivers? How many people die of lung cancer from breathing second-hand smoke? Given the painful consequences of those actions, why haven't we as a human race learned any better? Perhaps human beings need to study the wisdom of the elephants: When they learn a lesson, they never forget it.

The youth need to learn lessons from their elders, but, unfortunately, not all elders are wise. Some are outright foolish. They lack discernment of what is correct, and offer young people misguidance rather than guidance. In his book *Without Pretense*, Dr. Haraymiel Ben Shaleahk discusses this condition:

> *Another clear example for the need for discernment and the lack thereof, is illustrated by cigarette smokers. It's common knowledge that smoking kills people. It kills, not in a quick merciful manner (if any murder can be considered merciful) but slowly and agonizingly with great pain and the constant erosion of the quality of life.*
>
> *Despite this devastation, not only do people smoke, but they also give cigarettes to the people they love. Even doctors, who treat cancer patients and see first hand the misery suffered by smokers and their families, continue to smoke...*
>
> *They know they're slowly destroying themselves, but being totally void of discernment, they say, "you've got to die from something" and therefore smoke anyway. If this isn't bad enough, they pay their hard earned money for the privilege.*
>
> <u>Without Pretense, The Final Resolution of the</u>
> <u>Multiple Wife Controversy</u>, *Page 43*

In the wild, animals know that death can come at any moment, the consequence of carelessness, misjudgment, or failure to learn from an experience. Humans like to say that out of every species on the planet, they are the most intelligent. But most animals display more intelligence than human beings when it comes to decisions regarding self-preservation and survival. Humans purposely poison themselves. Does this sound like intelligence?

Human beings destroy life for reasons other than obtaining food. Human beings destroy the earth, the very earth that must sustain us all, or we all die. Human beings even kill their own children, the unborn children who represent whatever hope we have for a better future. Dr. Haraymiel Ben Shaleahk observes:

Another glaring example of no discernment is noted when we examine the issue of abortion. A heated debate has been raging for many years concerning this subject. What lies at the center of the abortion issue is the simple question of, when does life begin? Anti-abortion factions contend that it ranges from the time of conception to two or three months into the gestation period, depending on whom you're listening. The pro-abortion factions place the beginning of life anywhere from the fourth month until the actual birth, again depending on who's talking.

Both factions seem to miss the fact that when a man and a woman come together, the sperm cell he deposits is already alive and the egg cell from the woman, with which it unites, is likewise already alive. This being the case, how can there be an argument about when life begins? It should be obvious that life began long before the man and woman came together.

Without Pretense, The Final Resolution of the Multiple Wife Controversy, Page 49

Every new life created by a man and a woman has the potential to have a positive impact on other lives. Therefore, it is critical to obtain a certain level of wisdom by the time one reaches the stage where one can reproduce. In many cultures, the arrival of puberty is marked by some type of ceremony that impresses upon the mind of the adolescent that he or she has reached that important stage of physical development in which life can be reproduced.

It is essential that we teach our sons and daughters a deeper understanding of their power to create life. People who create life while in a state of ignorance will either kill the life they created or misshape that life into a person that causes harm to others.

Wisdom is defined as 1) The power of true and right discernment; 2) Good practical judgment; Common sense; and 3) A high degree of knowledge; learning.

We all have a responsibility to seek knowledge. To create a better future, we must gain wisdom, whether by learning from our elders or by learning from our elders' mistakes.

Seek Advice From A Wise Elder

Young people make mistakes in life often because they have no one to counsel them. A good adviser should demonstrate a certain level of personal maturity. If you are over 40 and you meet the following criteria, think of a young person you could advise. If you are under 40 and need counsel, seek an elder who:

1. Has had many life experiences. Someone who has never struggled through anything may not be able to empathize with your situation. A person who has seen and lived through many things - births, deaths, successes, failures, mistakes, achievements, etc. – has a wide range of experiences to draw on.

2. Is sane and sober. A person who is drunk or even slightly tipsy is not in his or her right mind. A person who has indulged in alcohol over a period of time has lost brain cells. Judgment may be permanently impaired. Most people who are chronic alcohol drinkers become so because of their own unresolved emotional issues.

3. Has had a happy marriage. Someone who is still bitter over a divorce, or was never able to trust anyone enough to commit to a marriage cannot advise you on how to be a good spouse or help you resolve a marital dispute.

4. Has raised emotionally healthy, productive children. As painful as it is to admit, our children are a direct reflection of our true household environment. People who behave well toward each other in their homes will generally produce good children.

5. Is patient and compassionate. Whether this person is your parent, grandparent, aunt, uncle, teacher or friend, they need to be willing to listen to you and not condemn you for your imperfections. They also need to be able to keep your conversations confidential and not gossip to others about what you discuss in private.

Conclusion
Raise a Better Human Being
Create A New World For Our Children

Years ago while on a field trip to the zoo with my daughter's first grade class, as we passed through a building with various pictures and maps on the walls, I noticed something rather puzzling. In the middle of the room, inside a large square glass enclosure was a tiny baby ape wearing a diaper.

As the children gawked in wonder at the round faced, big eared, wide-eyed creature rolling around its little cage, I turned to our tour guide, a petite young woman with brown hair and glasses.

"Why does the monkey have on a diaper?" I asked. "Is that how you always handle the primate babies?"

"No, usually a baby would be with its mother and she would keep him clean," she explained. "But this one is a gorilla, whose mother was born in captivity. She has never been a part of a community of gorillas in the wild. So, after she gave birth to the baby, she had no idea what to do with him. She just laid him over in the corner of her cage and left him alone. If we hadn't come and got him, he would have died. We put him in this incubator, where we can feed him and change him every day."

"She wouldn't nurse him or hold him or anything?" I asked, surprised.

"No. She didn't know what to do with him. If she had been born in the wild, she would have seen how other gorilla mothers take care of their babies. But, since she was born and raised in captivity, she never learned."

I looked sadly at the hairy little gorilla infant, its large innocent eyes almost lonely looking. It swayed back and forth, gazing at the children as they pointed and waved.

"Has anybody ever done any studies on the implications of this for human beings who are raised without parents – how they won't know how to take care of their babies?" I wondered aloud.

The zoo tour guide shrugged. "I don't know, but that might be a good idea."

Even among animals, instinct can only go so far in shaping survival skills. Children learn what they live. If they are not raised within a functioning family and community, they will not learn how to function in a family and a community.

The helpless gorilla mother born and raised in captivity is much like the teen mothers raised in homes where parents are absent, abusive, or emotionally detached. Girls get pregnant and have babies, but don't have a clue as to how to be mothers. Their children cry and, in frustration, ignorant mothers scream at them, beat them and in the worst cases, even kill them.

Maternal instincts don't just happen because someone gives birth. Motherhood is a skill that must be learned, by observing experienced mothers and imitating what they do.

A Mother's Love Shapes The Soul

Motherhood is more than a biological function. It is the shaping of a human soul. The decision to bring forth that living soul rests with the mother. There is no other being in a child's life that holds the same position as the mother. A mother's love is critical to the physical, mental and spiritual health of a child. It is the mother's treatment of the child that determines whether that child feels worthy of life and worthy of love. It is the mother who instills in the child the capacity to give love to others.

Years ago, companies that produce baby formulas marketed these formulas to new mothers by insisting that it was healthier to feed a newborn baby formula from a bottle than to breast feed. Many women, fearing that breast-feeding a child would lead to sagging breasts, chose to believe the baby formula companies. They would not breast feed their children, instead letting their own milk dry up and feeding babies from a bottle. Decades later, health care officials admitted that there is a special nutrient in breast milk that is not contained in baby formula, which enhances an infant's immune system. Formula-fed babies were found to suffer more from colds, ear infections, asthma, and other illnesses than breast-fed babies.

Today some mothers still prefer bottled formulas to breast milk, unknowingly depriving their children of the special nutrients that come only from them, making the child vulnerable to more physical illnesses.

In the past, some mothers believed that picking up a child too much would "spoil" the child, making the child too dependent. They would leave the child alone in a crib to cry and cry and cry, until the exhausted child finally fell asleep. Today, health care officials recognize that in order for the child to receive the brain stimulation necessary for intellectual development, a newborn must be held and cuddled. Touching and caressing infants and talking softly to them helps to stimulate brain activity. Studies showed that babies who were rarely held, rocked and cuddled developed intellectually at a slower rate than those babies who were often held, cuddled and given plenty of physical affection.

Today, some mothers still ignore their babies for long periods of time, unknowingly depriving their children of the special nurturing that comes only from them, making the child vulnerable to more spiritual illnesses.

Greed, selfishness, cruelty, dishonesty, envy, hatred – all are spiritual illnesses that prompt one to commit hurtful actions against others.

Every drug addict, alcoholic, thief, rapist and murderer was once an innocent child that came out of the womb of a woman. Look into the hearts of most angry, destructive men and women and you will find a sad and wounded child, deprived of love at some point in time, searching for a way to express the hurt and heal the pain.

"If we could read the secret history of our enemies, we would find in each man's life a sorrow and a suffering enough to disarm all hostility."
Henry Wadsworth Longfellow (1807-82)

Prison Industry Preys Upon Spiritually Weak and Wounded

Just as lions and wolves prey upon the physically weak and wounded in the wild, the criminal justice system has become the predator that preys upon the spiritually weak and wounded in our society.

The prison industrial complex is America's fastest growing industry. In the rural areas in some states, it has replaced family farms and factories as the highest employer of the people. If, while in a drunken rage, you happen to commit an act of violence against someone, you can go to jail. If you desire to get high on drugs to escape the pressure of your problems and you happened to be caught in possession of illegal drugs, you can go to jail. If you desire to appear to have more wealth than you actually have, and this desire prompts you to commit an act of theft and you get caught, you can go to jail.

Prison is big business. It is not meant to rehabilitate anybody. Just as the health care system is designed to profit from your physical illness, the criminal justice system is designed to profit from your spiritual illness.

The health care industry makes money by treating the symptoms of your illness. Doctors prescribe pills and medicines for high blood pressure, muscle pain, headaches, infections and other internal problems. A chemical imbalance is what causes the body to malfunction. If doctors truly had as their objective the complete and total healing of the body, efforts would be made to restore it to its natural balance, using the remedies provided by nature. But that doesn't happen.

In fact, natural herbal cures are often dismissed by the medical industry, are not covered by insurance, and are made so expensive that the average person cannot afford them. Healthy, unprocessed, organic food is made so expensive and unattainable that only the wealthy can afford to eat it regularly. But food filled with unhealthy chemical additives and preservatives is sold cheaply so that all may purchase it and suffer the resulting health problems – high blood pressure, diabetes, obesity, and other common illnesses.

Health care, just like every other industry, makes money on repeat business. Doctors can't afford to heal you. They make a living by repeatedly treating the symptoms of your physical illness.

Similarly, the criminal justice industry makes money by treating the symptoms of your spiritual illness. Judges prescribe fines and jail sentences for theft, assault, murder and other destructive acts. A spiritual imbalance is what causes this dysfunctional behavior. If the criminal justice system truly had as its objective the complete transformation of prison inmates so that they no longer engaged in crime, judges would be able to sentence criminals to programs that would lead to their rehabilitation. But the system is not designed to end crime. Police officers, lawyers, judges, and prison wardens get paid to punish wrongdoing. They, too, profit from repeat business.

Prayer, counseling, and other things requiring the love, patience and sensitivity needed to repair the damage to the human spirit are dismissed by politicians. Drug rehabilitation programs are practically non-existent, even though more than 80% of all criminal convictions are for drug related crimes. Education programs have been all but eliminated from most prison systems, even though nearly 85% of all those serving time are high school dropouts. The fastest growing industry in America today is the prison industry. Those who run the industry can't afford to heal you. They make a living by repeatedly treating the symptoms of your illness.

Knowing this reality, you must make a choice to heal yourself – both physically and spiritually.

> *"Love thy neighbor as thyself."*
> *The Holy Bible, Matthew 22:39*

Sometimes we cannot love others because we hate ourselves. Before we can love others, we must first learn to love ourselves. Sometimes we have to undo the emotional damage from parents who did not know how to make us feel worthy of love.

The Emotional Scars From Fatherlessness

Many sociological studies identify the epidemic of father-lessness as the root cause of today's social ills. However, pointing fingers of blame at men for not being in the home or pointing fingers of blame at women for not staying married does not heal their emotional scars.

In many families there are two or three generations of children that have suffered through the pain of divorce, or single parenthood because their mothers and fathers could not make a marriage work. Many children grew up feeling unloved and unwanted, and as a result, they suffer from low self esteem, insecurity, depression, chemical dependency, and erratic fits of temper that come from repressed rage. This makes it difficult for them to form healthy relationships in their adult lives.

Manhood is difficult to define in a society that continuously gives men mixed messages. Women demand strength, but also expect sensitivity. Women demand dependability, yet want to maintain their own independence. Many men were either raised without fathers, or did not have the kind of relationship with their fathers that allowed open, honest communication and positive direction. Constantly made to feel inadequate by the women in their lives, many men learned to mask feelings and repress pain in destructive ways. Without their fathers, many wander blindly into adulthood, still carrying the emotional wounds from childhood.

In his book, *He-motions,* author Rev. T.D. Jakes states:

We can spend a lifetime trying to determine the boundaries between who we are and the man who was our first and most influential role model. We constantly question what it means to be a man in relation to our father, and we have a constant need to connect with this man so we may discover who it is we really are.

Think back on your childhood and your attempts to get your daddy to notice you. Perhaps you performed and worked and strove to be a star athlete or a straight-A student. Perhaps you acted out and rebelled and tried to get his attention through angry words and illegal activities. But regardless of where you fall on the spectrum of action and reaction, you must begin to acknowledge the truth about your relationship with your father. You feel like you're a grown man and don't need your daddy's approval. You do. You may have experienced the absence of your biological father and struggled to find a worthy surrogate who could show you the way to your manhood, and you're still searching now. Even if you grew up with the extraordinary blessing of a good father who poured into you powerful streams of confidence, wisdom, faith and humor, my bet is that you will continue to crave connection with your father throughout your life.

<u>He-motions</u>, *page 105*

Fathers impact the lives of daughters as well as sons. When women have had strained relationships with their fathers, or have not had fathers in their lives at all, they must recognize the emotional wounds they suffer. In her book, *Whatever Happened to Daddy's Little Girl?* author Jonetta Rose Barras observes:

Losing our fathers, through death, divorce, or abandonment, stunted our growth. Consequently, we are still little girls. We can never become mature adult women until we honor that little girl in us; telling her, in language she understands, that she is without blame for the course her life took...

The search for our fathers is a real and necessary part of becoming accountable for our lives and what happens to us. It is a critical first step in bandaging, and later healing, that wound. While there are no organizations such as those that search for missing children, and no standard procedure for locating these lost men, there are methods that have been successful. Some women have used a simple telephone book approach: Look him up; dial the number. Others have relied on corporations with expertise in finding missing people. Still others have put to use the new technology now available to citizens throughout the world.

<u>Whatever Happened to Daddy's Little Girl?</u> *pages 212, 213*

The hostility that women spew out at men, whether they are the women's husbands, sons, neighbors, co-workers, employees, or complete strangers, is often a reflection of an unresolved father-daughter conflict. This has a greater impact on society than we realize. When we look at our schools across the nation, and see that women make up the majority of the teaching and administrative staff, we observe the high levels of suspension and expulsion of male students; we see male teachers routinely fired and not hired, preventing them from serving as one of the few positive male images in a fatherless child's life. In her book *The Isis Papers*, Dr. Francis Cress Welsing asserts:

> *It is little wonder that 98% of all the Black male children I talk with, who have reached the junior high school level, hate school. Schools and their personnel, like all other aspects of the racist system, do their share to alienate Black males from maximal functioning and thus further the ultimate alienation of Black males from themselves and their manhood. As a result of this pattern of socialization, Black males soon learn that it is easier to be a female child than a male child, and more promising to be an adult Black female than an adult Black male.*
>
> *In childhood, male children learn – whether at home or at school – that they can make mothers and female teachers happy (and they will shower you with smiles and affection) when they act like "females" rather than like boys."*
>
> <u>*The Isis Papers*</u>, *pages 88 and 89*

Many boys struggle with low self-esteem because their natural male aggression, rather than being positively channeled, is either condemned or suppressed by mothers. Many single mothers are too angry with the fathers of their children to instill in their sons a sense of pride in manhood.

Women have broken down barriers in employment, but what happens when they bring hostility toward men to the job with them? The female police officer, whose routine traffic stop escalates into the arrest of a man; the female bus driver who knowingly pulls off just as a man runs up to the bus's closing door; the female manager, whose promotion somehow results in the firing or demotion of every man in her department. When women are hurt, they sometimes make innocent men suffer.

Women are angry. They are angry because they are in pain. They are angry because they have been denied love.

Forgiveness Brings Healing

Learning how to be a good parent is like learning how to fly an airplane. It requires study, preparation, concentrated attention and mastered skills. It can evoke feelings of pride and a sense of great power; however, bad mistakes could result in the destruction of a lot of lives. And yet, as serious as the consequences of bad parenting are, there are few people who take the time to study how to raise children before they produce children. Many people had mothers and fathers with poor parenting skills.

Mothers and fathers are only human beings. They have faults. They make mistakes. Most of us have been wounded by the cutting words of a mother's sharp tongue or a father's scathing criticism when we did not measure up to parental expectations. Often, our parents' remarks are really a reflection of their own personal disappointments over their own perceived failures in life. Their fussing and cussing and put-downs of us are a reflection of their own low self-esteem. But as children, we don't know this. We only know that we have been made to feel worthless.

The first step to healing ones own damaged soul is to forgive ones parents. This is perhaps the most difficult, yet the most necessary thing to do. Forgive the parent who was physically or even emotionally absent from your life. They were struggling with their own unhealed wounds and simply did not have the capacity to give you what you needed. Forgive the parent who was verbally, or even physically abusive to you. If you think that confronting the parent will help you to heal, do so, but realize that the guilty party probably does not have the emotional capacity to admit any wrongdoing or give you the apology you would like to hear. Express your feelings honestly and openly, then let it go.   Their weakness, their illness, is not your fault.

If you think that someone has committed a crime of abuse against you that should be prosecuted, in order to prevent that person from committing a crime against another innocent child, have the courage to seek legal help and prosecute. You should also seek counseling, to help you heal from your own emotional wounds. The spiritually correct thing to do is to try to prevent another wrong from being committed whenever possible.

Women who are emotionally wounded from physical and psychological abuse often cannot recognize the damage they are doing to their own children. They sometimes take their anger and frustration out on their children, berating them and beating them in the name of "discipline." They unconsciously select men that mistreat them and their children, repeating the same cycle of pain and hurt, and creating angry, rebellious children that grow into violent, cruel, self-destructive adults.

A society that raises men to treat women as if they have no value will continue to produce children who do not value themselves or other human life.

A Lesson From the Animal Kingdom: Form Families

The greatest lesson we can learn from observing the animal kingdom is that animals form families and communities. They instinctively know that this is necessary for survival.

We are not individuals on this planet. We are a collective, and our actions affect each other every single day. If we are to survive as a human species, we can no longer raise our children to think irresponsibly and to commit careless acts that destroy the lives of others. The bloody wars that are being fought around the globe are a reflection of the selfishness, insensitivity, greed and cruelty in the human being that develops during childhood.

The root of every civilized society is the family. We must form families. We must make permanent commitments through marriage. We must teach our sons and daughters how to be good husbands, wives and parents. Young people who desire to get married and raise healthy, well-adjusted children in a positive, nurturing environment must be allowed to do so. Our culture must be reformed to encourage them to do so.

Some community and faith-based organizations hold classes for couples that are either considering marriage, are newly married, or have been married for some time, to help them learn how to maintain healthy relationships. This is a positive approach that religious leaders of all faiths should follow, to compensate for the large percentage of people raised in broken or dysfunctional homes where there were no examples of happy, loving couples raising good children.

Young men and women today are afraid of marriage. They have seen too many failed relationships. They have experienced too many disappointments. They are afraid of losing their "freedom." They don't trust others enough to make a lifetime commitment. They don't know what to look for in a spouse.

Some women feel trapped in relationships that serve as a means of financial security but are physically or emotionally abusive. They believe that they must sacrifice personal happiness in order to keep their families together. This is not the case.

Marriage is meant to be a source of peace and comfort for both men and women. If a woman finds herself in an abusive relationship, it is because she lacked the ability to detect the meanness in her spouse before marriage.

The females in the baboon clans of east Africa demonstrate how to avoid selecting abusive males in the first place. Perhaps human females can learn something from observing their methods.

In the baboon clan, some males are loud and aggressive in their anxiousness to declare their dominance over other males. They even get a little violent with the females, hitting and biting them trying to force the females to display a submissive posture.

But other males in the clan are quiet and peaceful. They will even play with the baboon children, showing them gentleness and affection. Though these males will defend themselves if challenged by another male, they never, ever show violence toward the females or the children.

Female baboons with children will bring their children to a male baboon and watch his response. If he is gentle with the children and willingly watches over them, she knows he will make a good father.

So when it comes to selecting mates, whom do all the females choose? The gentle baboon male that shows fatherly tenderness toward children. The loud and aggressive baboons end up by themselves, with no mates. They do not produce any offspring. In fact, they tend to develop diseases and die earlier than the peaceful baboon males that the females choose to father their children.

Violent displays of temper, insensitivity, selfishness and impatience with children are early warning signs that a man is not good marriage material. Women have to thoroughly examine a man's character, not just his looks, his money, or his status. Like the female baboon, a woman must recognize ahead of time when a man does not have the proper temperament to head a family.

Often women feel that they are more powerful and in control if they refuse to make a commitment to marriage. This only adds to a culture of uncommitted, undefined sexual relationships in which men learn irresponsibility for children. Women unknowingly teach their daughters not to expect marriage. They teach their sons to avoid marriage. By their own example they are preparing the next generation to be selfish men and women.

"If you're not part of the solution, you're part of the problem."
Malcolm X (El Hajj Malik El Shabazz)

Our society is in a mess and it is we, the women, who have made this mess. We have created men who abuse women. We allow our sons to mistreat their young girlfriends. We allow men into our lives who don't like our children and don't want to be husbands or fathers. We use sex to compete with one another for the attention of men. We try to seduce other women's husbands, and destroy other women's families.

Give Every Woman An Opportunity For Marriage

Marriage is a spiritual commitment between a man and a woman, a promise to their Creator to be responsible for each other and for the children they create and raise together. Nature has provided a means for all of us who desire a good husband to have one.

In cases where there is a severe shortage of good men, women must have the honesty and integrity to form family groups in which a man, with the approval of his wife, may marry additional women and make them his lawful wives. Each wife is to be respected in her own right. There are to be no secret lovers or mistresses or out-of-wedlock children. There are to be no intimate relationships between men and women outside the bounds of an official marriage.

Polygyny is a system that prevents the kind of exploitation of women that occurs when women engage in sex without the benefit of marriage or commit adultery in the hopes of stealing another woman's husband. A small change in the marriage laws can enable women to reverse the effects of centuries of exploitation.

When women react with alarm at the thought of sharing their husband with another woman, it is because they don't understand the spiritual purpose of marriage.

We are souls inside a physical body. Our purpose for living is to develop our souls in preparation for our transition at the end of this physical life. We mature spiritually through our life experiences. Our goal is to become better human beings. Marriage is a step toward that goal. Marriage is the only institution in which individuals make a promise to God to unite as family.

Developing a lifetime partnership with another human being is a spiritual struggle. Going through the process of learning how to listen to, respect, and live in harmony with another person helps us develop spiritual qualities such as love, compassion, forgiveness, patience, tolerance, understanding, and wisdom. Rev. Willie Taplin Barrow points out in her book, *How To Get Married...And Stay Married:*

274   *The Female Solution*

There are many ways marriage can make us better people. We learn a greater appreciation for partnership. We recognize our limitations and strengths. We become better people as we carry out God's intentions. To do this, you must operate in life with purpose. Together in marriage, partners are called to run God's world according to His intentions. That means you respect the uniqueness of your spouse. That means you respect each other's intellect because it comes directly from God. Learning a deeper respect for your partner and God's purpose will surely make you a better person.
                    <u>*How To Get Married...And Stay Married*</u>*, page 28*

If we know that there is a great numerical imbalance be-tween men and women, for various reasons (death, imprisonment, etc.), and it is physically impossible for every woman who desires to get married to find a compatible man who is single, then we have to have to adopt a marriage system that makes sense. If we do not provide a means for women to get married, we are denying them the right to grow spiritually in a sacred, legally recognized union that enhances their physical and emotional well-being.

If we deny women the right to share husbands legally, they will continue to do it illegally in the form of adultery, or they will continue to have sex outside of marriage, creating irresponsible, immature men who won't marry anybody.

Chicago Sun-Times newspaper columnist Mary Mitchell, in her October 22, 2000 column, observed how the numerical imbal-ance between men and women causes many women to accept marital infidelity as a necessary evil and to simply look the other way when their husbands have extra marital affairs:

You really don't have to be a mathematician to figure out why that is. How can a society lock up 1.8 million people—the vast majority of them black men—and there not be a man short-age? In Illinois, 90 percent of drug offenders admitted to prison in 1996—the last year for which complete numbers were available— were black. And the rate for incarceration for all crimes in Illinois is 14 times greater for black men than for white.

Add to that the large numbers of men who are substance abusers and alcoholics or are homosexuals, then you understand why so many women are out here alone—or sharing someone's husband...

By and large, women have tried to ignore this problem. Our refusal to confront man-sharing openly has allowed men to play by their own rules. And that means there really are no rules at all, just a marriage filled with betrayal and deceit.

When the cheating is exposed, marriages are torn asunder, children are often left fatherless, and one's faith in human decency is shattered... Maybe we should skip the vows and adopt some form of polygamy.

If that proposition sounds farfetched, consider what is at stake. It is no secret that sexually transmitted diseases, including HIV/AIDS, have exploded in the black community. Unfortunately, some of the victims were infected by their husbands or boyfriends who swore they were being faithful...

And preaching about moral values and the sin of adultery isn't working. Churches are filled with women on Sunday morning who are seeking forgiveness for sleeping with someone's husband the night before.

Don't get me wrong. I still believe in marriage. We just need to update the rules.

<u>*Chicago Sun-Times*</u>*, October 22, 2000*

The Women's Movement, while it assisted women in achieving some necessary education and employment goals, also created very unrealistic expectations. Society sends signals that it expects successful women not to need male companionship, but to be independent and self-sufficient. If women desire to have children, society expects economically self-sufficient women not to need husbands to help them.

The growing number of single parent families sends signals to the younger generation that marriage is optional, but is not a necessary component for raising children.

Women have spent the past few decades convincing themselves that marriage is not important, that children can be raised without the input of fathers, that work outside the home is more important than child rearing in the home, that sex outside of marriage is a sign of freedom and liberation for women.

We are paying a heavy price for our mistaken beliefs, in the form of absent, irresponsible fathers and angry, rebellious children. Marriage is a civil union that protects women and children from exploitation and neglect. In their confusion, women are rejecting the very institution that upholds their dignity and honor.

Women that have children outside of wedlock often don't realize the disadvantage they have created for their children until the father of the children dies, and they are unable to produce legal documents that enable them to share death benefits from insurance policies. They are unable to gain access to bank accounts and other financial assets owned by the father of their children.

Women that have relationships with other women's husbands discover that, when the men die, they get none of the respect given to a grieving widow, even though they may be just as grief stricken. Rather than receiving sympathy for their loss, they sometimes find themselves facing hostility from the man's family, as if they are a shameful reminder of what should not have happened.

The Law of Cause and Effect

Many social problems in the society can be eliminated if all of us as women agree to make one simple decision: Select only good men to marry us and help raise our children. Good marriages produce happy families. Happy families create good children. Good children grow up to make positive contributions to society. Unhappy children become a destructive force in society.

Child rearing is a science. When scientists conduct physical or chemical experiments they study physical changes or chemical reactions and try to determine the causes. Scientific discoveries are based on the scientist's ability to identify cause and effect. A scientist asks, what are the causes that created these effects?

Where did we go wrong with our children? A scientist might express it this way:

Cause:	*Effect:*
* A woman has sex with a man who is not emotionally ready to be a father.	* The woman has a daughter by the man who did not want to be a father.
* A man who did not want to be a father does not visit his daughter.	* The daughter develops low self-esteem and does not value herself
* A girl has low self esteem, does not value herself and needs reassurance from a male that she is loveable.	* The girl, seeking male love and affection, has sex with a boy who does not value her.
* A girl gets pregnant and has a son by a boy who did not want to be a husband or father.	* The boy who did not want to be husband or a father does not marry the girl or visit his son.
* A son is raised with no father in the home and no positive male role model.	* The son develops low self-esteem and becomes unruly and defiant.
* An unruly and defiant young man commits a crime.	* The unruly and defiant young man goes to jail.

If women are able to make good choices, and can select good men who are emotionally mature enough to become stable husbands and fathers, they can prevent the cycle of crime stemming from fatherlessness.

Think of all the individuals and families that are hurt by crime and violence. Have you been the victim of crime? We can blame drugs, alcohol, guns, cars, whatever we want to blame, but inanimate objects don't commit destructive acts; people do.

How do parents feel when they have taken pains to raise a good, honest, intelligent, obedient child, only to have that child's life snuffed out by an angry, violent child whose parents failed to instill the child with love, high self esteem, and respect for others?

The children with low self-esteem have begun to take over the schools. They disrupt classrooms, they fight, they get drunk, they use drugs. They are angry because they are in pain. They are in pain because they feel rejected and unloved. Often they feel unloved because a parent has left the home or disappeared from their lives. Sometimes the children have been neglected or abused. When marriages fail, the greatest damage is done to our children.

The high divorce rate in today's society is a sign that men and women do not know how to stay married. If they came from broken homes, they often have no idea how to resolve the conflicts that arise in their own homes.

Most marriages that end in divorce could have been saved if the husbands and wives had the necessary tools to repair the damage. It's just like if a plumber comes to your home to fix the stopped up sink. He may need a wrench to loosen the drainpipe. But if all he has is a hammer, what can he do? Bang on the pipe to try to loosen it? More than likely, the pipe will break, and then the sink is not usable at all.

When men and women grow up in broken homes, the only model they have for ending marital conflict is to break up the marriage. They need to see the process of resolution: calming down from an argument, discussing the situation, admitting error on the part of both parties, forgiveness on the part of both parties, and planning how to properly address such situations in the future.

When children grow up in broken families, or in families that were never formed, they tend to create more broken families or unformed families when they reach adulthood. We have created a culture of divorce and non-marriage. If we want a better future, we must create a culture of happy, life-long lasting marriages. We must create extended families that provide proper protection and nurturing. Then we can raise better children.

Choosing Men Fit to Father the Future

In just 50 years, we can eliminate the problems of today's world. We can end crime, violence, war, and poverty. We can create a peaceful society in which all of humanity lives in harmony. All we have to do is one thing:

Raise a better human being.

In order for a woman to give the kind of love and nurturing to a child that produces a peaceful, secure, happy human being, she must be loved and nurtured herself. She must be secure in a committed relationship where she is valued, enabling her to freely express the love she is capable of giving.

When a woman engages in premarital sex with a man, she destroys his incentive to continue his development to emotional maturity; she destroys his capacity to perceive sexual intimacy as a permanent spiritual bond; she destroys his natural paternal instincts to protect the life of his offspring; and she sets him on a course of selfish immaturity that may render him unfit for fatherhood.

When we, the women, abstain from premarital sex and allow men to mature, they will become fit to be good husbands and fathers. Then we can raise children who are intelligent, industrious, compassionate, generous, respectful, obedient, and committed to the betterment of the human family.

How can a woman know whether a man is fit to be a good husband and father?

Men carry the seeds of life. Before a man engages in the act of pro-creation, he must first have a personal relationship with his Creator. He must know the sacredness of this act, and must respect himself, his seed, and the woman with whom he will create life. Before engaging in this act, he must make a vow to his Creator to be responsible for the life that he creates and for the woman who will bring forth that life. This is what marriage means.

In short, before a man "knows" a woman, he must first know God. If he has no relationship with God, he is capable of any act of deception, selfishness, meanness, and cruelty towards a woman, because he feels accountable to no one.

Having a personal relationship with God is not the same as being religious. Some of the cruelest men on earth have been religious zealots who were willing to flog, stone, and behead anyone who disagreed with their ideas. Some who claim to be very religious have been leaders of nations; they started wars and murdered multitudes. Some "religious" men beat their own wives and children. How can such men ever be decent husbands or fathers?

A woman must look for far more than just a man who professes religious beliefs. A woman should seek a man who knows his Creator, talks to his Creator regularly through prayer, a man who has repented of his wrongdoings and seeks his Creator's help in correcting himself, a man who has love in his heart and compassion for his fellow beings. Such a man is worthy to create life. Look into the eyes of such a man, and you will see the light of God – not the bloodshot haze from last night's drunken stupor, or the glassy glaze of yesterday's drug induced high.

Would you be attracted to a man who never washed his body? Even if he was wealthy and handsome, if he never bathed himself, never touched water, you would find him repugnant.

A man who has never washed his soul is just as repugnant.

Every human being is imperfect. We all have faults, weaknesses, and imperfections in our character. But when deprivation of love causes us to lie, cheat, steal, and intentionally commit acts that harm other human beings, we become spiritually unclean.

Being spiritually unclean, just like being physically unclean, does not have to become a permanent state of existence. Even if a person wallows in mud and becomes extremely filthy, that same person can take a long hot shower with soap and water and become totally clean.

"Verily, verily, I say unto thee, Except a man be born again, he cannot see the kingdom of God."
                                        The Holy Bible, John 3:3

People who have been denied love are suffering from deep spiritual wounds. Love has the power to heal a wounded soul.

Just like plugging an electrical appliance into a wall socket connects it to electrical energy, prayer is the cord that connects us to the positive spiritual energy of the Creator, the source of love to which we are all connected and without which we cannot survive.

The spiritually cleansing experience of meeting God, described in Biblical scriptures as being "born again" is an indescribable sensation that transcends theology. It transcends religion, race, culture and nationality. It is every soul's journey toward the ultimate joy and peace that is found in the presence of the Divine.

Those who see life as a shallow pursuit of personal gain suffer from spiritual blindness. They commit wrong acts in order to acquire things. They misuse others for the sake of selfish personal pleasure. Still, they are not satisfied, because their souls are starving for true love, the love that only comes from knowing God.

The powerful presence of God, summoned through sincere prayer, can literally rock ones soul, sending one into a convulsion of weeping. The soul pours out its pain to the Creator, and tears of sadness turn to tears of joy as the heavy burden of anger and hatred is lifted. The stains from past hurts, bad memories and negative influences that have misshaped ones character are washed away by the Creator's healing hand. Once this happens, even men and women who have struggled to overcome some of the worst faults are transformed. They discover what true love really is: the unselfish love that comes from God, the love that is to be shared with all creation. They have no desire to violate any living soul.

Unless a man's eyes have been thus opened and he has become a spiritual man, he is subject to make selfish decisions in his personal life, oblivious to the pain he is causing women.

It is a woman's responsibility to recognize whether a man is truly a spiritual man. His love for God and humanity would be reflected in his actions, in his treatment of her, their family, neighbors, friends, and even total strangers.

A spiritual man loves and respects his mother. A man's relationship with his mother lays the foundation for his attitude toward all women.

> *"Heaven lies at the feet of thy mother."*
>   **The Holy Prophet Muhammad**

A woman should observe the way a man talks about his mother and the way he treats his mother. A man that has anger and resentment toward his mother will express that anger and resentment in his relationships with all women, until he is able to forgive his mother for whatever shortcomings she had that may have negatively affected his life.

A spiritual man has a sense of humor. He is able to laugh and have fun. He is able to appreciate the innocence of children and to enjoy their presence. A man who is so stern and rigid that he cannot laugh does not reflect the joy that comes from a relationship with God.

A spiritual man is industrious. He knows that he must strive for what he wants and for what his family needs. He knows that others depend upon him for their survival and that as a man, he is responsible for the care of his wife and children. Laziness and indolence are signs of selfishness. A man who is content to let a woman struggle alone to take care of their children is a man of low moral character who will not make a good husband or father.

A spiritual man is involved in some positive way in his community. He is not a hermit or a recluse, refusing to talk to his neighbors. He demonstrates love for humanity through small acts of kindness, even simple things such as shoveling the snow in front of an elderly neighbor's home, helping a neighbor jump-start a stalled car, or contributing money to a school fundraiser. A woman should observe the way a man interacts with his neighbors. A grouchy, miserly, stingy person does not reflect a loving spirit.

No human being is perfect. But it is our job, as women, to seek out those men who, out of love for their Creator, are striving to remove their shortcomings so that they will be good husbands and fathers. When good women marry good men, they can work together to raise better human beings.

A Challenge and An Opportunity

Every child that is born is another chance granted by our Creator to correct our past mistakes and fashion a better world. We must value the lives that have been entrusted to us.

The women who are of childbearing age face both a challenge and an opportunity. There is a great opportunity to create stronger families and more harmonious communities. The challenge is to overcome a culture of disrespect for marriage and family and to be willing to explore new family structures that will provide greater protection and provision for children.

We will not be respected as women until we first respect ourselves. We have suffered oppression, but we are not helpless victims. It is we who raise boys to become men. It is we who set the standard for what is acceptable treatment for women.

Some women, approaching their forties and nearing the end of their childbearing years, have become desperate. After enduring the frustration of failed relationships, some decide to simply have a child out of wedlock, either with a boyfriend who refuses to commit to marriage, or with the aid of a donor to a sperm bank. They resign themselves to a lifetime of single parenthood.

This is sad. Women deserve viable options for marriage and motherhood. Children deserve both mothers and fathers.

We can love ourselves enough to select good men to marry us and father our children. We can love ourselves enough to allow these good men to have a positive effect in the lives of other women and children as well, by allowing mature, responsible men to marry more than one wife. We can love ourselves enough to make this small sacrifice in order to receive a greater benefit in the long run. The greater benefit is the decrease in crime, violence, teen pregnancy, drug addiction, and a host of other social ills exacerbated by the epidemic of fatherlessness.

Intelligent, talented women should not have to remain alone for the rest of their lives because of a shortage of compatible single men. They should not have to resort to immoral acts of adultery in order to enjoy the love and companionship of a man.

We, the women, hold the keys to the future of the human race. Let us create a new, better world, by creating a new, better human being. Let us select men who respect themselves and others, men who will not betray a woman's trust, men who will not abandon their children, men who will keep their bodies and minds clean, men who are worthy to father the next generation. Let us raise our sons to be good, moral men, let us raise our daughters to be good, moral women. Let us model the proper behavior for our children by accepting only the best treatment for ourselves.

Those who are approaching puberty must be prepared for adulthood in a different manner than the generation before them. They must be equipped with a deeper understanding of their roles as future husbands, wives, and parents. They must be instilled with respect for the power to create life and the responsibility that comes with that power. Their decisions will have a critical impact on the world that they and their children will inherit long after the adults in this present generation are gone.

Today's world is in a state of crisis. We who are raising children now, and will be raising children in the years to come, must take responsibility for changing mankind's direction.

We have an opportunity to transform the whole global society in the next fifty years. Fifty years from now, the earth will be populated by a new generation of adults, many of whom are yet unborn. Our mission is to nurture them in childhood with love, guidance and protection, and to raise them in healthy, happy families. If we impart values of compassion, generosity, and respect for fellow human beings, they will create a world where people can live together in peace.

This is our goal. This is our responsibility. Every woman, by the choices she makes, is shaping the destiny of the human family. So, to ensure our survival as a human species and to enable our future generations to ascend to the highest level of moral and spiritual development, let every woman everywhere become a part of the female solution.

About The Author

Naimah Latif is Vice President of Latif Communications Group, Inc., a multi-media promotions firm specializing in book publishing, newspaper publishing and video productions.

She is co-author of the book *Slavery: The African American Psychic Trauma*. This 384-page history and sociology textbook, written in collaboration with her husband Sultan Abdul Latif, is used in elementary schools, high schools and colleges throughout the United States and abroad.

Naimah is Executive Producer and Co-host of *The Media Connection*, a weekly television show broadcast on Cable TV Channel 19 in Chicago, Illinois. The show features a variety of journalists, activists, educators, elected officials and business people who discuss the impact of current events on the community.

She is an Editor for *Money Matters Financial News Journal*, a national news magazine that provides wealth management tips on financial investments and retirement income.

A supporter of youth career development, she teaches a special course in video production for students at Betty Shabazz International Charter School and at DuSable Leadership Academy in Chicago. She is Writer and Co-Producer of the musical docudrama *A Hip Hop Journey With The Ancestors*. She is a member of the National Association of Black Journalists.

An activist in the cause of building stable families, she conducted parenting classes for women inmates at Cook County Jail in Chicago. A strong supporter of multi-lingual education, she continually studies to improve her fluency in sixteen languages: German, French, Italian, Portuguese, Spanish, Twi, Yoruba, Wolof, Zulu, Swahili, Hebrew, Arabic, Urdu, Chinese, Japanese and American Sign Language for the Deaf. She is developing an international culture and language studies course for English speaking people.

She is a member of the Ahmadiyya Movement in Islam, an international Muslim Missionary organization that provides social services in more than 180 countries worldwide.

A resident of Chicago, Naimah and her husband Sultan have one daughter, Zakiyya Amirah Latif.

Bibliography

Thanks to all of the authors quoted in this book whose research provided valuable information and documentation. These books are highly recommended reading.

Books

Ahmad, Hazrat Mirza Ghulam, *The Philosophy and Teachings of Islam*

Baird, Robert M. and Rosenbaum, Stuart E., *Pornography: Private Right or Public Menace?*

Bassoff, Dr. Evelyn Silten, *Between Mothers and Sons,* The Penguin Group, 375 Hudson Street, New York, New York, 1994

Barras, Jonetta Rose, *Whatever Happened to Daddy's Little Girl?*

Barrow, Rev. Willie Taplin, *How To Get Married...And Stay Married,* Cool Springs Publishing, Inc., Colorado Springs, CO, Chicago, IL, 2004

Bassim, Dr. Behrooz, *Thus Speaks Zarathustra,* 2000

Berry, Mary Frances and Blassingame, John W., *Long Memory: The Black Experience in America*

Blankenhorn, David, *Fatherless America, Confronting Our Most Urgent Social Problem,* Basic Books, A Division of Harper Collins Publishers, Inc., New York, NY, 1995

Boyles, Salynn, *Where Do Kids Learn Abut Sex, Web MD with AOL Health*, September 29, 2002,

Brownmiller, Susan , *Against Our Will, Men Women and Rape*, Bantam Books, Inc., New York NY 1975

Cornish, Dr. Grace, *10 Bad Choices That Ruin Black Women's Lives,* Three Rivers Press, New York, NY, 1998

Daniels, Dawn Marie and Sandy, Candace, *Souls of My Brothers,* The Penguin Group, 375 Hudson Street, New York, New York, 2003

Deckard, Barbara, *The Women's Movement, Political, Socioeconomic and Psychological Issues*, Harper & Row, Publishers, Inc., New York, NY, 1975

Eastman, Charles Alexander (Ohiyesa), *The Soul of the Indian*

Friday, Nancy, *The Power of Beauty*, Harper Collins Publishers, Inc. New York, NY, 1996

Gratch, Dr. Alan, *If Men Could Talk...,Here's What They'd Say,* Little, Brown and Company, Boston, New York, London, 2001

Jakes, Rev. T.D., *He-Motions* G. P. Putnam's Sons, a member of Penguin Group (USA) Inc., 375 Hudson Street, New York, New York, 1994

Kelly, Joe, *Dads and Daughters*, Broadway Books, a Division of Random House, Inc., NY, NY, 2002

Kunjufu, Jawanza, *State of Emergency: We Must Save African American Males*, African American Images, Chicago, IL 2001

Leving, Jeffery M., *Father's Rights*

Madhubuti, Haki, *Black Men, Obsolete, Single, Dangerous? The African Family in Transition, Essays in Disovery, Solution and Hope,* Third World Press, Chicago, IL, 1990

Nave, Dr. Kenneth, *A Season of Afflictions,* Lumen-us Publications in conjunction with Western Griot Communications, Richton Park, IL 2005

Rogers, J.A., *Sex and Race in the New World*, J.A. Rogers, New York, NY, 1942

Russell, Dr. Diana, *Against Pornography: The Evidence of Harm,* *www.csus.edu/indiv/m/merlonos/dianarussell.html*

Shaleahk, Dr. Haraymiel Ben, *Without Pretense: The Final Resolution of the Multiple Wife Controversy*, Global Images International Press, USA, 2004

Stewart, Gail B., *The Other America: Gangs,* Lucent Books, San Diego, CA,

Szumski, Bonnie, *America's Prisons, Opposing Viewpoints,*Greenhaven Press, St. Paul MN, 1996

Wassil-Grimm, Claudette, *Where's Daddy? How to Provide What's Missing When Dad is Missing*, The Overlook Press, Woodstock, New York, 1994

Weiner, Jonathan, *Planet Earth*

Welsing, Dr. Francis Cress, *The Isis Papers*

Winters, Paul A. *At Issue, Child Sexual Abuse,* Greenhaven Press, San Diego, CA 1998

Wrangham, Richard, *Demonic Males*

Newspapers, Magazines and Websites

Awake! Magazine, July 22, 2003, Watchtower Bible and Tract Society of New York, New York, NY

Business Week Magazine, October 20, 2003

Chicago Defender, Bill Cosby, Thursday June 10, 2004, Chicago, IL

Chicago Sun Times, Mary Mitchell, October 22, 2000, Chicago, IL

Chicago Sun Times, Editorial Page, June 5, 2005, Chicago, IL

Glamour Magazine, August 2003

Parenting Magazine, April 2004

Psychology Today, May 21, 2003

Resident's Journal, November/December 2004, Chicago, IL

Associated Press, Laura Meckler, September 26, 2002

Religious Texts and Reference Books

The Holy Bible, King James Version, The Original African Heritage Study Bible, James C. Winston Publishing Company, Nashville, TN 1993

The Holy Quran, Arabic Text and English Translation With Commentary, Ahmadiyya Movement In Islam, London Mosque, London, England 1981

Film and Television

Nature, PBS TV, 2004, 2005

Family Lost, Family Found, ABC-TV, June 2005

The Lion King, Walt Disney Pictures, 1995

The Most Extreme, Animal Planet, 2004, 2005

The Oprah Winfrey Show, May 12, 2004, Harpo Studios, Chicago, IL

Index

Other Books Published by Latif Communications Group

Slavery: The African American Psychic Trauma
By Sultan Abdul Latif and Naimah Latif
Published by Tankeo, Inc. in conjunction with
Latif Communications Group, Inc., Chicago, IL,　1994
$14.95

When Nations Gather
By Sultan Abdul Latif
Published by Nadia's House Publishing Company in conjunction
with Latif Communications Group, Inc., Chicago, IL,　2001
$16.95

For more information, call (312) 849-FILM (3456)
Or visit www.latifmedia.com